WARRING OVER VALOR

I0880271

WAR CULTURE

Edited by Daniel Leonard Bernardi

Books in this series address the myriad ways in which warfare informs diverse cultural practices, as well as the ways cultural practices—from cinema to social media—inform the practice of warfare. They illuminate the insights and limitations of critical theories that describe, explain, and politicize the phenomena of war culture. Traversing both national and intellectual borders, authors from a wide range of fields and disciplines collectively examine the articulation of war, its everyday practices, and its impact on individuals and societies throughout modern history.

Tanine Allison, *Destructive Sublime: World War II in American Film and Media*
Brenda M. Boyle and Jeehyun Lim, eds., *Looking Back on the Vietnam War: Twenty-First-Century Perspectives*
Jonna Eagle, *Imperial Affects: Sensational Melodrama and the Attractions of American Cinema*
H. Bruce Franklin, *Crash Course: From the Good War to the Forever War*
Aaron Michael Kerner, *Torture Porn in the Wake of 9/11: Horror, Exploitation, and the Cinema of Sensation*
David Kieran and Edwin A. Martini, eds., *At War: The Military and American Culture in the Twentieth Century and Beyond*
Delia Malia Caparoso Konzett, *Hollywood's Hawaii: Race, Nation, and War*
Nan Levinson, *War Is Not a Game: The New Antiwar Soldiers and the Movement They Built*
Matt Sienkiewicz, *The Other Air Force: U.S. Efforts to Reshape Middle Eastern Media Since 9/11*
Jon Simons and John Louis Lucaites, eds., *In/visible War: The Culture of War in Twenty-First-Century America*
Roger Stahl, *Through the Crosshairs: The Weapon's Eye in Public War Culture*
Simon Wendt, ed., *Warring over Valor: How Race and Gender Shaped American Military Heroism in the Twentieth and Twenty-First Centuries*

WARRING OVER VALOR

How Race and Gender Shaped American Military Heroism in the Twentieth and Twenty-First Centuries

EDITED BY
SIMON WENDT

RUTGERS UNIVERSITY PRESS
New Brunswick, Camden, and Newark, New Jersey, and London

Library of Congress Cataloging-in-Publication Data

Names: Wendt, Simon, editor.
Title: Warring over valor : how race and gender shaped American military heroism in the twentieth and twenty-first centuries / edited by Simon Wendt.
Description: New Brunswick : Rutgers University Press, [2018] | Series: War culture. | Includes bibliographical references and index.
Identifiers: LCCN 2017060240| ISBN 9780813597546 (cloth : alk. paper) | ISBN 9780813597539 (pbk. : alk. paper) | ISBN 9780813597553 (epub) | ISBN 9780813597577 (web pdf)
Subjects: LCSH: Heroes—United States—History—20th century. | Heroes—United States—History—21st century. | United States—Armed Forces—Minorities—History—20th century. | United States—Armed Forces—Minorities—History—21st century. | United States—History, Military—20th century. | United States—History, Military—21st century.
Classification: LCC E745 .W39 2018 | DDC 355.00973/0904—dc23
LC record available at https://lccn.loc.gov/2017060240

A British Cataloging-in-Publication record for this book is available from the British Library.

This collection copyright © 2019 by Rutgers, The State University of New Jersey
Individual chapters copyright © 2019 in the names of their authors
All rights reserved
No part of this book may be reproduced or utilized in any form or by any means, electronic or mechanical, or by any information storage and retrieval system, without written permission from the publisher. Please contact Rutgers University Press, 106 Somerset Street, New Brunswick, NJ 08901. The only exception to this prohibition is "fair use" as defined by U.S. copyright law.

∞ The paper used in this publication meets the requirements of the American National Standard for Information Sciences—Permanence of Paper for Printed Library Materials, ANSI Z39.48-1992.

www.rutgersuniversitypress.org

Manufactured in the United States of America

CONTENTS

WARRING OVER VALOR

INTRODUCTION

Reconsidering Military Heroism in American History

SIMON WENDT

In the history of American military heroism, the patriotic white warrior hero seems to tower above everybody else. In fact, military heroism continues to be a key symbol of what tends to be regarded as a heterosexual, masculine, white nation. Unfortunately, scholars who have explored the cultural history of U.S. soldiers primarily describe this truism, failing to fully explore the complex interrelationships between war, heroism, gender, race, and the nation.[1] Similarly, although numerous books on the patriotic military service of racial minorities and women have appeared in recent decades, they likewise neglect the ramifications of these complexities. The vast majority of these studies merely attempt to unearth the "unsung" heroism of previously neglected groups of soldiers, implicitly or explicitly imploring readers and the public at large to acknowledge their exploits on and off the battlefield.[2] As laudable as such efforts are, they tend to obscure the fact that heroism is a cultural construct that can both affirm and challenge social and political hierarchies. By implying that heroism is "real," historians and other academic writers frequently miss chances to shed light on how tributes to martial valor stabilize and, occasionally, disrupt U.S. society.

Addressing these historiographical shortcomings, this volume seeks to provide fresh perspectives on the history of U.S. military heroism in the twentieth and twenty-first centuries. It focuses on the question of how the idea of heroism on the battlefield helped to construct, perpetuate, and challenge racial and gender hierarchies in the United States, complicating existing scholarly accounts of the white warrior hero. At the same time, it sheds light on the ways in which the meaning of martial valor changed between World War I and the present, a period characterized by both the introduction of an array of new military decorations for valor and fundamental challenges to traditional notions of martial heroism. More specifically, this book examines how minorities such as African Americans, Asian Americans, Native Americans, women, and gay men were affected by America's military heroism discourse, and how they used that discourse in their quest for full membership in the nation. In addition, the volume's contributors explore the processes of construction that shaped, sustained, and sometimes ran counter to the entrenched ideal of the white warrior hero. Given that military heroism serves as a major discursive battleground on which dominant notions of race, gender, and national identity are fought over, this collection of essays provides new insights into the interrelationship between America's wars and U.S. society, the malleability of heroism, and the ambiguous functions that heroism has served in American history.

Any study of military heroism has to begin with an attempt to define its subject, an endeavor that requires scholars to consider its constructed nature and historical contingency. Most importantly, it is worth reiterating that heroes as such do not exist. Rather, they are the product of an intricate communication process in which some people are elevated to the status of heroes through reoccurring iterations about what people believe to be heroic at a certain point in time.[3] Although heroism is a social and cultural construct, it serves important functions in human societies. In general, heroes and heroines embody the norms, values, and beliefs of social groups—making them key components in the formation of collective identities—and become role models whose behavior people seek to emulate. As symbols of dominant norms and identities, they become sources of authority and are frequently used to legitimize social, cultural, and racial hierarchies. Heroism thus tends to be a stabilizing force in society, but it is constantly debated, reevaluated, and revised, reflecting struggles over norms, values, and claims to group membership.[4]

In the history of American military heroism, we can discern continuities and discontinuities with regard to the importance accorded to martial valor, the particular attributes that were ascribed to war heroes, and the norms and values these heroes were believed to embody. In Western cultures, the warrior hero first emerged in ancient Greek mythology, which teemed with tales of daring fighters who ventured into the unknown, risked their lives during extraordinary feats, and triumphantly returned home to be praised, honored, and commemorated. In many cultures, such heroic warriors were depicted as half-divine men with superhuman strength, and they received lavish praise in epics, songs, and oral traditions. Throughout the Middle Ages, battle-hardened knights were similarly lauded for their valor by chivalric and noble orders. Heroic military leaders came in for just as much veneration because they, in the words of historian Sidney Hook, assumed the aura of "event-making" men who changed the course of history because of their extraordinary intelligence, will, and character. In general, however, heroic status remained reserved for European nobility until the late eighteenth century.[5]

It was during the nineteenth century that interpretations of war heroes and heroic military leaders underwent unprecedented change, which also affected the attributes that people associated with martial valor. In a closely intertwined process, whose earliest manifestations could be observed in the United States, heroism was simultaneously nationalized and democratized. As new nation-states emerged in Europe and North America, warrior heroes and heroic leaders became revered symbols of nationhood. After the American Revolution, for instance, heroic general and first U.S. president George Washington became an almost mythical figure who seemingly embodied the new republic. More importantly, official recognition of valor on the battlefield, which had long been confined to the upper echelons of the military hierarchy, was increasingly extended to ordinary soldiers for their willingness to die for the nation. During the War of Independence, the War of 1812, and the Mexican-American War, common servicemen received praise for successfully defending the young republic, although few military decorations existed to match that sentiment, since many Americans believed that medals for military valor smacked of European aristocracy. The Civil War and the Spanish-American War eventually transformed ordinary soldiers who had fought courageously on the battlefield into icons of U.S. nationalism. In part, this iconization was reflected in the introduction of the Medal of Honor in 1862, the first permanent American award for valor on the battlefield.[6]

As in the past, servicemen who received this coveted award were admired as daring risk takers who embodied manly honor, but their recognition as national heroes was now contingent upon their willingness to sacrifice their lives for the United States. The hundreds of monuments that were built to commemorate southern and northern Civil War soldiers around 1900, as well as countless nineteenth-century school textbooks that lavished praise on American fighters of the past, hammered home the message that men's heroic deaths on the battlefield constituted the highest form of patriotism.[7] By the beginning of World War I, Americans thus tended to associate war heroes with a catalogue of attributes that revolved around cherished masculine qualities and national loyalty. "True" heroes were devoted to honor, duty, and the nation; showed physical courage, endurance, and strength in the face of mortal danger; deliberately risked their lives to save comrades in battle; or fought against impossible odds to defeat the enemy.[8]

In this context, the Great War marked an important turning point with regard to the U.S. military's willingness to officially recognize such heroic qualities, leading to the introduction of a number of new awards for valor on and off the battlefield. Although the United States had been among the first nations to honor common soldiers with military decorations, many military officials remained skeptical of their usefulness. Consequently, the Medal of Honor and the Certificate of Merit, which was established in 1847, were America's only permanent military decorations for martial heroism in the nineteenth century.[9] What initiated the process that led to the creation of additional awards after World War I was a growing chorus of critics who charged that the award criteria for the Medal of Honor were too arbitrary. During the Civil War era, for instance, Union soldiers had won the award for deeds such as stealing Confederate battle flags and escorting the body of martyred Abraham Lincoln to his final resting place, and for actions that no one but the recipients themselves had witnessed. Reacting to these critics, Secretary of War Russel A. Alger in 1897 announced stricter standards, as well as more uniformity and transparency in the U.S. military's efforts to determine soldiers' eligibility for the Medal of Honor. According to these new guidelines, "incontestable proof" for "most distinguished gallantry in action" needed to be furnished, which required official reports, eyewitness reports, and recommendations by officers. Applying these new guidelines, an official review board assembled in 1916 to reassess the 2,625 Medals of Honor that had been awarded since 1862, and rescinded more than one-third of them, including those given to Lincoln's honor guard.[10] Thereafter, the award was given only to members of the U.S. armed forces for "conspicuous gallantry and intrepidity at the risk of life above and beyond the call of duty" in battle.[11] These stricter award criteria ultimately prompted the U.S. military to create additional awards that recognized deeds deemed praiseworthy but less heroic than those required for obtaining the Medal of Honor. American soldiers' distinguished service during World War I seemed to make such additional decorations even more imperative. In 1918, new awards such as the Distinguished Service Cross were officially created, and more awards for valor were established in the following decades. That same year, military officials also introduced the so-called Pyramid of Honor, a ranking system of U.S. military decorations that continues to be in use in the twenty-first century.[12]

If debates about what constituted "true" heroism led to an increase in the number of permanent U.S. military awards in the post–World War I period, the changing nature of modern warfare and the perceived need to boost soldiers' morale in these new types of conflict also contributed to this process. For example, while support forces had always played a role in warfare, their numbers rose exponentially in the large-scale military conflicts of the twentieth century. Similarly, during the Cold War, modern strategic weapons systems such as intercontinental missiles required highly trained noncombat personnel, but like support troops, these servicemen had few opportunities to distinguish themselves through heroic feats on the field of battle. To recognize the service and the achievements of such noncombat forces, the military introduced numerous awards that were given for heroism in peacetime, meritorious service, participation in particular wars or campaigns, or particular proficiency with weapons and equipment. Today, there are fifty-seven different military decorations that can be given to members of the U.S. armed forces.[13]

The fact that only a small number of these various awards are given for martial valor—combined with the virtual flood of medals and ribbons that inundated soldiers in the post-1918 period—somewhat blurred the line between martial heroism and military service. In general, the number of official awards given for combat heroism gradually decreased over the course of the twentieth century, while the number of decorations given for meritorious service or mere participation in certain wars or campaigns soared to unprecedented levels. During World War I and World War II, millions of decorations were given to U.S. soldiers for merely taking part in these conflicts, but the most conspicuous example of this award inflation was the U.S. invasion of Grenada, which took place in 1983. After this three-day military campaign, whose goal it was to depose the country's military government and to evacuate several hundred U.S. citizens, the Pentagon awarded almost 9,000 decorations to fewer than 7,000 American soldiers who had participated in or assisted the campaign.[14] Simultaneously, the number of awards established to honor combat valor waned; the most conspicuous decrease has occurred in the twenty-first century. According to the military analyst Eileen Chollet, "20 times fewer valor decorations have been awarded during the Iraq and Afghanistan wars than during Vietnam and Korea." Chollett argues that this decrease is due to a combination of factors, including the introduction of new military technologies such as drones, and military officials' growing concern since the 1990s that too many awards had been bestowed in a haphazard fashion.[15] The historian Donald Baucom believes that these intertwined developments had profound consequences for the U.S. military's awards and decorations system, which put unprecedented emphasis on service and thus "yielded much of its traditional function of recognizing those who demonstrated extraordinary courage in combat."[16]

For this volume, the debates about what constitutes "true" heroism and whether military service undermined or simply transformed what people deem heroic are important because they underscore the fact that heroism is a historically contingent construct that not only reflects and shapes dominant norms and values, but also serves as a symbolic marker of inclusion and exclusion. Although the U.S. military introduced seemingly "objective" criteria to distinguish between various degrees of heroism on and off the battlefield, the selection process continued to be highly subjective and tended to favor white men. Just as importantly, discussions about who deserved to be called a hero were not confined to the U.S. military, demonstrating that related beliefs about race and gender were deeply entrenched in American society. In fact, for much of the twentieth century, only white men were believed to be capable of the type of heroic behavior that would earn them coveted awards such as the Medal of Honor and the Distinguished Service Cross. Most Americans believed that neither white women nor citizens of color could ever be war heroes.[17]

The gendered and racial stereotypes that undergirded white Americans' thinking on martial heroism were inextricably intertwined with ideas about nationalism and citizenship. Nationalists claim that a unique and sovereign nation exists, that its members have a common destiny and a national "homeland," and that the nation trumps all other collective and individual loyalties. Although the nation is as much a construct as heroism, its members believe it is real, and constantly debate the question of who belongs to it and who does not. To analyze these inclusionary and exclusionary functions of nationalist ideologies, scholars tend to differentiate between civic and ethnic nationalism. In the case of civic nationalism, people are accepted as members of the nation because they pledge allegiance to its political institutions and values. In the case of ethnic nationalism, membership qualifications are tied to a specific racialized ancestry and notions of national culture that are purportedly shared by all members of the nation. Consequently, even if people who are regarded as an "alien" race have formal citizenship, they are not necessarily deemed legitimate members of the nation.[18] In the twentieth century, as Gary Gerstle has demonstrated, American nationalism constantly veered between civic and ethnic nationalism in ambiguous and often contradictory ways. For example, although U.S. politicians frequently invoked America's civic creed, various ethnic and racial groups were either barred from citizenship or regarded as detrimental to the nation's progress. White women faced similar forms of discrimination. Debates about soldiers' martial valor or the perceived lack thereof reflected such ambivalent ideas about who belonged to the American nation.[19]

During the first half of the twentieth century, however, marginalized groups began to push back against the notions that underpinned these discriminatory and exclusionary ideologies, seeking to prove that they were no less valorous than white servicemen. Yet, it was only the various social movements that jolted the United States in the post–World War II period that led people to finally reconsider the preeminence of the white warrior hero. Especially during the 1960s and 1970s, African Americans, Native Americans, Latinos, women, and gay rights activists demanded full membership in the nation, forcefully challenging long-held stereotypes that portrayed them as unheroic cowards or projected tales of nonwhite and female heroism that justified rather than challenged centuries of subjugation by reserving heroic status only for those who accepted the racial and gendered status quo. At the same time—as a result of antiwar activism and America's humiliating defeat in the Vietnam War—a growing number of people began to question the validity of martial heroism itself.[20] As the twentieth century came to an end, an increasingly integrated all-volunteer army engaged in new forms of warfare that offered fewer opportunities for combat valor, but questions of whose heroism needed to be acknowledged, who was capable of "true" heroism, and what martial valor actually stood for continued to vex military authorities, the U.S. government, and American society at large.[21]

This volume's contributors shed light on this complex history between World War I and the present, utilizing various methodologies to probe its racial and gender dimensions, while also explaining how these analytical categories intersected with nationalism and the changing nature of warfare in the new millennium. The various case studies that are assembled here should not be regarded as a definitive account of American military heroism, but taken together, they do provide two key insights.

First, this volume reveals a precarious ambiguity in the efforts of racial minorities, homosexual men, and women to be recognized as heroic soldiers. Their quest for full membership in the American nation was inextricably intertwined with the argument that they were as heroic as white, heterosexual men. Fighting for official recognition of their valor on the battlefield could thus yield real and tangible results in the struggle for civil rights. In addition, heroic military service frequently helped to strengthen racial pride and could affirm certain group-specific norms and values. Ultimately, however, official acknowledgments of their heroic service required an embrace of the dominant ideal of the masculine warrior hero and the nationalist ideology with which it was entwined. Any direct critique of or deviation from this ideal undermined marginalized groups' claims to membership in the pantheon of official war heroes and, by extension, the nation. In the case of racial minorities, the patriotic imperative of America's military heroism discourse silenced or muffled more militant voices that faulted the state for lauding heroes of color while ignoring the entrenched traditions of racism that these decorated soldiers continued to face as civilians. Feminine heroism fared even worse, if it was acknowledged at all, since women who demanded recognition of their sacrifices either were expected to conform to traditional notions of femininity or felt they needed to abandon or obscure their female identity. An openly gay hero, too, seemed incompatible with the heroic warrior archetype. Similarly problematic, white stereotypes of racial minorities such as Japanese Americans and Native Americans facilitated their recognition as heroic soldiers but also contributed to the perpetuation of those stereotypes. Paradoxically, then, America's heroism discourse allowed racial minorities, homosexual men, and women to press their case for full membership in the nation, but doing so simultaneously validated the dichotomous interpretations of race and gender they repudiated. Military heroism thus became and continues to be a stabilizing force in U.S. society, which generally serves to maintain the social and political status quo.

The ambiguous role of marginalized groups in war-related hero-making processes also testifies to this volume's second general insight, which acknowledges the durability and tenacity of the masculine warrior hero in U.S. society and culture. The efforts of minorities and women to make American military heroism more inclusive indirectly helped to sustain this ideal, which persevered in the face of changing representations of heroism and military conflicts that called into question its triumphalist aura. As Amy Lucker shows in this volume, for instance, realist war photography of the twentieth century captured moments on the battlefield that seemed to belie uplifting tales of soldierly courage. In a similar fashion, the carnage of World War I, as well as U.S. soldiers' morally questionable behavior during the Vietnam War, prompted many Americans to reconsider the idea that martial valor, manliness, and honor were intertwined, if not synonymous. The period of contemplation that followed the Vietnam War also influenced generations of filmmakers who questioned rather than celebrated war heroes in their works. Yet, even though certain segments of U.S. society briefly expressed unease about traditional interpretations of martial valor and were exposed to portrayals of heroism that were at odds with these traditions, the ideal of the masculine warrior hero survived such crises almost unscathed and was repeatedly affirmed by state-sponsored acclamations, as well as in popular culture.

The following essays allow us to draw these two general conclusions, and each case study offers additional insights into the intricacies of military heroism in the United States in the twentieth and twenty-first centuries. The first four chapters focus on the interwar period and World War II, although they also consider the Vietnam Era. Chapter 1, George Lewis's "The End of Military Heroism? The American Legion and 'Service' between the Wars," calls attention to the fact that while America's wars in the first half of the twentieth century generally affirmed the ideal of the white masculine warrior hero, they also led some people to challenge it. In the case of the American Legion, a powerful veterans organization whose members had personally experienced the carnage of the Great War, the interwar period saw a surprising attempt by the organization's leadership to redefine military heroism. Shunning earlier generations' adulation of manly soldiers who had proved their patriotism by willingly risking their lives for the nation, the Legion advocated a heroic ideal that revolved around people's patriotic "service" for the United States. Only those citizens who strove to protect American democracy and "Americanism" in their daily lives, its leaders asserted, ought to be regarded as heroes; this interpretation potentially allowed virtually every citizen to attain that status. The Legion's reinterpretations, which echoed the ideal of the politically active citizen-soldier, were an attempt to highlight the collective nature of U.S. soldiers' efforts to defend the nation and indirectly salvage members' manhood, since few men had been able to conform to the traditional hero archetypes in the increasingly mechanized battles of the Great War. Ultimately, however, neither the Legion's vision of heroic pluralism nor its focus on civic service as a heroic alternative to martial valor proved durable. When the next world war loomed on the horizon, the American Legion reverted to pre–World War I models of heroism, even though its calls for "preparedness" rhetorically veiled its evocations of such models. While the example of the American Legion shows that the ideal of the white warrior hero was challenged during the 1920s and 1930s, it also testifies to the tenacity of that ideal, which was rekindled during World War II.

Although World War II helped reinforce the ideological stature of the white warrior hero in U.S. society, it also presented opportunities, as well as challenges, for minorities in their efforts to repudiate entrenched racial stereotypes and to gain civil rights. In what historian John Dower has called a "race war," Japanese Americans in particular faced an uphill battle, as Ellen D. Wu shows in the second chapter, "GI Joe Nisei: The Invention of World War II's Iconic Japanese American Soldier."[22] Surprisingly, though, despite being regarded as "enemy aliens" and incarcerated in remote prison camps for the duration of the war, this group managed to utilize public acknowledgements of Japanese American soldiers' heroic service on the battlefield to convince white America of its members' patriotism and willingness to assimilate into American society. Military heroism thus became part and parcel of a process of gradual racial liberalization that characterized the post–World War II period. However, the benefits of white tributes to their martial valor were debated vehemently among Japanese Americans, and ultimately served to simultaneously erode and strengthen racial hierarchies. Especially, the Japanese American Citizens League sought to convince white America that Japanese Americans were loyal patriots, readily joining arms with the federal government to disseminate the image of the heroic "GI Joe Nisei" as widely as possible. Yet, although this campaign proved successful and prompted policymakers to end the most egregious forms of discrimination against this minority, it constrained dissent and projected a "model minority" tale that perpetuated rather than challenged racism and racial stereotypes. For Japanese Americans, then, military heroism proved a double-edged sword, because it bolstered the idea of civic nationalism but indirectly sustained the racial hierarchies that ethnic nationalism entails.

For African Americans, military heroism proved similarly ambiguous, as shown in chapter 3, Simon Wendt's "Instrument of Subjugation or Avenue for Liberation? Black Military Heroism from World War II to the Vietnam War." Examining how the U.S. military, the federal government, and African Americans shaped and used interpretations of martial valor in World War II, the Korean War, and the Vietnam War, Wendt argues that although acknowledgments of black heroism afforded citizens of color important opportunities to claim full membership in the American nation, they also served as a discursive means of social control for white authorities to strengthen blacks' loyalty to the nation. In the face of growing black protest against racial discrimination in the 1940s and 1950s, the U.S. military and the White House readily recognized black citizens' valorous service during America's wars in the past and the present. However, such official acclaims were primarily meant to soothe African American discontent, rather than to educate white citizens about black soldiers' intrepidity or to eliminate racial discrimination. With regard to African Americans' reactions to these forms of white praise, black journalists in particular used heroes of color and the stories of their feats to counter deep-seated stereotypes of black cowardice and to demand full citizenship rights, but their combative articles also tended to reflect a steadfast trust in white definitions of martial heroism and the related ideal of the masculine citizen-soldier. Prestigious official awards such as the Medal of Honor were portrayed as coveted prizes that white authorities had deliberately denied to nonwhite soldiers, which reflected a general acceptance of America's purported civic creed and the legitimacy of the patriotic service that male citizens were expected to perform. Neither the nonviolent civil rights revolution of the 1950s and the early 1960s nor the subsequent turn toward more militant activism and the vocal antiwar movement that emerged after 1965 fundamentally altered the black media's faith in the validity of the heroic citizen-soldier ideal. Wendt's chapter thus suggests that the concept of the masculine warrior hero resonated with many African Americans who viewed it as a path toward full equality. At the same time, white authorities deliberately used it to convince citizens of color that fighting heroically on the battlefield would help them to gain full membership in the American nation.

Compared with Japanese Americans and African Americans, Native Americans have similarities but also significant differences with regard to military heroism, as Matthias Voigt demonstrates in the fourth chapter, "'Warriors in Uniform': Race, Masculinity, and Martial Valor among Native American Veterans from the Great War to Vietnam and Beyond." As a minority whose members enlisted in the U.S. military in greater numbers than any other ethnic group in the twentieth century, American Indians were frequently decorated for valorous service on the battlefield. However, Voigt argues, their service more often reflected ancient tribal warrior traditions and a commitment to Native American nations and communities than steadfast loyalty to the United States. Similarly, although there was some ideological overlap between tribal accolades for returning veterans and modern notions of military heroism, Native Americans' understanding of what constituted heroism differed significantly from Western ideas about the heroic—a term for which there is no equivalent in Indian languages. While they honored Indigenous warriors for masculine valor in battle, killing enemies was seen as less important than assuring the well-being of the tribe. Significantly, rather than using official awards for martial valor to call for full inclusion in the American nation, most

Indigenous communities—especially those whose ancestors had lived on the Great Plains—used military heroism to strengthen tribal identities and Native cultural practices. By contrast, white Americans, conceiving of Native Americans as a "martial race," believed that Indigenous men had a seemingly natural propensity for heroic action in battle. White citizens' admiration not only perpetuated racial difference by relying on entrenched stereotypes, it was also part and parcel of their expectation that Indians readily assimilate into white society. Hence, Native American military heroism was only tangentially related to Native Americans' determination to prove their patriotism; instead, it served mostly to affirm Indigenous masculinity and to support tribal nation building, while also bolstering racist ideas among white citizens.

The following three chapters shed light on the Vietnam War and its legacy. In chapter 5, "My Lai: The Crisis of American Military Heroism in the Vietnam War," Steve Estes focuses on the major challenge that the Vietnam War posed for traditional notions of martial valor and its gendered implications. Estes argues that the debates about William Calley, the commanding officer at My Lai, and Hugh Thompson, a helicopter pilot who tried to prevent the 1968 massacre and subsequently testified against Calley, attest to an unprecedented disruption in the history of martial heroism and related ideas about white masculinity. Atrocities such as the indiscriminate killing of civilians that took place at My Lai called into question the long-standing image of the morally upright American soldier who heroically defended freedom and democracy during World War II and the Cold War. At the same time, Americans were divided on whether My Lai justified such reconsiderations, which testifies to the ambiguities of heroism and the ideological strife over the nation's war aims in the late 1960s. While opponents of the war denounced Calley as an unheroic villain, numerous prowar citizens pinned that label on Thompson, whom they considered an unpatriotic traitor. In fact, during the first half of the 1970s, U.S. culture was suffused with examples of hero worship of Calley. By the 1990s, however, as more critical assessments of the Vietnam War began to dominate the memory of the conflict, Thompson reemerged as a heroic figure, and he was belatedly decorated for his courageous efforts to save civilians at My Lai. Significantly, while standing up to fellow soldiers' transgressions during the Vietnam War, the rediscovered hero never questioned the war or its goals.

If Estes reminds us of the challenges that the Vietnam War posed for traditional notions of military heroism, the sixth chapter, Simon Hall's "Leonard Matlovich: From Military Hero to Gay Rights Poster Boy," sheds light on some of the Vietnam era's gendered continuities. Examining the unsuccessful efforts in the 1970s of the decorated war hero Leonard Matlovich to serve as an openly homosexual soldier in the U.S. Army, Hall's analysis highlights the tenacity of the warrior hero ideal, which remained a symbol of manly courage, patriotism, and heterosexuality. For that reason, Matlovich's unexpected rise to fame as a champion of gay liberation presented a quandary for gay rights activists, some of whom hesitated to embrace a patriotic war hero. Although he loved men, Matlovich advocated conservative values and supported both the U.S. military and the Vietnam War. Consequently, while debunking the stereotype of homosexuals as effeminate cowards, he was also seen as a supporter of an institution that perpetuated the dominance of heterosexual masculinity. Many gay rights activists eventually hailed him as a heroic champion of their cause who would help them gain acceptance in U.S. society, but Hall reminds us that such uses of military heroism as a form of protest also muted more assertive activists within the movement and limited their ability to call for more fundamental change. As in the case of ethnic minorities, the gay liberation movement's embrace of martial valor certainly advanced its cause for full equality, but simultaneously helped to safeguard the social status quo.

In the following chapter, "Displaying Heroism: Media Images of the Weary Soldier in World War II, the Korean War, and the Vietnam War," Amy Lucker complicates our understanding of the white warrior hero by examining visualizations of the heroic and unheroic between the 1940s and 1970s. Focusing on photographs of "weary" soldiers on the covers of the popular weeklies *Time* and *Life*, she sheds light on the tensions between tales of heroic courage and the bleak reality of modern warfare. While many articles and captions lauded the heroism of the servicemen whose faces looked into the camera, photographs of exhausted, frequently frightened, and sometimes crying men tended to run counter to uplifting tales of masculine valor. Especially during the Korean War and Vietnam War, doubts about the heroic nature of soldiers' missions could be sensed when looking at magazine covers, and such doubts also gradually emerged in some of the texts that accompanied the images. War photography thus seemed to challenge traditional notions of military heroism and related ideas about what constituted strong masculinity, while the U.S. government and the U.S. military tried to uphold these traditions by decorating numerous soldiers for heroic conduct on the battlefield. It is difficult to determine whether realist photography disrupted ordinary Americans' interpretations of martial valor, but Lucker's chapter does call attention to the important fact that visualizations of military heroism constitute an important source that scholars need to examine more thoroughly to fully understand the evolution of the American warrior hero in the twentieth century.

The volume's last three chapters give insight into military heroism in the twenty-first century. Chapter 8, Sarah Makeschin's "'From Louboutins to Combat Boots'? The Negotiation of a Twenty-First-Century Female Warrior Image in American Popular Culture and Literature," investigates whether and how women's changing roles in the U.S. military around 2000 translated into more visibility and recognition of female heroism. Makeschin stresses that entrenched notions of hegemonic masculinity in the U.S. military contributed to the perpetuation of the idea that women were capable of serving only in supporting roles, regardless of the fact that distinctions between support troops and combat troops became increasingly blurred in the wars of the late twentieth and early twenty-first centuries. In public debates over whether women should be allowed to serve in combat, many officials argued that women were biologically incapable of becoming "true" warriors, while others questioned their willingness to use violence on the battlefield. Still others feared that women constituted a risk because they were believed to be defenseless against sexual violence when captured by enemy troops. Makeschin argues that these ideas about women in combat, bolstered by the fact that U.S. media largely ignored female soldiers who displayed "heroic" behavior in battle, were reaffirmed in American popular culture. Many Hollywood movies from the 1990s prominently featured female soldiers, but ultimately suggested that the majority of women could not conform to masculine warrior hero standards. By the early twenty-first century, cinema and television productions on war-related themes had reverted to male warrior heroes as the main protagonists, further marginalizing female soldiers. However, according to Makeschin, the second decade of the twenty-first century saw the emergence of a new interest in the figure of the female warrior in popular culture, which was a result of both the lifting of the ban on female combat troops in 2013 and the increasing use of high-tech weaponry in modern warfare. While these developments offered women new opportunities to gain heroic status, the chapter's analysis of Marines officer Jane Blair's autobiographical account of her combat experience in the Iraq War suggests that women's new roles ultimately served to uphold traditional interpretations of the masculine warrior hero. In her memoir, Blair portrays herself as a warrior who could act as heroically on the battlefield as her male counterparts, but she also suggests that doing so is only possible if women fully embrace the U.S. military's masculine warrior hero ethos and conform to its particular standards. Makeschin's chapter thus suggests that the idea of female military heroism continues to be at odds with the ingrained warrior paradigm in the U.S. military and American society at large.

In the ninth chapter, "From Warrior to Soldier? Lakota Veterans on Military Valor," Sonja John elaborates on the peculiar role of Native Americans in the history of military heroism in the United States. Focusing on Lakota veterans in the twenty-first century, she confirms Matthias Voigt's findings that racial stereotypes about "natural" Indian warriors help maintain racial hierarchies and likewise stresses that Indigenous notions of what constitutes martial heroism are distinct from white ideas about the heroic. In particular, Lakota interpretations of warriors' virtues emphasize their duty toward relatives and the community, as well as their ability to survive military conflict rather than dying a hero's death on the battlefield. More significantly, John's interviews with Lakota veterans reveal that in contrast to academic and popular interpretations of Indian soldiers as "natural" warriors whose willingness to fight for the United States is intertwined with ancient tribal traditions, most of these men joined the military for economic reasons, including the chance to finance their education. Western ideas of masculine valor tended to have little appeal among Lakota men, who sought to be providers for their families and communities, but saw no use in the white warrior hero archetype. According to John, white expectations that Lakota and other Native American soldiers adhere to seemingly "authentic" codes of Indigenous bravery obscure the heterogeneity of interpretations of the heroic among different tribal communities and ultimately strengthen racial hierarchies, in spite of a twenty-first-century heroism discourse that professes color blindness and inclusionary nationalism.

If the real-life warrior hero has lost some of its luster at the beginning of the new millennium, the volume's concluding chapter, Carrie Andersen's "Virtual Warfare: Video Games, Drones, and the Reimagination of Heroic Masculinity," provides evidence that ongoing transformations of martial heroism may fundamentally upend traditional ideas about the heroic and related notions of gender. Focusing on the influence of video games and computer games on popular representations of martial valor in battle, Andersen argues that, at least in the popular game *Call of Duty*, twenty-first-century military technology has served to challenge traditional interpretations of "militarized masculinity" in the gaming world. Emphasizing the close relationship between the military and the entertainment industry in the United States, she shows that the increasing use of drones in the borderless War on Terror has affected representations of martial heroism insofar as it is reinterpreted as an ability to expertly control lethal technological power. Although the *Call of Duty* series—like politicians' rhetoric in the War on Terror—evoked echoes of heroic and manly hunters who use their instincts and skills to kill their prey, traditional heroic qualities such as strength and valor no longer feature prominently in its narrative, since drone pilots who hunt down terrorist enemies incur no risk of capture, injury, or death. To be sure, conventional notions of the heroic warrior continue to inform popular interpretations of military heroism, but Andersen's analysis hints at gradual changes in these interpretations, fetishizing military technology and conceptualizing it as a new symbol of masculine might.

Addressing an array of topics, *Warring over Valor* sheds light on important aspects of American military heroism that scholars have either neglected or treated in a cursory manner. However, this volume makes no claim to topical or chronological comprehensiveness, and may raise as many questions as it answers. Indeed, there are a number of issues future research could and should address. For example, while this volume's authors address the efforts of several racial minorities to inscribe themselves into dominant hero narratives in the United States, Hispanics are conspicuous by their absence. Given their growing cultural and political importance in U.S. society, historians should investigate whether and how this heterogeneous group was able to claim hero status, and what role its members played in debates on martial valor in the twentieth and twenty-first centuries. A closer look at other ethnic groups could also yield new insights into the role of race and ethnicity in American hero-making processes, while an analytical focus on lesbian women and transgender persons might allow scholars to shed fresh light on the complex interplay between heroism, gender, and sexuality. A different chronology, too, would help historians better understand the particular dynamics of heroism in the United States. This volume focuses on the period 1918 to the present, because it was characterized by the growing importance of martial heroism within the U.S. military and in American society more generally, as well as by particularly visible challenges to America's social, cultural, and political status quo. But examining the pre-1918 period with a similar analytical perspective is likely to add just as much to our understanding of the continuities and discontinuities in America's history of military heroism.

Future studies should also pay more analytical attention to class, a perspective that is only hinted at by some of this volume's contributors. As Kimberlé W. Crenshaw has emphasized, racial hierarchization and discrimination intersect not only with gender, but also with class.[23] Such an intersectional analysis can reveal much about the discrepancy between public perceptions of heroism and honorees' lived socioeconomic reality. Even though popular representations of military service frequently suggest that it is a combination of masculinity and patriotism that prods male soldiers to engage in heroic behavior, many of these men join the U.S. military for economic reasons, and thus can become "accidental" heroes during dangerous situations they regarded as simply part of their job as professional soldiers. While the class dimensions of male and female military service were evident before and during the Vietnam era, the introduction of the all-volunteer army in the second half of the 1970s accelerated the transformation of America's armed forces into one of the most important employers in U.S. society, a fact that scholars need to take into account when studying military heroism. Especially since the beginning of the twenty-first century, the history of martial valor and its representations in American popular culture reflect conspicuous tensions between traditional tales of manly fighters who want to serve their country and the mundane reality of economic necessity.[24] At the same time, the professional expert soldier, who has become a coveted employee because of his superior knowledge of and particular skill in using lethal technology, similarly clashes with heroic orthodoxy. It remains to be seen whether and how such contradictions will affect the powerful warrior hero paradigm and popular understandings of martial heroism more generally.

Finally, Carrie Andersen's chapter calls attention to the ways in which twenty-first-century warfare and military technology may reshape popular understandings of military heroism and related notions of masculinity and femininity. In the new millennium, warfare no longer consists of traditional battles, and increasingly relies on remote-controlled technologies to observe and kill the enemy, which has led to novel interpretations of what constitutes soldierly heroism. Drones in particular appear to leave little room for the display of the character traits or skills that are traditionally associated with heroic conduct. Some commentators have argued that this new military technology contributed to a conspicuous decrease in the number of military awards for heroism since 2000.[25] It remains to be seen whether such qualities as the ability to skillfully operate complex military technology might ultimately be added to the catalogue of attributes that the American military and U.S. society associate with martial heroism. Such ideas have already become prominent in popular culture, and the U.S. military's announcement in 2016 that it planned to bestow official awards upon drone pilots who contribute to the success of combat missions hints at changing interpretations of heroism and military service among the higher echelons of America's armed forces. However, since previous plans to award Distinguished Warfare Medals to drone pilots have also drawn vehement rebukes from veteran groups, whose leaders argue that such citations would diminish the heroism—and, presumably, the manliness—of decorated combat soldiers, it is unlikely that debates over what constitutes "true" military heroism will die down in the twenty-first century.[26] Examining these wars over valor in a manner that goes beyond merely accounting for the "unsung" heroism of neglected groups of soldiers will help us to better understand the historical evolution of this construct and its social, political, and cultural implications in the past and the present.

NOTES

1. See, for example, Andrew J. Huebner, *The Warrior Image: Soldiers in American Culture from the Second World War to the Vietnam Era* (Chapel Hill: University of North Carolina Press, 2008); Christina S. Jarvis, *The Male Body at War: American Masculinity during World War II* (DeKalb: Northern Illinois University Press, 2004); Edward Tabor Linenthal, *Changing Images of the Warrior Hero in America: A History of Popular Symbolism* (New York: Edwin Mellen Press), 1982.

2. See Scott McGaugh, *Honor before Glory: The Epic World War II Story of the Japanese American GIs Who Rescued the Lost Battalion* (Boston: Da Capo Press, 2016); Linda Hervieux, *Forgotten: The Untold Story of D-Day's Black Heroes, at Home and at War* (New York: Harper, 2015); Marc Wilson, *Hero Street U.S.A.: The Story of Little Mexico's Fallen Soldiers* (Norman: University of Oklahoma Press, 2009); Deanne Durrett, *Unsung Heroes of World War II: The Story of the Navajo Code Talkers* (Lincoln: University of Nebraska Press, 2009); Bill Yenne, *Rising Sons: The Japanese American GIs Who Fought for the United States during World War II* (New York: Thomas Dunne Books, 2007); Robert Asahina, *Just Americans: How Japanese Americans Won a War at Home and Abroad* (New York: Gotham, 2006); Brenda L. Moore, *Serving Our Country: Japanese American Women in the Military during*

World War II (New Brunswick, NJ: Rutgers University Press, 2003); Gail Buckley, *American Patriots: The Story of Blacks in the Military from the Revolution to Desert Storm* (New York: Random House, 2002); Susan H. Godson, *Serving Proudly: A History of Women in the U.S. Navy* (Annapolis, MD: Naval Institute Press, 2002); Robert Edgerton, *Hidden Heroism: Black Soldiers in America's Wars* (Boulder, CO: Westview Press, 2002); Elizabeth M. Norman, *We Band of Angels: The Untold Story of American Nurses Trapped on Bataan by the Japanese* (New York: Random House, 1999); Thomas A. Britten, *American Indians in World War I: At War and at Home* (Albuquerque: University of New Mexico Press, 1998); Lettie Gavin, *American Women in World War I: They Also Served* (Boulder: University Press of Colorado, 1997). With regard to scholars' tendency to merely highlight the "unsung" heroism of women and racial minorities in the U.S. military, Douglas W. Bristol Jr.'s and Heather Marie Stur's edited volume *Integrating the US Military: Race, Gender, and Sexual Orientation since World War II* (Baltimore: Johns Hopkins University Press, 2017) is a notable exception. Although it does not explicitly focus on heroism, its contributors shed light on the complex ways in which minorities sought to protest against discrimination in the U.S. armed forces, showing that receiving official acclaim for valorous conduct does not necessarily erase racial and gender hierarchies.

3. Susan J. Drucker and Robert S. Cathcart, "The Hero as a Communication Phenomenon," in *American Heroes in a Media Age*, ed. Susan J. Drucker and Robert S. Cathcart (Cresskill, NJ: Hampton Press, 1994), 3–5; Lance Strate, "Heroes and/as Communication," in *Heroes in a Global World*, ed. Susan J. Drucker and Gary Gumpert (Cresskill, NJ: Hampton Press, 2008), 19.

4. Orrin Klapp, "The Creation of Popular Heroes," *American Journal of Sociology* 54, no. 2 (September 1948): 135–141; Janice Hume, "Changing Characteristics of Heroic Women in Midcentury Mainstream Media," *Journal of Popular Culture* 34, no. 2 (2000): 9; Drucker and Cathcart, "The Hero as a Communication Phenomenon," 3–5; Tristram Potter Coffin and Hennig Cohen, introduction to *The Parade of Heroes: Legendary Figures in American Lore*, ed. Tristram Potter Coffin and Hennig Cohen (Garden City, NY: Anchor Press, 1978), xxiii; Lance Strate, "Heroes: A Communication Perspective," in *American Heroes in a Media Age*, 15; William J. Goode, *The Celebration of Heroes: Prestige as a Control System* (Berkeley: University of California Press, 1978), 7–8, 151–152.

5. Bernhard Giesen, *Triumph and Trauma* (Boulder, CO: Paradigm Publishers, 2004), 15; Karl Kerényi, *Die Heroen der Griechen* (Zurich: Rhein-Verlag, 1958), 12–24; M. Gregory Kendrick, *The Heroic Ideal: Western Archetypes from the Greeks to the Present* (Jefferson, NC: McFarland, 2010), 5; Joseph Campbell, *The Hero with a Thousand Faces* (1949; repr., London: Fontana Press, 1993), 30–37; David T. Zabecki, "Medals and Decorations," in *The Encyclopedia of World War I: A Political, Social, and Military History*, ed. Spencer Tucker, vol. 1 (Santa Barbara, CA: ABC-CLIO, 2005), 767; Sidney Hook, "The Eventful Man and the Event-Making Man," in *Heroes and Anti-Heroes: A Reader in Depth*, ed. Harold Lubin (San Francisco, CA: Chandler, 1968), 132–137.

6. Karen Hagemann, "Of 'Manly Valor' and 'German Honor': Nation, War, and Masculinity in the Age of the Prussian Uprising against Napoleon," *Central European History* 30, no. 2 (1997): 219; René Schilling, *"Kriegshelden": Deutungsmuster heroischer Männlichkeit in Deutschland, 1813–1945* (Paderborn, Germany: Ferdinand Schöningh, 2002), 26; Barry Schwartz, "George Washington and the Whig Conception of Heroic Leadership," *American Sociological Review* 48, no. 1 (1983): 20–24; Barry Schwartz, *George Washington: The Making of an American Symbol* (New York: Free Press, 1987); John Pettegrew, "'The Soldier's Faith': Turn-of-the-Century Memory of the Civil War and the Emergence of Modern American Nationalism," *Journal of Contemporary History* 31, no. 1 (1996): 49–73; "Awards,

Decorations, and Honors," in *Encyclopedia of American War Heroes*, ed. Bruce H. Norton (New York: Checkmark Books, 2002), xxvii.

7. Goode, *The Celebration of Heroes*, 167–179; Ute Frevert, "Vom heroischen Menschen zum Helden des Alltags," *Merkur* 63, no. 9–10 (2009): 803–812; Ute Frevert, "Männer und Heroen: Vom Aufstieg und Niedergang des Heroismus im 19. und 20. Jahrhundert," in *Erfindung des Menschen: Schöpfungsträume und Körperbilder, 1500–2000*, ed. Richard van Dülmen (Vienna: Böhlau, 1998), 323–344; Michael Kammen, *Mystic Chords of Memory: The Transformation of Tradition in American Culture* (New York: Knopf, 1991), 115; Linenthal, *Changing Images of the Warrior Hero in America*, 27.

8. Joshua S. Goldstein, *War and Gender: How Gender Shapes the War System and Vice Versa* (Cambridge, UK: Cambridge University Press, 2001), 265–266; Edward Madigan, "Courage and Cowardice in Wartime," *War in History* 20, no. 1 (2013): 4–6; William C. Cockerham, "Green Berets and the Symbolic Meaning of Heroism," *Urban Life* 8, no. 1 (1979): 98–99; Jeffrey W. Anderson, "Military Heroism: An Occupational Definition," *Armed Forces & Society* 12, no. 4 (1986): 601–604.

9. John E. Strandberg and Roger James Bender, *The Call of Duty: Military Awards and Decorations of the United States of America* (San Jose, CA: R. James Bender Publishing, 1994), 13–16.

10. Editors of Boston Publishing Company, *The Medal of Honor: A History of Service Above and Beyond* (Minneapolis, MN: Zenith Press, 2014), 12–15, 47–49, 53, 49, 94–95.

11. "Awards, Decorations, and Honors," xvii.

12. Editors of Boston Publishing Company, *The Medal of Honor*, 94–95; Strandberg and Bender, *The Call of Duty*, 14.

13. Zabecki, "Medals and Decorations," 767–768; Donald Baucom, "Awards, Decorations, and Honors," in *The Oxford Companion to American Military History*, ed. John Whiteclay Chambers II (New York: Oxford University Press, 1999), 67–68; Bruce Peabody and Krista Jenkins, *Where Have All the Heroes Gone? The Changing Nature of American Valor* (New York: Oxford University Press, 2017), 79.

14. Strandberg and Bender, *The Call of Duty*, 149, 208; Peabody and Jenkins, *Where Have All the Heroes Gone?*, 79.

15. Eileen Chollet, "'Gallantry and Intrepidity': Valor Decorations in Current and Past Conflicts," *Joint Force Quarterly* 72, no. 1 (2014): 62, 64.

16. Baucom, "Awards, Decorations, and Honors," 68.

17. On this issue, see, for example, Bobby A. Wintermute, "'The Negro Should Not Be Used as a Combat Soldier': Reconfiguring Racial Identity in the United States Army, 1890–1918," *Patterns of Prejudice* 46, no. 3–4 (2012): 277–298; Simon Wendt, "Nationalist Middle-Class Women, Memory, and Conservative Family Values, 1890–1945," in *Inventing the Modern American Family: Family Values and Social Change in 20th-Century United States*, ed. Isabel Heinemann (Frankfurt: Campus, 2012), 31–58.

18. John Breuilly, *Nationalism and the State* (Chicago: University of Chicago Press, 1993), 2; Craig Calhoun, *Nationalism* (Buckingham, UK: Open University Press, 1997), 4–5; Michael Billig, *Banal Nationalism* (London: Sage, 1995); Benedict Anderson, *Imagined Communities: Reflections on the Origin and Spread of Nationalism*, rev. ed. (New York: Verso, 1991); David Brown, "Are There Good and Bad Nationalisms?," *Nations and Nationalisms* 5, no. 2 (1999): 281–302; Andreas Fahrmeir, *Citizenship: The Rise and Fall of a Modern Concept* (New Haven, CT: Yale University Press, 2007), 2–4.

19. Gary Gerstle, *American Crucible: Race and Nation in the Twentieth Century* (Princeton, NJ: Princeton University Press, 2001).

20. On the various social movements of the 1960s, see, for example, Maurice Isserman and Michael Kazin, *America Divided: The Civil War of the 1960s*, 2nd ed. (New York: Oxford

University Press, 2004); David Farber, ed., *The Sixties: From Memory to History* (Chapel Hill: University of North Carolina Press, 1994); Terry H. Anderson, *The Movement and the Sixties* (New York: Oxford University Press, 1995).

21. On the history of the all-volunteer military and the debates over the memory of martial valor, see, for example, Beth Bailey, *America's Army: Making the All-Volunteer Force* (Cambridge, MA: Belknap Press, 2009); Kristin Ann Hass, *Sacrificing Soldiers on the National Mall* (Berkeley: University of California Press, 2013).

22. See John W. Dower, *War without Mercy: Race and Power in the Pacific War* (New York: Pantheon, 1986).

23. Kimberlé W. Crenshaw, "Mapping the Margins: Intersectionality, Identity Politics, and Violence against Women of Color," *Stanford Law Review* 43, no. 6 (1991): 1241–1299.

24. On these developments, see Bailey, *America's Army*; Ahu Tanrisever, *Fathers, Warriors, and Vigilantes: Post-Heroism and the U.S. Cultural Imaginary in the Twenty-First Century* (Heidelberg: Winter, 2016).

25. Chollet, " 'Gallantry and Intrepidity,' " 63.

26. "Military Honors Will Be Given to Drone Operators," *New York Times*, January 7, 2016, A15.

1 • THE END OF MILITARY HEROISM?

The American Legion and "Service" between the Wars

GEORGE LEWIS

World War I wrought chaos on the Western heroic ideal. Not only were long-standing tropes of masculine, military heroism questioned in its aftermath, but so, too, was the very notion of heroism itself. On one side of the Atlantic, for example, Winston Churchill returned from the western front ready to question whether communities could dispense with "great men" and "hero worship." If the questions reflected gendered assumptions that had long been made about heroes in general, and by Churchill in particular, the need to ask them was rooted in shifts in both modern warfare and modern society. "Modern conditions do not lend themselves to the production of the heroic," Churchill surmised. "The heroes of modern war lie out in the cratered fields, mangled, stifled, scarred; and there are too many of them for exceptional honours." On the other side of the Atlantic, heroism's viability and trajectory were under equal scrutiny. In Sidney Hook's analysis, the key differentiation to be made in understanding heroism was between the "eventful man" and the "event-making man," the latter of whom was more likely to fulfil the requirements of heroism. For Hook, however, it was not modernity's mechanization of the battlefield that threatened the hero, but the expansion of participatory democracy. His "event-making man" was defined by an ability to redetermine the course of history. By the time in which he was writing, that power was increasingly deemed to lie not with a small coterie of individual men, but with the enfranchised citizenry of a democratic community, now regardless of gender. For Hook's putative hero, the "processes of democracy" were likely "a fetter upon his calling."[1]

While Churchill continued to cast around for a solution to military heroism's place in the modern world, by the end of the interwar period Hook believed that he had scented one. Modern society should not confine its definition of the heroic life to the "grandeur and nobility" most commonly associated with careers and actions that reeked with "blood and suffering." For heroism to reemerge and survive as a valuable concept, Hook argued, it should be reimagined, although, notably, not in a way that would alter its gender dynamic: "a hero," he concluded, should be "any individual who does his work well and makes a unique contribution to the public good." Developing his theme, Hook declared that "a democracy should contrive its affairs, not to give one or a few the chance to reach heroic stature, but rather to take as a regulative ideal the slogan, 'every man a hero.' We call this a 'regulative ideal,'" he summarized, "because it would be Utopian to imagine that it could ever be literally embodied."[2]

That "regulative ideal," however, did not have to remain "Utopian." For the entire interwar period, it was adopted, developed, and resourced by the American Legion. The Legion occupied a privileged position in the discourse of military heroism, not least because its members had each had personal experience of modern warfare as a prerequisite of membership, but also because of the intricate local, national, and, indeed, international network of posts of which it was comprised, and the significant lobbying operation that it developed. As will be argued here, the Legion's stance on heroism is surprising and counterintuitive, and had a major impact on the shape and tenor of discourses of American heroism—and masculinity—in the interwar period. In its view of heroism, the Legion negotiated a pathway between the complex concerns of both Churchill and Hook. It concurred with Churchill on military heroism, for example, but for subtly different reasons: where, for Churchill, the mechanical horrors of modern warfare meant that military heroism could not be celebrated, the Legion argued that it should not be. More significantly, however, and in line with Hook's "regulative ideal," the Legion strove to disassemble conventional theories of military heroism, relegating them below a sublimated ideal of heroism as "service," by which it meant the collective endeavor of citizens to build and protect both democracy and what it defined as "Americanism" in civic society. Such activity should take place, the Legion believed, with a sense of sacrifice and fervor equal to that with which veterans had fought on the battlefield for the same ideals.[3]

The Legion, in other words, sought a seismic shift in the collective American understanding of the heroic: acts of military heroism were purposefully omitted from Legion discourse. In addition, they were consciously replaced with the privileging of service to civic democracy as the new, modern heroic ideal. Reimagining heroism not as something that was achieved via hypermasculinized military bravery, but as citizenship-oriented civic service, thus effectively severed what earlier commentators have referred to as the "inherent" and "underlying theme" of the "continuing universal appeal of the myth of the warrior hero."[4] Moreover, it also brought with it an important by-product, for—at least in theory—it also effectively served to democratize heroism: under such a schema, all citizens, and not just physically strong and martially skilled white men, gained access to the potentially heroic. In that sense, the Legion's activity in the interwar era forces a further reconceptualization of American military heroism, for it suggests flaws in the mooted model of "transcendent national citizenship" that, it has been claimed, was fostered by the U.S. military along heterosexual, masculine lines.[5] Despite the importance and, above all, the scale of its work, however, the Legion's attempts to reshape American notions of heroism in the interwar period have been subjected to what might be termed symbiotic neglect—the few organization histories that do exist of the Legion fail to acknowledge its impact on the heroic ideal, and the historiography of American heroism simply fails to recognize the Legion.[6] As a result, the rationales that lay behind the Legion's position, the way in which it put that theoretical position into practice, and the effect that practice had on American notions of military heroism, gender, and identity are in need of explanation and explication.

As would be expected from such a large organization with such a multifaceted membership, those motivating factors were often complex, but can nonetheless be understood as practical, pragmatic, political, experiential, and ideological. The decision to reimagine heroism was born largely of the experiential, but also had pragmatic and ideological elements. Most decisively, the Legion shared Churchill's reading of the nonheroic nature of modern warfare: war was hell rather than heroic, and to pretend otherwise was an affront to the battlefield experience of Legionnaires, and also increased the likelihood of a return to conflict in the future.[7] Thus, for example, one Legionnaire wrote in a regular Legion publication that a mooted international agreement aimed at "more humane warfare" was, of course, "a contradiction in terms." Another, asked to identify his first "thrill" in the war, mentioned not the excitement of basic training, or embarkation, or transatlantic travel and arrival on the exotic shores of Europe, or the first close shell explosion he witnessed at the front. Rather, he realized that "I was scared, not thrilled," and said the first thrill he could recall was his eventual return—safe—to the peacetime tranquility of the New Jersey shoreline.[8]

As ideological and pragmatic corollaries, the Legion's focus on battle as a collective endeavor and its need to represent each of its members equally also led it to eschew military heroism as traditionally conceived. Thus, for example, the postwar vogue for ruminating on and ranking the "greatest" battles and "most heroic" acts of war was summarily dismissed. As an *American Legion Weekly* editorial surmised, such comparisons were odious. Soldiers fought equally as hard in side skirmishes as they did in battles that decided "the fates of a nation and of ideas," and reducing these activities to a cleanly ordered list of battles was highly inappropriate. Such a formula was "so much cold mathematics," the editorial noted, before concluding somewhat ruefully that, in the modern age, "much of war" in general was "cold mathematics and no more."[9] In terms of pragmatism, the Legion recognized that it needed to represent a diverse cross-section of members, given that the prerequisite for joining was personal experience of battles waged for the preservation of American ideals of democracy, albeit in carefully selected wars. It would, therefore, have been counterproductive to alienate vast swathes of that membership by elevating only a small number of military "heroes" in its ranks, thereby implying that the military service of all other Legionnaires had not been recognized as heroic, or, indeed, had been identified as nonheroic. That situation was all the more delicate given that a majority of the soldiers who joined the U.S. Army in 1917 to 1918 did not have the opportunity to leave the nation's shores for the European theater before an end to hostilities was declared. For those who were involved in fighting, the modern battlefield was a mechanically democratized arena, and it was a reflection of the collective nature of the Legion's response that—jarringly, as it soon turned out—Legionnaires referred to one another as "comrade." So, too, was the sense of collective military responsibility: frequent were the Legion's assertions, for example, that single regiments should not receive plaudits for particular battles, for all who served contributed an equal share.[10]

That collectivism should also be understood more broadly, however, for it also explicitly included women, and implicitly included nonwhite citizens. Indeed, a women's section was established at the very first Legion convention in 1919, although it is notable that it was labelled the "Auxiliary" and was tasked with traditionally gendered assignments such as fund-raising and children's welfare. Nonetheless, its continual growth was such that by the end of the interwar period it boasted more than 520,000 members, and the Legion's forward-thinking postwar ethos of the value in civic service, rather than a backward-looking gaze toward past battlefield heroism, allowed—at least in theory—the new version of heroism to appreciate the input of female members as much as male. In practice, Auxiliary members were often hidebound by traditionally gendered roles within that service, although the equally gendered historiography on the subject often obscures even those limited roles.[11]

Indeed, the evidence from here and elsewhere suggests that the Legion's extending to women access to possible heroism as part of a drive to reimagine heroism as civic rather than martial was a reflection of internal schisms within the organization, or—at the very least—of the extent to which the many different parts of the Legion worked at such different speeds that they were often in tension with one another. Thus, it was an unintended consequence of the "collective" aspect of heroic civic service that it repeatedly turned out to be selective. For example, although it proclaimed all citizens to be "united in a common purpose," a schools educational award initiated by the Legion outlined the judging criteria for boys as honor, courage, scholarship, leadership, and service; girls could also be judged on courage, scholarship, and service, but honor and leadership were replaced by companionship and character.[12] That should not be taken as evidence of an organization that was simply failing to reflect modernizing attitudes toward gender roles, but rather of one in which the aspiration for a more modern approach had yet to manifest itself in real change across its membership. The tension between the two positions exemplified the difficulties of enforcing a unified position on such an amorphous and sprawling organization as the Legion, and especially one so reliant upon the work of volunteers. Where, for example, the entrenched conservatism of the "kingmakers" of the Legion's central command clung to the idea of heroism as the preserve of a very masculine construction of warfare, other branches of the Legion structure, notably the National Americanism Commission (NAC), took a more forward-looking view of service that at least offered a bridge to a more egalitarian future. It was one that reflected the more participative role played by women in World War I, but was useful only if Legion posts and members were willing to take it up.

Nowhere were those tensions more graphically illustrated, and the positives that could be wrought from the adoption of service over heroism more obviously demonstrated, than in the internal confusion at the end of the 1920s that surrounded a war novel prize which was cosponsored by the Legion and the Houghton Mifflin publishing company. After rancorous internal debates between the judges, the decision was made to award the prize jointly to two authors, one of whom was Mary Lee, for her novel *It's a Great War!* The idea for running the prize grew from the obvious success of one of the Legion's main tactics to ensure the successful dissemination of its service strategy—a series of annual school essay writing competitions on self-consciously "patriotic" topics. Those competitions saw 50,000 school children take part in 1922, 330,000 just two years later, and a staggering six million students from four thousand communities in 1934. While the judging of those contests remained firmly under the Legion's control, the mixed economy of judges from the literary, publishing, and Legion worlds that was assembled for the war novel competition exposed the organization's continuing internal divide over gender. Lee emerged as a compromise winner. Her book, which was originally titled *The Farce*, described in 574 pages of disjointed, jolting, staccato prose a battlefield that was chaotic rather than controlled, and also had women at the heart of the theater of war. Most pointedly, perhaps, Lee's main protagonist encountered soldiers so disillusioned with the very process of war that the novel threatened not only the idea of a martial hero, but also the collectivist ideal of camaraderie. It was a view of warfare that collided headlong with the conservatism of many in the Legion's national leadership structure who wished to continue to curate a view of heroism as a masculine martial act. At the same time, it reinforced the strategic need for the adoption of service as a means to obviate the internal tensions surrounding gender, memory, and heroism that continued to exist in Legion ranks.[13]

It is in the context of the collective sense of responsibility that the sublimation of heroic "service" at the expense of a more traditional, martial heroism had its most significantly gendered impact. On one hand, for those who continued to view heroism as attainable only in a male, martial domain, "service" allowed the heroic ideal to be more easily attainable by women. On the other hand, it offered an avenue for rescuing male veterans' postwar manhood, for, viewed through the classical lens of a hypermasculinized military heroism, it was increasingly clear that many soldiers were being emasculated by what they were—and were not—able to achieve on the modern battlefield, due to war's growing mechanization and expansive scale. That battlefield, which had long offered the greatest arena in which manhood could—and should—be performed, instead threatened manhood's ideals and the possibilities of its performance, as exemplified by the decision of psychiatrists to diagnose and treat shell shock as "the result of insufficient manliness."[14] Transferring the heroic from the martial to the civic therefore offered—at least theoretically—positive opportunities to both men and women.

In a strategy that brought all of its various objectives together, the Legion directed its energies at a program that sought to celebrate and institutionalize the idea of "service," while simultaneously both developing a usable alternative to the narratives of military heroism from which it sought to distance itself and allowing itself to harness the collective ethos that had been forged in wartime. The main strategy by which the Legion sought to transfer its shifting aspirations from military heroism to heroic civic service was to maintain the collective ethos that had underpinned Legionnaires' war efforts, but to do so for civic rather than martial ends; this was, in the Legion's phrase, "carrying on." That signal shift has been routinely missed by those who have focused on the high political stakes of the Legion's lobbying efforts in Washington, D.C., and by those who have sought to understand the organization's work by studying only those parts of its machinery that kept, or sought to keep, a national profile, in particular the "kingmakers" of its command structure and the *American Legion* magazine, which first appeared weekly and then monthly. Such a focus offers a top slice of an organization of far greater complexity, texture, and depth. Many Legionnaires, for example, paid more attention to the NAC's publication of *The Huddle,* which looked inward to reflect the rank-and-file membership of the organization in a more thoroughly democratic and representative way than did the glossier, outward-looking *American Legion Monthly.* As the very first issue of *The Huddle* made clear, "We have 'made the world safe for democracy.'

Now to keep democracy safe for itself."[15] Once more, Legionnaires saw themselves as being in a unique position to oversee this transformation in the way heroism was understood; after all, in the words of National Commander Raymond J. Kelly, their organization was composed of those who "had taken their post-graduate course in citizenship" whilst fighting in the forces.[16] So enthusiastically was that point made that it overlooked a central tenet of Legion identity. Referring to them as "ex-service men" was "a misnomer," for they were still dedicated to providing service: "civilian service, to be sure, but service just as effective and far-reaching in our battle for the preservation of American ideals and principles as wartime service."[17]

In order to ensure that its core message—that active civic service was both comparable to, and a direct replacement for, traditional notions of heroic military service—was transmitted to as wide a constituency as possible, the Legion poured its considerable resources into a series of initiatives, ranging from the redevelopment of school curricula to the reshaping of public commemorations of wartime service and sacrifice. In addition to *The Huddle* and a slew of handbooks, official magazines, populist newsletters, lectures, and pronouncements from its annual conventions, NAC chairman Garland W. Powell produced a book-length study in 1924, *"Service" for God and Country,* which was originally intended as a high school text but soon found wider appeal.[18] The ideas of "carrying on" and "service" were paramount in Powell's endeavor, as was the development of the theme that service had become so essential because it was the United States alone that had safeguarded "civilization." As citizens, Powell wrote, Legionnaires had "finally" and "most gloriously" taken up "the defense of civilization and thereby saved, to the best of our knowledge and belief, the civilization of the world." With news of the death of former president Wilson, who, having passed on, was described as sleeping "with the thousands who died for democracy's fulfillment," and with the passage of time diminishing the number of both Civil War and slouch hat–wearing Spanish-American War veterans, the Legion increasingly believed that its members, and only its members, could perform the heroic act of safeguarding democratic civilization. Thus, Legionnaires' active engagement would remain central to civilization's future once the war had ended: "They are devoted to the service of the nation, having offered themselves against its enemies."[19]

At first glance, the Legion's strategic privileging of civic service over traditional notions of heroic military service jarred with its desire to establish itself as the controlling force of public commemoration of wartime service and sacrifice. To elide its priorities smoothly, the Legion deployed significant capital outlay in reshaping public understanding of the process of wartime commemoration, emphasizing commemoration's role as central to the idea of civic service via sections of the *Service* handbook, articles and editorials in its more regular publications, and executive strategy documents emanating from its annual national conventions. In particular, the Legion strove to take ownership of Armistice Day, which its national Americanism director referred to openly as "the Legion's own holiday," and Memorial Day, the observance of which, one of its publications noted, "is becoming largely a responsibility of the American Legion as each year the ranks of Civil war [*sic*] veterans grows thinner," and at which thousands of Legion posts took an active annual part.[20] Throughout the 1920s and the early 1930s, the Legion made strenuous efforts to ensure that those days' activities reflected the organization's ethos of service and, equally, avoided the temptation of privileging heroism. Preparing for the tenth anniversary of the signing of the armistice, for example, NAC director Dan Bowers declared that "The day should be made to convey a lesson in patriotism and Americanism to the entire community and should bring home the fact that after ten years the men who fought in the World War still hold true to the ideals and purposes for which they served." A three-page "Armistice Day—After Ten Years" special produced by the Legion included suggestions for a lavishly detailed program of celebrations that drew deeply on camaraderie and remembrance, and glossed over wartime heroism entirely.[21] By the end of the decade, the Legion used the build-up to Armistice Day not only to remind its posts of the day's significance, but also to remind Legionnaires to use the day "to show the people of its community that it is an all-inclusive organization of World war veterans, banded together to maintain the comradeship of the war and to continue in peace-time service to community, state and nation." When legislation was finally passed, in 1938, to enshrine Armistice Day as a national public holiday, the Legion's lobbyists took full credit.[22]

The Legion, it became clear, wished to be instrumental in shaping the tone, register, and tenor of the nation's wartime commemoration, to ensure that it would center around community service rather than the elevation of heroes.[23] It was equally clear that, wherever possible, the organization wished to transform national holidays into commemorative events that were in line with its own agenda. With Arbor Day, for example, the Legion took steps to bring uniformity to an event that had traditionally fallen on different days in different states, depending upon local climatic conditions, and which tended not to be linked to military commemoration. Under the Legion's aegis, it was to become a day on which trees would be planted to represent those comrades who had "fallen for the cause of world freedom," and which should therefore simultaneously commemorate that loss and celebrate the democratic freedom for which they fell. Each community should plant trees to commemorate its dead "citizens," and should do so by "planting, with suitable ceremonies, groves or avenues of trees which should serve as incentives to civic progress and betterment."[24] Elsewhere, Legion posts proclaimed themselves to be "the logical organization to lead the community" in celebrating the Fourth of July, because Legionnaires had "proved their patriotism in a way beyond all dispute" and were "the recognized leaders in patriotic activities," and "other citizens naturally look to them for leadership in the observance of the greatest patriotic holiday of the year."[25] Perhaps more obviously, Flag Day became, in the Legion's eyes, core to commemorating war as "the price that has been paid for human liberty," leading to a zealous promotion of its own Flag Code, of which 386,956 copies were distributed in a single year.[26] At almost every turn, the prescriptive guidelines that the Legion routinely produced for commemorative events tied to these national holidays included a reference to the reading of the Gettysburg Address, which, of course, preempted the Legion's view that all those who gave their lives in devotion for the freedom of the nation should be honored collectively, rather than remembered piecemeal for individual acts of heroism.[27]

When the Legion did make qualitative distinctions between wartime service, it was not between the heroic and the nonheroic, but between those who had been willing to give such service—patriots, all of whom were worthy of Legion membership—and the few "slackers" who did not. Indeed, it became a core tenet of Legion discourse and strategy in the interwar period to continue to identify and deride slackers long after the armistice, as part of the process of sublimating all service, rather than just the heroic. This culminated in drives to ensure the identification, capture, and adequate sentencing of those who had refused to serve.[28] The fact that the Legion fine-tuned its understanding of the slacker by creating distinct subcategories of the genre further exemplifies the importance of its view of service. Indeed, because peacetime civic service had been identified by the Legion as the replacement for wartime heroism, radical, alien, or religious slackers filled the oppositional void created by the armistice, while being fueled by the social, political, economic, and migratory dislocations of the immediate postwar era. Slacker groups and individuals were identified by the Legion in two ways: either as primarily radicals who exhibited a slacker ethos secondarily because pacifism was one of many ideological positions that they espoused, or as primarily slackers whose "slacker ethic" was key to defining their radicalism.[29]

The most obvious manifestation of those identified as "secondary" slackers by a multitude of printed Legion materials was the influx of "new wave" immigrants who were the target of much of the nativism that pervaded the immediate aftermath of the war. Many in the Legion chose to describe interwar radicalism as a foreign-born threat, which allowed them to argue, for example, that neither slackerism nor radicalism were part of the ideology of Americanism, and therefore had no place in the civic democracy that the organization was trying to uphold.[30] Far more important were the "primary" slacker groups, the clearest example of which was the Women's Peace Union (WPU), which, due to its single-minded push for the political outlawing of war, was identified as the Legion's bête noir. The case of the WPU also sheds light on the way the

Legion's treatment of martial heroism intersected with contemporary gender concerns. For the Legion, service was required to preserve civilization, and the WPU's pacifism threatened anarchy. An official report to the fifth annual convention of the Legion noted the symbiotic relationship between government and governed: indeed, a "contract" had been formed whereby the former guaranteed the latter benefits including security, while the latter's obligations included support and maintenance of the former. "Forgetfulness or disregard of this obligation," the Legion report noted, "is the greatest menace to the American State and to American civilization today." Thus, the antiwar pledge designed by the WPU "is anarchy pure and simple." In the wake of a presidential executive order that saw "political prisoners" including "slackers," pacifists, and draft dodgers from the war era released, the Legion's Americanism commissioner was blunt. "To my mind," he noted, "there is an exact analogy between releasing a war criminal and releasing a murderer; to give the former his liberty after the war in which his offense is committed seems identical to releasing a murderer merely because his victim is dead and cannot be killed again."[31]

It was not insignificant that when it came to formalizing an active and political response to the slacker ethos of the Women's Peace Union, the task was designated to the Legion's Women's Auxiliary, which organized a conference, "National Defense as Peace Insurance," with the primary purpose of combating the "Slacker's Pledge" of the WPU.[32] The role of women on either side of the debate was complex. The progressive notion that women were just as capable of providing heroic service (under its new terms) as men was often undermined by the specifics of the role that the Auxiliary was asked to play, for the service it was allowed to provide was often deeply gendered, being limited to, for example, fund-raising drives via "strawberry festivals" with much of the raised funds earmarked for limited use in youth work, child welfare, and rehabilitation. Likewise, although in theory the Legion's co-option of Mary Roberts Rinehart to its "service" campaigns appeared to be a positive development for the equality of gendered roles—since she had served as the *Saturday Evening Post*'s correspondent on the Belgian front during World War I—in practice, Rinehart's attraction for the Legion lay mainly in her other work, including her 1920 essay "Isn't That Just Like a Man!," which the Legion quoted in one of its publications: "We need men, not only prepared to defend this country in case of war, but physically fit and disciplined to be efficient citizens in time of peace."[33]

Such a view, too, lends itself to a reading of the Legion's economic response to the Depression, which at least attempted to rescue manhood for those who, on the one hand, had been denied the opportunity of traditional military heroism by the mechanization and brutality of modern warfare, and, on the other, were further emasculated by their economic inability to provide for their families. Thus, for example, as part of its emphasis on civic service, after the onset of the

Depression the Legion initiated a "Find a Buddie a Job" campaign that called upon the same "high civic duty" that had underlined Legionnaires' wartime service. "The responsibility for that civic duty has reached a peak," National Commander Ralph T. O'Neil noted in December 1930, "and should be met with the same fortitude and courage that was displayed during war time."[34] It left a complicated gender situation, balancing the potentially energizing masculinity to be gained by one Legionnaire knowing that he could once again be a provider with the potentially emasculating knowledge that such a role was possible only because of the beneficence and charity of a comrade, who, in turn, could draw upon the masculinity associated with "saving" a comrade. In such a circumstance, altering the prism through which heroism was viewed in order to include fulsome civic service—which could be carried out with or without gainful employment—offered a positive escape to the emasculated, even if its theoretical promise rang hollow for women.

The promise of egalitarianism that the Legion offered to women who subscribed to its view of service may have been hollow in absolute terms, but as contemporary critics were wont to suggest, its progressivism was significant in relative terms. Indeed, as the ideological terrain of the 1930s became more complex, satirizing the gender views of Legion opponents became a useful tool for the organization's adherents. A number of Legionnaires had evidently long found it galling, for example, that the move away from the valorization of martial heroism had allowed the organization to be depicted as a pacifist force, not least because many of its most obdurate foes on the radical Left were pilloried because of their pacifist, slacker ethos. As a second global conflict began to appear increasingly inevitable in the second half of the 1930s, Legion ideology tangibly shifted. Now, elements within the organization's hierarchy began to turn once again to the needs of the battlefield, although they did so by couching their concerns in language describing the necessities of "preparedness" rather than any opportunity for martial glory. Such a linguistic shift provided the comfort of clear water between the position of the Legion and that of many of its ideological foes, who returned instead to accusing its members of being little more than warmongering lobbyists. In response, Frederick Palmer, who maintained a regular profile in the Legion's interwar publications (having served as a press officer to the American Expeditionary Force), sought to draw further distinctions between Legionnaires and their critics on the radical Left by undermining the gender politics of such groups in general, and the Communist Party of the United States of America (CPUSA)—sponsored American League Against War and Fascism (ALAWF) in particular. In a long essay, Palmer carefully reported the way Legionnaires had been portrayed in ALAWF publications: in a scene imagined by ALAWF propagandists as a second global conflict loomed, it fell to the Legionnaire father to tell his young sons, each of whom had been too young to have been conscripted in previous wars, not to worry, for "You'll have your chance yet, to be in a war." The ALAWF's take on the role of the Legionnaire's wife was wholly at odds with any sense of the egalitarianism offered by the Legion's civic service. Perhaps one of their sons would not return with "more wound stripes" than his father, the ALAWF had her musing, but might be killed heroically. "Then think how your grave will be covered with flowers on Decoration Day," continued the mother, "and your name will be on a bronze plaque in the Town Hall—and how proud I shall be to be a Gold Star mother!"[35]

Military heroism as classically understood—individual feats of death-defying bravery most often carried out by white men—had been threatened for some time by the modernization and mechanization of warfare, but in the interwar decades, the close memory of techniques of mass, indiscriminate, and remote slaughter left the very idea of military heroism in jeopardy. If, in the American consciousness, that change had begun with the American Civil War, the Legion's realization that the parameters of heroism should be altered away from the battlefield and toward civic service represented clear evidence of the apparent finality of that shift. It was a shift that intentionally widened the parameters of those able and, indeed, expected to offer "service" to their nation, although the significant effects it had on interpretations of gender were largely unintentional. In that context, the development of the idea of service represented a strategic move to sustain the momentum of wartime patriotism and camaraderie, while simultaneously avoiding the increasingly contested and fractious view of wartime heroism that was liable to raise its head in internal debates such as those about the positioning of gender, or those that followed the 1929 war novel imbroglio. Finally, although the organization's impact on the contemporary discourse surrounding gender remains a matter of scholarly neglect, as does the historical and historiographical understanding of the United States's largest veterans organization, it is clear from the evidence that both were of signal significance in real terms: the Legion had the power to lobby for legislation that aided it in its reimagining of the idea of service, and did so; it had the power to alter the broader public understanding of the commemoration of wartime service and sacrifice, and did so; it had the power to remodel the nation's understanding of gender in its relationship to heroism explicitly, but it did not. Nonetheless, its interwar campaigns fractured any possibility of a single, smoothly arcing trajectory in the narrative discourses of U.S. military heroism.

NOTES

1. Winston Churchill, "Mass Effects in Modern Life" (speech, 1925), National Churchill Museum, http://www.nationalchurchillmuseum.org/mass-effects-in-modern-life.html; Sidney Hook, *The Hero in History: A Study in Limitation and Possibility* (London: Secker

and Warburg, 1945), 157, 158, 164–165. Hook's study was first published in the United States in 1943.

2. Hook, *The Hero in History*, 164–165.

3. In some senses, then, the Legion sought to adhere to Theodore P. Greene's 1970 characterization of the "new style hero" as one motivated not by the attainment of personal fame, which was common to iterations of nineteenth-century Napoleonic traditions of heroism, but rather by the effects his heroic actions might have on others. The emphasis on civic service, too, brought Legionnaires closer to Greene's "hard working organizer type," although they were far from the "new bureaucratic hero" that he identified as key to heroism's World War I incarnation. Theodore P. Greene, *America's Heroes: The Changing Models of Success in American Magazines* (New York: Oxford University Press, 1970), 319–320, 324, 335.

4. This is Goffman's view, as discussed in William C. Cockerham, "Green Berets and the Symbolic Meaning of Heroism," *Urban Life* 8, no. 1 (1979): 96.

5. Holly Allen, "Gender, Sexuality, and the Military Model of U.S. National Community," in *Gender Ironies of Nationalism: Sexing the Nation*, ed. Tamar Mayer (New York: Routledge, 2000), 309–310.

6. For works on the American Legion, see William Pencak, *For God & Country: The American Legion, 1919–1941* (Boston: Northeastern University Press, 1989); Thomas A. Rumer, *The American Legion: An Official History, 1919–1989* (New York: M. Evans and Company, 1990); and Raymond Moley Jr., *The American Legion Story* (New York: Duell, Sloan and Pearce, 1966). None mention the National Americanism Commission's *The Huddle*, which was an essential driving force for its campaigns to promote heroic service. Stephen R. Ortiz, *Beyond the Bonus March and GI Bill: How Veteran Politics Shaped the New Deal Era* (New York: New York University Press, 2010) focuses on the Legion as a lobbying force in matters pertaining to political economy and neglects the organization's parallel work on service. For a cross-section of works on heroism that fail to acknowledge the Legion's role, see, for example, Greene, *America's Heroes*; Hook, *The Hero in History*; Anthony Synnott, *Re-Thinking Men: Heroes, Villains and Victims* (Farnham, UK: Ashgate, 2009); Michael Kimmel, *Manhood in America: A Cultural History*, 3rd ed. (New York: Oxford University Press, 2012); Frank J. Barrett, "The Organizational Construction of Hegemonic Masculinity: The Case of the U.S. Navy," in *The Masculinities Reader*, ed. Stephen M. Whitehead and Frank J. Barrett (Cambridge, UK: Polity Press, 2001), 77–99; E. Anthony Rotundo, *American Manhood: Transformations in Masculinity from the Revolution to the Modern Era* (New York: Basic Books, 1993); John Lash, *The Hero: Manhood and Power* (New York: Thames and Hudson, 1995); George Lipsitz, "The Culture of War," *Critical Survey* 18, no. 3 (2006): 83–91; Selwyn W. Becker and Alice H. Eagly, "The Heroism of Women and Men," *American Psychologist* 59, no. 3 (April 2004): 163–178.

7. Tellingly, even an advertisement for a lamp with a base fashioned from a statue of an American "doughboy" soldier, which was tailored to the readership of an official Legion publication, sought to capture an audience with the strap line, "It Was Hell!" *American Legion Weekly*, February 2, 1923, 24. Copies are available to researchers at the American Legion Library (hereafter cited as TAL Library), American Legion National Headquarters, Indianapolis.

8. "ENS" of Hartford, Connecticut, letter to "Voice of the Legion" letters page, *American Legion Weekly*, July 14, 1922, 1; Edward M. Cobb, letter to "More Greatest War Thrills" column, *American Legion Weekly*, February 23, 1923.

9. Editorial, *American Legion Weekly*, September 26, 1924, 8.

10. Thus, when Legion posts were asked to prepare for an upcoming anniversary of the Battle of Belleau Wood, which historians termed "the turning point of the war," a Legion

publication noted that in written accounts, "the glory has always gone to the Marines," yet in a democratizing gesture that was common to its postwar publications, the Legion added the caveat that Legionnaires, at least, knew that "the infantry did its equal share." "An Idea for June Meeting," *The Huddle* 3, no. 5 (1930): 3. Copies of *The Huddle* are available to researchers at TAL Library. On the proportion of soldiers who did not travel overseas, see Steven Trout, *On the Battlefield of Memory: The First World War and American Remembrance, 1919–1941* (Tuscaloosa: University of Alabama Press, 2010), 26.

11. "The Legion: What It Is Doing, What It Has Done," *American Legion Weekly*, February 1, 1924, 8–9. There is no mention of the Auxiliary in William Pencak's academic monograph *For God and Country: The American Legion, 1919–1941* (Boston: Northeastern University Press, 1989). For a typically gendered general history, see, for example, Moley, *The American Legion Story*, where he explains Americans' response to Pearl Harbor as one in which "their ill-equipped manhood [was] tried and found flint-hard, resourceful and manly" (241). J. Edgar Hoover contributed a foreword and a blurb for the dust jacket.

12. "United for a Common Purpose," *The Huddle* 6, no. 3 (1933): 2–3. When this award was first announced at the end of the 1920s, it was to celebrate "the highest purpose" to which the Legion could "devote" itself, namely, "the cultivation of high character and wholesome ideals in the youth coming to citizenship." "The Legion School Award," *The Huddle* 2, no. 2 (1929): 3.

13. For the essay contests, see "2nd National Essay Contest," May 25, 1923; "State Winners in American Legion's National Essay Contest Are Announced," January 18, 1924; "Youth Speaks to America," July 4, 1924; "Puncturing the Windy Bag of Communism," May 22, 1925; Norman L. Marks, "The American Legion Looks at Youth," October 29, 1935, all in the *American Legion Monthly*. For the war novel contest, see Mary Lee, *It's a Great War!* (New York: Houghton Mifflin, 1929); Trout, *On the Battlefield of Memory*, 103–105.

14. Kimmel, *Manhood in America*, 99.

15. "Why the Post Should Interest Itself in a Good Government Campaign," *The Huddle* 1, no. 1 (1928). For a study that concentrates on the political economy of veteran politics and the Legion's lobbying, see Ortiz, *Beyond the Bonus March and GI Bill*, esp. ch. 1.

16. Raymond J. Kelly, "Let's Outlaw It," *American Legion Monthly*, March 1940, 16–17, 44.

17. "Armistice Day Suggestions," *The Huddle* 6, no. 10 (1933): 2. As *The Huddle* sought to remind those who might have forgotten, "When the World war ended, the citizen soldiers in the armed forces of the United States, men who fought and suffered and risked their all for the preservation of our ideals of government, formed The American Legion for the purpose of carrying on their unselfish service in peace time. Their objectives were to uphold and promote those ideals to the end that citizenship, democracy and American institutions would be advanced. They adopted a code of patriotism to define their purposes and for their guidance. A part of that code reads, 'To safeguard and transmit to posterity the principles of justice, freedom and democracy.' These three principles embrace all that is best in American national life." "Why Junior Baseball?," *The Huddle* 4, no. 2 (1931): 3.

18. Garland W. Powell, *"Service" for God and Country* (Indianapolis, IN: Cornelius Printing Company, 1924).

19. Powell, *Service*, 64–65; National Commander, "Memorial Day—Its Inner Meaning," *American Legion Weekly*, May 30, 1924, 6. As well as the ideological side to Powell's efforts, there was a harder edge of pragmatism, too. Keen to distance the organization from claims in some quarters that, at its inception, it represented little more than a "money-hungry band of mercenaries" intent upon a single-issue campaign of adjusted compensation for World War I veterans that amounted to "a selfish national conspiracy to get a 'bonus,'" the Legion increased its emphasis on its service work. The adjusted compensation campaign,

it claimed, was just one plank in a wider platform, just as Cantigny and Château-Thierry were single battles rather than the entire war effort. Thus, in the same year Powell issued *Service*, the *American Legion Weekly* published the article "The Legion: What It Is Doing, What It Has Done," with the clear conclusion that "Instead of being simply a compensation-chasing organization, the Legion has become recognized as a dividend-paying investment for the whole country and particularly for every community which has a Legion post" (February 1, 1924, 8–9). The Legion also maintained that much of the drive for war had been fueled by motives of profit rather than a desire for heroism. With that in mind, the labelling of Legionnaires as money-grabbing proved particularly irksome. See, for example, Senator Arthur Capper, "Compensation and a Nation's Honor," *American Legion Weekly*, September 9, 1921, 7; Editorial, *American Legion Weekly*, January 6, 1922, 12; Editorial, *American Legion Weekly*, February 29, 1924, 10.

20. "Memorial Day," *The Huddle* 1, no. 4 (1928): 2; Dan Bowers, (untitled article), *The Huddle* 1, no. 9 (1928): 1.

21. Bowers, *The Huddle* 1, no. 9 (1928): 1.

22. "Armistice Day," *The Huddle* 2, no. 8 (1929): 1. On the Legion's role in the passage of Public Law No. 510, see "Report of National Legislative Committee," *Reports to the Twentieth Annual National Convention of The American Legion, Los Angeles, Calif., September 19, 20, 21, 22, 1938*, 1930s Convention Reports & Digests, TAL Library.

23. The Legion listed 148 possible "Community Service Activities" in 1928, for example, including "Establishing World War Museum" and building a "Memorial Archway at Cemetery Entrance," but made no mention of heroes, heroism, or their commemoration. See "Community Service Activities," *The Huddle* 1, no. 1 (1928): 4.

24. Powell, *Service*, 64; "Arbor Day," *The Huddle* 3, no. 3 (1930): 1.

25. "The Fourth of July," *The Huddle* 2, no. 6 (1929): 3.

26. National Adjutant's Report including "Flag Education," *Reports to the Twentieth Annual National Convention of The American Legion, Los Angeles, Calif., September 19, 20, 21, 22, 1938*, 73–74, 1930s Convention Reports & Digests, TAL Library.

27. "Observe the Birthdays of Washington and Lincoln," *The Huddle* 4, no. 2 (1931): 4.

28. There was, as Powell put it in the foreword to *Service*, "a great deal of insincere flag-waving" during the war, alongside "a lot of talk which meant nothing but vague, useless chatter." Powell, *Service*.

29. On the Legion's aggressive attempts to prosecute slackers, see, for example, the separate chapters on "Slackers" in *Report of the National Legislative Committee to the Third National Convention of The American Legion, October 31, November 1, 2, 1921, Kansas City, MO*, 228–230, and *Report of the National Legislative Committee to the Fourth National Convention of The American Legion, October 16, 17, 18, 19, 20, 1922, New Orleans, La.*, 214–215; both in 1920s Annual Convention Reports & Digest, TAL Library. On the distinctions among and gradations of slackers, see, for example, Will Irwin, "How Red Is America?," *American Legion Monthly*, October 1926, 14–17, 56–58; Roger Sherman Hoar, "Out of Their Own Mouths," *American Legion Monthly*, May 1939, 10–11, 42; Powell, *Service*, 144–147.

30. See especially "Providing for the Deportation of the Alien Slacker," *Summary of the Proceedings of The Second National Convention, The American Legion, Cleveland, Ohio, September 27, 28, and 29, 1920*, 43–44, 1920s Annual Convention Reports & Digest, TAL Library.

31. See "Anti-War Pledges" and "War Criminals" sections in *Fifth Annual Convention, The American Legion, San Francisco, October 15–19, 1923, Reports of National Officers, Americanism Commission, Legislative Committee, Legion Publishing Corporation, Rehabilitation Committee*, esp. 45, 47, 1920s Annual Convention Reports & Digest, TAL Library.

32. "Extreme Pacifism," *Reports to the Seventh Annual Convention of the American Legion, Omaha, Nebraska, October 5, 6, 7, 8, 9, 1925*, esp. 12, 1920s Annual Convention Reports & Digest, TAL Library.

33. Irwin S. Cobb and Mary Roberts Rinehart, *Oh! Well! You Know How Women Are! and Isn't That Just Like a Man!* (New York: George H. Doran, 1920), which includes the line, "How many hours do you think were wasted by the new Army practicing salutes in front of a mirror . . . ?"; "Mary Roberts Rinehart Is Dead; Author of Mysteries and Plays," *New York Times*, September 23, 1958, 1, 33; *The Huddle* 1, no. 5 (1928): 2.

34. "Legion Posts Urged to Aid in Employment Problem," *The Huddle* 3, no. 11 (1930): 4.

35. Palmer painstakingly sought to differentiate between pacifism (lowercase) and Pacifism (uppercase). Adherents of the former, Palmer carefully noted, wanted to prevent war but were realistic in that endeavor, and were "not in favor of our disarming until other nations will meet us at least half way"; he therefore included the Legion as "the largest pacifist organization of this class." Supporters of the latter, however, were "noisy, dreamy, exhibitionist, narrow and intolerant" Pacifists, who, despite the Legion's clear record of patriotic service, commemoration, and sacrifice, routinely depicted the organization as "glorifiers of war" and "racketeers of war." Frederick Palmer, "Peace, the Reds and the Rest of Us," *American Legion Monthly*, May 1936, 12–13, 44–47.

2 • GI JOE NISEI

The Invention of World War II's Iconic Japanese American Soldier

ELLEN D. WU

Military heroism figured centrally in rearranging the racial order of the United States in the middle decades of the twentieth century. Indeed, military heroism facilitated the spread of racial liberalism—the belief that the country's racial diversity could be most ably managed through the assimilation and integration of nonwhites into the white middle class. Minority groups, including those of Asian ancestry, found unprecedented opportunities for recognition and acceptance as bona fide Americans during and after World War II.

The astonishingly rapid evolution of Japanese Americans from "enemy aliens" to loyal citizens to "model minority" between the 1940s and the 1960s forcefully illustrates the centrality of soldierly valor to the realignment of America's racial order. In the tense weeks immediately following Japan's bombing of Pearl Harbor on December 7, 1941, President Franklin Delano Roosevelt issued Executive Order 9066. With it, he authorized the removal and imprisonment of some 120,000 persons of Japanese ancestry residing on the Pacific Coast for the sake of "military necessity," despite the absence of evidence of fifth column activity. In authorizing, executing, and defending the constitutionality of mass removal and imprisonment, the state effectively classified each and every ethnic Japanese in the United States as "enemy aliens."[1]

Yet, quite unexpectedly, by the war's end in 1945, many Americans lauded Japanese Americans for their courageous sacrifices on and off the battlefield. Some 33,000 Nisei (second-generation ethnic Japanese immigrants)[2] served in various capacities, including the Women's Army Corps, Air Force, Quartermaster Corps, the Military Intelligence Service Language School, Army Map Service, Office of Strategic Services, and Office of War Information. The

Army's all-Nisei 442nd Regimental Combat Team, one of the most decorated units in U.S. history, amassed a combined 7 Presidential Unit Citations, 18,143 individual citations, and 9,486 casualties, totaling over 300 percent of its original infantry strength.[3]

In effect, the impressive contributions of Nisei in uniform—consummate patriots—supplanted conventional assumptions of Japanese Americans as subversive foreigners. The heroic Japanese American soldier, in turn, served as a pivotal foundation for the rise of the new, widespread typecasting of Japanese Americans as a "model minority" by the mid-1960s: an exceptional racial group distinct from the white majority but celebrated as well assimilated, upwardly mobile, politically nonthreatening, and *definitively not-black*. Since then, the model minority stereotype has been a fixture of the nation's racial topography and a pillar of racial common sense.

How exactly did this happen? That is, how did the heroic Nisei warrior become the public face of Japanese America in this period? What were the social, cultural, and political contexts, along with the public relations machinery, that allowed the *idea* of Japanese American martial patriotism—defined as unwavering loyalty to the nation demonstrated through soldiering[4]—to gain traction and circulate widely throughout the United States? Moreover, what impact did these ideas have on the postwar trajectory of the community? Delving into the process of iconizing the Japanese American soldier offers productive insight into the internal divisions, disagreements, and dynamics within the Nikkei (ethnic Japanese) community as its members grappled with the high stakes of responding to their collective incarceration by the state during World War II.

Just as vitally, this chapter explores the long-term, far-reaching benefits and costs of fashioning Japanese Americans as martial patriots. The invention of "GI Joe Nisei" underscores the historically contingent ways that race is produced and reproduced in relation to military service. At the broadest level, this history accentuates the fundamental role of war in both maintaining and eradicating human distinctions of various kinds—often simultaneously and in tension with one another. The racial order of the "post–civil rights" decades, in short, cannot be fully understood without locating its origins in the global, armed conflicts of the mid-twentieth century.

THE JAPANESE AMERICAN CITIZENS LEAGUE, MARTIAL PATRIOTISM, AND THE BIRTH OF THE NISEI SOLDIER

The iconic (male) Nisei soldier was the brainchild of the Japanese American Citizens League (JACL), the most influential Japanese American organization between the 1940s and 1960s. Select second-generation Japanese Americans born in the United States founded the JACL in the 1920s to address their collective predicament under the regime of Asiatic exclusion—the web of laws, ideas, and social practices designed to shut out "Orientals" from meaningful participation in American life. From the mid-nineteenth century through the 1960s, persons of Asian ancestry encountered myriad, stringent constraints, including prohibitions on entering the United States, naturalized citizenship, property ownership, and interracial marriage; segregated homes and schools; severely limited job prospects; and cultural dehumanization. By and large, the state and society considered ethnic Asians "aliens ineligible to citizenship": threatening, disgusting, indelibly foreign, and *definitively not-white*. Even those of the second generation, born on American soil and thus U.S. citizens by birth, had little hope for mainstream acceptance and socioeconomic advancement. From the outset, then, the JACL stressed Americanism and public relations to counter racist obstacles and improve the life opportunities of all Nikkei in the United States.[5]

Once the United States declared war against Japan on December 8, 1941, the issue of national loyalty loomed as an inescapable conundrum for each and every Japanese American. As the FBI rounded up the community's immigrant leaders, the JACL stepped into the power vacuum and acted as a self-appointed spokesorganization for all Nikkei. The League's national headquarters denounced Japan and pledged Japanese America's "fullest cooperation" with the United States. Much to the chagrin of other Nikkei, the JACL's visionaries also pushed vigorously for military enlistment as a means for Japanese Americans to prove their faithfulness to the nation. In March 1942, the War Department forbade any further induction of West Coast Nisei into the armed forces, and by July, the Selective Service System had officially designated all ethnic Japanese as "4C," or enemy aliens, rendering them ineligible for military service. JACL visionaries, anxious to reopen the doors of this important venue for proving Japanese American patriotism, pressed federal authorities to end this "unwarranted and unjust discrimination" that placed their "loyalty and allegiance" under suspicion.[6]

Such a calculation made sense given the JACL's previous success in pressing for the passage of the Nye-Lea Act (1935), which granted naturalization rights to World War I veterans of Asian ancestry. The passage of the Nye-Lea Act had shown that martial patriotism had the power to eclipse racial nativism, if only momentarily, and under circumscribed conditions. JACL officers also must have been keenly aware of the role that taking up arms in defense of the nation-state had played in assimilating myriad European ethnic groups.[7] Thus, the JACL could reasonably imagine that soldiering might again counter racial animosity and be used as proof of Nikkeis' fitness for national belonging. Enlistment would afford Japanese Americans the immediate opportunity to fulfill this highest obligation of citizenship, and hopefully force Americans to recognize Nisei as their own.

Federal authorities were persuaded by the JACL's lobbying. The liberal government officials of the War Relocation Authority (WRA), the agency that ran the internment camps, saw the war as an opportunity and a necessity to assimilate Japanese Americans into the white middle class. To them, military service seemed an especially foolproof way for internees to prove their unswerving loyalty to the nation—not to mention a visible means to counter the Japanese propaganda that the United States was fighting a "race war." Failure to provide for the reentry of Japanese Americans into mainstream society, they feared, would play right into the hands of the Axis powers. More generally, liberal thinkers and leaders invested racial reform with grave urgency: the failure of the nation to live in accordance with its professed democratic ideals endangered the country's aspirations to world leadership. Following this logic, internment could not be a permanent condition, but rather a stepping-stone to Americanization and citizenship.[8]

Upon learning the news of this plan, vocal, angry protests erupted within the camps. Sixty-three inmates at the Poston camp sent letters of protest directly to President Roosevelt stating that they would be willing to serve only when the federal government reinstated their rights as U.S. citizens. Some bitterly denounced the proposed "Jap Crow" (segregated) regiments. Others made death threats against JACL officers.[9]

Despite the objections, the Army approved the formation of an all-Nisei volunteer combat team on January 1, 1943.[10] In order to muster the troops, the WRA devised a system to differentiate between "loyal" and "disloyal" inmates whereby authorities administered a loyalty questionnaire, officially known as the "Application for Leave Clearance," to all internees over the age of seventeen to determine who among the population would be suitable for military service or for "resettlement" to new homes away from the Pacific coast. The most controversial parts of the appraisal were questions 27 and 28: "Are you willing to serve in the armed forces of the United States on combat duty, wherever ordered?" and "Will you swear unqualified allegiance to the United States of America and faithfully defend the United States from any or all attack by foreign or domestic forces, and forswear any form of allegiance or obedience to the Japanese emperor, or any other foreign government, power or organization?" Both questions sparked widespread upheaval and protests among internees, who feared the unknown consequences regardless of their responses.[11]

Among allegedly loyal internees, reaction to opportunity for military service was less than enthusiastic. Many who answered yes to both questions declined to sign up. The recruitment drive in the ten camps yielded only 1,181 volunteers, far short of the 3,000 anticipated by the War Department. After a protracted debate, the department announced the reinstatement of the draft for Japanese Americans in January 1944. Draftees would serve as replacements for the 442nd.[12]

Tensions ran high in the camps. News of the severe casualties suffered by the 100th Battalion (comprised of Hawaiian-Nisei men, and later folded into the 442nd) in Italy further eroded internee confidence in the WRA-JACL plan. The resumption of the draft was itself an admission that the volunteer combat team had failed to inspire support. Of the 315 Nisei who refused compliance, 263 were convicted and jailed, including the 63 resisters known as the Heart Mountain Fair Play Committee.[13]

The skepticism, resistance, and outright hostility toward military service within Nikkei circles, then, posed a serious stumbling block to the JACL's blueprint for guaranteeing Japanese American acceptance and assimilation. Quickly, JACL stewards realized that they would need to persuade their own community members to buy in to martial patriotism in order to see their plan come to fruition.

THE BIRTH OF "GI JOE NISEI"

To neutralize their opposition, JACL partnered with the federal government to launch an urgent publicity campaign centered around "GI Joe Nisei." The operation unfolded along two tracks. First, *within* the ethnic community, the organization needed to convince Japanese Americans themselves that military service was the key to their collective future in the United States. Given their ongoing incarceration, this was of course a highly controversial position to advocate. Second, the JACL sought to convince the nation as a whole that Japanese Americans were patriotic and loyal—as evidenced by their military service under the most extraordinary of circumstances—and thus deserving of recognition as full, entitled citizens. Both objectives (internal and external public relations) met considerable opposition, calling into question the JACL's claims to represent all Japanese Americans.

The JACL turned to intracommunity public relations to defuse the prevalent unrest among internees, especially after the 442nd began active duty in June 1944. The JACL's official organ, *Pacific Citizen*, devoted ample space to reporting Nisei combatants' exploits.[14] Another tactic was the utilization of individual soldiers to speak before camp audiences. According to the JACL, the purpose of these tours was to educate friends and family members about the "facts" of Japanese American soldiers' experiences overseas, as well as to quash rumors that Nisei soldiers were being used as "cannon fodder."[15] Yet, inmates' responses, ranging from lukewarm to antagonistic, suggest that these efforts had only limited appeal.[16]

Meanwhile, the JACL simultaneously directed its publicity efforts outward to tell the nation about Japanese Americans' battlefront contributions. In fact, the League, fearful that the war's impending shift to the Pacific front would likely lead to "greater hatred" against Nikkei, named public relations its top priority for 1944. One project that the JACL pursued with particular zeal was its use of Army Air Corps technical sergeant Ben Kuroki to personalize the Nisei soldier. The League distributed 15,000 copies of *Ben Kuroki's Story*, detailing his Nebraska upbringing and his fifty-eight completed missions as an aerial gunner over North Africa and Europe. In it, Kuroki argued that there were "two battles to fight—against the Axis and against [in]tolerance," a statement reminiscent of African Americans' "Double V" campaign. Reminding his audience of Nisei currently in the service, he proclaimed, "I do believe that loyal Americans of Japanese descent are entitled to the democratic rights which Jefferson propounded, Washington fought for, and Lincoln died for."[17]

In many ways, the interests of the JACL and the state merged in publicizing the contributions of Nisei soldiers. JACL national secretary Mike Masaoka personified this intersection. As public relations officer for the 442nd, he generated more than 2,700 stories about his comrades in action during his tenure. Masaoka recalled that his primary objective as the regiment's media contact was to highlight their "volunteer[ism] as an example of democracy in action . . . a chance to prove our Americanism."[18]

Federal officials, too, had a vested interest in touting the accomplishments of Nisei troops in the face of formidable stakes. In addition to their desire to offset international criticisms that the nation was fighting a race war, political leaders remained wedded to using internment and resettlement as vehicles for Nikkei assimilation. State narratives framed Nisei service as heroic efforts to save democracy in order to prime whites to welcome Japanese Americans as fellow patriots and future colleagues, neighbors, and friends. Take, for example, the informational booklet *Nisei in Uniform*, issued in October 1944 by the Department of the Interior (the WRA's parent agency) in conjunction with the War Department. Prefaced by President Roosevelt's declaration that "no loyal citizen of the United States should be denied the democratic right to exercise the responsibilities of his citizenship, regardless of his ancestry," *Nisei in Uniform* embraced racial liberalism's tenets, emphasizing that "men whose parents come from Japan are showing that devotion to America and gallantry in action are not determined by the slant of the eyes or color of the skin." It noted that the Nisei fought not only to defeat the Axis, but also to "prove" that there was no difference "in attitude or loyalty" between Japanese Americans and other citizens. Scores of photographs displayed "American soldiers with Japanese faces"—including the famous Ben Kuroki—in the field, at rest, and on leave. In addition to the 442nd and 100th, the publication also featured Marines, Coast Guard, and Women's Army Corps members juxtaposed with newspaper and magazine snippets from around the country praising enlisted Nisei.[19] The overall effect was not only to Americanize the Nisei but also, more grandly, to elevate all Japanese American wartime service to the level of national heroism.

The popular press proved amenable to this campaign. Just days after the military announced that it would begin to draft Nisei, *Life* featured "American hero" Yoshinao "Turtle" Omiya, a Hawai'i-born veteran blinded in combat. The same week, both the *Los Angeles Times* and *Time* ran celebratory profiles of Ben Kuroki, emphasizing his Americanism. *Crisis,* the magazine of the National Association for the Advancement of Colored People (NAACP), editorialized that "our fellow citizens of Japanese ancestry . . . deserve every line" of this publicity, lamenting only that African American soldiers were not receiving the same type of favorable reporting. These depictions indicate that the liberal notion of accepting Japanese Americans as heroic members of the national community had started to gain a toehold among white and black Americans during the latter part of the war.[20]

Still, significant numbers of Americans remained hostile to these messages. Paradoxically, one of the most visible opportunities for alerting the public to Japanese American sacrifice stemmed from an attempt to deny recognition to Nisei soldiers. In November 1944, the Hood River, Oregon, post of the American Legion removed the names of Nisei enlistees from the town's honor roll. The erasure generated a flurry of local and national criticism, with some 300 GIs writing to the *Hood River News* in protest. New York City's American Legion Brooks post extended an invitation to the deleted Nisei to join their ranks.[21] In denouncing the Hood River post's decision, mainstream publications reminded readers of the exemplary patriotism of Nisei in the military and their deservedness of full membership in the nation.[22]

Nisei soldiers could not avoid being identified on the basis of race. But the second half of the war marked a turning point when many whites did not automatically construe the differences that they perceived between themselves and Japanese Americans as negative or threatening. Journalists, social observers, and state authorities increasingly identified singularizing characteristics among Nisei as strikingly complimentary. Racial liberalism's arrival had opened up the possibility not for expunging racial distinction but, rather, for recasting the alien into assimilable racial Others. The *American Mercury* (1945) did precisely that in finding the Nisei to be uniquely set apart from other troops by virtue of their "superior soldiership," evinced by the unusual phenomenon of "AWOL-in-reverse"—wounded men who left their hospital wards to resume fighting before having fully recuperated.[23] In July 1946, thousands turned out to witness the 442nd parade through the streets of Washington, D.C., en route to receiving one of the first Presidential Distinguished Unit Citations from President Truman. The same year, Mississippi journalist Hodding Carter received a Pulitzer Prize for "Go for Broke," his essay foregrounding the valor of Nisei troops in a passionate plea to the nation to accept Japanese Americans as equals.[24] What had been unthinkable at the time of the Pearl Harbor bombing was now surprisingly within reach.

MEMORIALIZING THE NISEI SOLDIER

Martial patriotism successfully revamped the public image of Japanese Americans by the end of World War II, but this turnaround alone did not ensure Nikkei equal treatment as full citizens as they resumed their lives outside the camps. Many struggled to locate housing, find employment, and recreate their households and community networks in the face of racial antagonism. Japanese Americans returning to rural areas on the Pacific coast, especially, confronted shootings and arson attempts by white vigilantes. Nativists sought to rekindle anti-Japanese animosity with Proposition 15, which would have made the Alien Land Law (originally passed in 1913 to deny Japanese immigrant farmers the right to purchase land) a permanent fixture of the California state constitution.[25]

Fearing backlash, the JACL redoubled its external public relations efforts to jumpstart legislative reforms to secure the social and political footings of Japanese Americans. The League pursued the repeal of race-based exclusions in immigration and naturalization law, reparations for losses incurred during incarceration, nullification of discriminatory legislation targeting Japanese and other racial minorities, and statehood for the territory of Hawaiʻi, where Japanese comprised the largest ethnic group. The JACL hoped to convince lawmakers to undo the remaining vestiges of exclusion by lobbying for Issei (first-generation immigrants from Japan) naturalization rights and other forms of inclusion as the reward for Niseis' undeniable sacrifices on the battlefield. To do so, they coordinated a host of commemoration activities: rechristening the Army troop ship *USAT Wilson Victory* as *USAT Pvt. Sadao Munemori* in honor of the posthumous Nisei recipient of the Congressional Medal of Honor; staging memorial services at the first burial of Japanese American war heroes at Arlington National Cemetery (1948); and designating October 30 as "Nisei Soldier Memorial Day."[26]

Incidences of discrimination continued to present additional opportunities to energize narratives of Japanese American martial patriotism. Cemeteries bound by racially restrictive covenants in Orange County, California, Denver, Washington, D.C., and Chicago declined to bury Nisei veterans. The JACL countered by emphasizing the soldiers' entitlement to equal treatment in death as in life. In the case of Distinguished Service Cross recipient Kazuo Masuda, denied burial in Santa Ana, California, the JACL effectively called on Army general Mark Clark to pressure the offending cemetery to relent.[27]

Journalist Drew Pearson drew national attention to the issue during an ABC radio broadcast in January 1949. Pearson remarked, "Now the bodies of the heroic 442nd regiment are being shipped home, and the once big-hearted city of Chicago today refuses to give these men a final resting place. These men were good enough to die for their country. But because of Chicago's after-death discrimination law, they are not good enough to be buried in Chicago." The *Chicago Daily News* quickly sided with Pearson. The Mayor's Commission on Human Relations immediately moved with the JACL and the Chicago Council Against Racial Discrimination to rectify the situation, with the latter coordinating a letter-writing campaign to area graveyard operators and city and state officials. Within weeks, the pressure persuaded Mount Hope Cemetery to permit deceased Nikkei veterans—although other owners, notably, remained unwilling.[28]

The pinnacle of the JACL's public relations blitz was *Go for Broke!* (1951), the Metro-Goldwyn-Mayer movie that chronicled the valor of the famed 442nd all-Nisei battalion on the European front. Tellingly, Masaoka served as "special consultant" during production. The moral of the tale was that Japanese Americans had proved beyond a doubt their Americanism through their "baptism of blood." The movie opened with great fanfare in Washington, D.C., Honolulu, Los Angeles, and Tokyo. The mayor of Cincinnati, Ohio, even declared a "Go for Broke" week in May to honor the city's Nisei veterans. Metro-Goldwyn-Mayer advertised the movie heavily and even distributed lesson plans to schools to enhance students' viewings. In a descriptive and prescriptive review for the Japanese American magazine *Scene* (1951), *Pacific Citizen* editor Larry Taijiri proclaimed, "The picture is a heartwarming tribute to a group of young Americans who went to war to fight two foes, the enemy in the field and racial bigotry at home—and won both battles."[29]

The figure of the brave and loyal Nisei soldier wound through all of the JACL's postwar lobbying efforts. As the JACL's Washington representative and public relations guru, Masaoka testified before President Harry S. Truman's Committee on Civil Rights, numerous congressional hearings, and in amicus curiae briefs filed with the Supreme Court on behalf of the organization and Japanese America as a whole. Without fail, he shrewdly conjured up Nisei martial patriotism to suggest that continued discrimination against Japanese Americans would "threaten those fundamental concepts of decent living that so many fought for overseas." As a complement to GI Joe Nisei, Masaoka often invoked the plight of immigrant "Gold Star mothers"—women who selflessly sacrificed their sons to war, yet were still barred from naturalized citizenship, property ownership, and other rights—to buttress his calls for Japanese American equality. The recognition of Gold Star mothers provided a compelling, if secondary, means for Japanese American *women*—alongside their men—to claim full citizenship as virtuous maternal nurturers of family and nation.[30]

These arguments won over many policy makers and organizations, as well as countless ordinary Americans. The JACL led the push for a string of legal and legislative victories, including the defeat of California's Proposition 15 (1946), which would have made the 1913 Alien Land Law a permanent fixture of the state constitution; the passage of Public Law 213 (1947), allowing Japanese war brides to enter the United States; Public Law 863 (1948), conceding to Japanese nationals the right to petition the attorney general to suspend deportation orders; *Oyama v. California* (1948) and *Takahashi v. California Fish and Game Commission* (1948), both of which upheld the application of the Fourteenth Amendment for Issei "aliens ineligible to citizenship"; the Japanese American Evacuation Claims Act (1948), granting modest compensation for imprisonment-related losses; and the JACL's crown jewel, the McCarran-Walter Act (1952), which finally allowed ethnic Japanese to become naturalized citizens and the resumption of immigration from Japan.[31]

The JACL similarly mobilized the warrior icon to champion the admission of Hawai'i to statehood—a gesture that the League's spokesmen believed would elevate the territory's residents (the majority of whom were of Asian ancestry) from second- to first-class citizenship. The JACL stressed that the Nisei of Hawai'i had earned statehood for their home through their participation in the armed forces. As Mike Masaoka asserted before the Senate Committee on Interior and Insular Affairs in 1953, "They have purchased with their blood . . . equal status not only as individual Japanese-Americans but also for their homeland, the Territory of Hawaii." Statehood should thus be "a recognition of the magnificent gallantry in combat which won for them the admiration of every group with whom they were associated."[32]

That prominent political leaders, including successive secretaries of the interior, military officials, representatives, and senators, continually glorified the "splendid" combat performance of Nikkei in World War II and Korea throughout the statehood debates suggests a burgeoning accord on their racialization as praiseworthy, loyal heroes in arms. Its salience in these testimonies also presaged the symbol's enduring power, utility, and flexibility—all traits that enabled it to reach beyond the immediate concerns of Japanese Americans to impact the nation's racial order as a whole.

THE JAPANESE AMERICAN SOLDIER AND THE ORIGINS OF THE MODEL MINORITY MYTH

The persistence of racial liberalism in the 1950s and 1960s constituted the conditions for GI Joe Nisei to keep reappearing in popular discourse. The Japanese American veteran and his family and community seemed to confirm the efficacy of martial patriotism, government intervention, and assimilation for dissolving "the color line"—what thinker W.E.B. Du Bois had presciently dubbed the foremost problem of the twentieth century.[33]

By the mid-1950s, the Nisei soldier icon occupied a prominent place in the spate of mass-market periodical "success stories" detailing Japanese Americans' recovery from the traumas of internment. *Reader's Digest* (1956) cheered the group's "amazing turnabout" that saw Japanese Americans "enjoying a prestige, a prosperity, and a freedom from prejudice that even the most sanguine of them had never hoped to attain within a lifetime." Notably, this rebound was made possible in large part by military service. As the *Saturday Evening Post* (1954) suggested, enlistment had allowed Nikkei the chance not only to prove their loyalty to the United States and upset existing notions of their "character," but also to gain access to socioeconomic mobility through the GI Bill. "As a direct result of the Pacific war, Japanese residents of California have lifted themselves higher in a few postwar years than they had done in the preceding half century. And agitation against them has almost been silenced," the *Post* triumphantly declared. *Newsweek* (1958) proclaimed internment a "disguised blessing," reporting that former internees were "glad" to have been "pushed into the mainstream of American life."[34]

Such narratives redeemed the nation's wartime missteps, allowing for Americans to express optimism in the ability of democracy to right its wrongs. At a time when the United States sought to convey its credibility as a world leader to win the Cold War, this was particularly important to project abroad. These "success stories" also reinforced liberalism's tenets. In intimating that the federal government had effectively shepherded Japanese American integration, these examples offered evidence to quell contemporary anxieties surrounding state-mandated desegregation in the wake of the Supreme Court's momentous decision in *Brown vs. Board of Education*.[35]

Firmly entrenched, the Nisei soldier icon came to serve as the basis of the emerging racial common sense that Japanese Americans were politically moderate, patriotic Americans who had legitimately earned their right to national recognition and belonging. This consensus among social scientists, culture watchers, journalists, political leaders, and countless ordinary folk had broad implications for the national racial order. In the context of the black freedom movement of the 1950s and 1960s, stakeholders mythologized Japanese Americans as a "model minority" in explicit contrast to stereotypes of African Americans, who were widely assumed to be unruly, criminal, and undeserving of state welfare entitlements. In short, Japanese Americans had come to be racialized as *definitively not-black*.[36]

Daniel Inouye, the consummate Nisei soldier, most famously embodied this contradistinction. As a member of the famed 442nd Regimental Combat Team, he rose to the rank of captain and earned numerous decorations (Purple Heart, Distinguished Service Cross, Bronze Star). While in action, Inouye lost his right arm, a sacrifice unfailingly mentioned by reporters ("Asked if he would fight to defend America, he holds up his empty sleeve, says, 'The country can have the other one, too.'") The injury extinguished his aspirations to a medical career, and Inouye turned instead to law and government. After attending the University of Hawai'i and George Washington University Law School on the GI Bill, the veteran practiced as an attorney and deputy prosecutor in Honolulu, then secured a seat in the Territorial House as part of the 1954 "Democratic revolution." He won reelection in 1956 before moving to the Territorial Senate in 1958, and then on to Capitol Hill the following year as the state's inaugural delegate to the House of Representatives.[37] In 1962—the same year he was named by *Life* magazine as one of the 100 most influential young members of the "take-over generation"—Inouye defeated the scion of one of the islands' most elite families to capture Hawai'i's open Senate seat.[38]

As one of Washington's rising stars, Inouye delivered the keynote address at the turbulent 1968 Democratic National Convention in Chicago. In it, he pointedly acknowledged the increasingly commonplace comparisons between Nikkei and African Americans: "As an American whose ancestors come from Japan, I have become accustomed to a question more recently asked by a very prominent businessman who was concerned about the threat of riots and of the resultant loss in life and property. 'Tell me,' he said, 'why can't the Negro be more like you?'" "You" in this statement functioned as rhetorical shorthand, referring both to Inouye as an individual and Inouye as a stand-in for all Japanese—if not all Asians—in the United States. Furthermore, without the need for elaboration, "you" conjured up and braced the embryonic stereotype of "Orientals" as patriotic, mild-mannered, industrious, and eager to blend into the white middle class. This moment distilled the new position of Japanese Americans in the national racial order by the late 1960s. Japanese Americans had become "good minorities" in contrast to "bad minorities," a recasting that observers would mobilize frequently to defend the political and racial status quo.[39]

AFTERLIFE[40]

GI Joe Nisei undoubtedly facilitated the dismantling of Japanese exclusion laws and social practices in the mid-twentieth century. But it did so at a price. As narratives of Japanese American military heroism gained widespread traction in the postwar period, they crowded out competing representations of Nikkei. These included zoot-suiters, draft resisters, citizenship renunciants, leftists, and others who disagreed with the JACL's martial patriotism, assimilationist politics, and racial liberalism more broadly. The hegemony of the Nisei soldier ideal and the attendant growth of the JACL's influence left little room for debate and impactful dissent within the Japanese American community. It also rendered invisible the difficulties that real-life Nisei soldiers and veterans faced during and after their tours of duty, including psychological, interpersonal, and financial troubles, among others.

Significantly, the JACL's invention of the iconic Nisei soldier resulted in a momentous, if inadvertent, spin-off: the racialization of Japanese Americans as *definitively not-black* model minorities amidst the urgent press for civil rights and Black Power by African Americans in the 1960s. As the nation scrambled to respond to what was then called the "negro problem," many people found it politically expedient to compare the "successes" of ethnic Japanese to the "failures" of African Americans.

Ultimately, the "work" of model minority mythology has been to deny systemic racism, not only against African Americans and other nonwhite groups, but also against Asian Americans themselves. A January 1972 television broadcast of the CBS network's newsmagazine *60 Minutes* tellingly revealed this dynamic, even as it glimpsed the pushback by Japanese Americans highly critical of the stereotype. Introducing the segment "100% Americans," correspondent Mike Wallace recited the proverbial narrative: " 'The model minority,' they are called. They have scrambled into the American middle class from the economic ruin of the concentration camp. Yankee ingenuity, the will to work, a respect for learning and the law—all of them clichés one has to repeat about those super-Americans, the Japanese-Americans. They've become the very model of the way that white Americans like to think of themselves." Visiting Southern California, home to the largest mainland concentration of Nikkei, Wallace observed a thriving community of overachievers melding their ethnic heritage and "Japanese ethic" with the influences of Americanization.[41]

Yet, *60 Minutes* also aired the tension between the success image and its discontents—drawing attention, ironically, to problems encountered by Japanese Americans in the military. When prodded by Wallace about whether he had ever "*really* suffered from white racism," a young man recalled his military experience in Vietnam, where he was not only subjected to racial epithets ("gook") but also singled out by officers and fellow soldiers as an example of the enemy. Wallace skeptically countered with the suggestion that "the Japanese-American has it made" compared to blacks and Chicanos. Another interviewee disagreed, arguing that a "good stereotype" was nonetheless an infringement of Nikkei's "human dignity," because it denied people the right to be treated as individuals. Unconvinced, Wallace suggested that well-to-do Nisei parents "like the box they're in," taking pleasure in the material rewards of their industriousness and facing "little real sense of racial discrimination."[42]

Nearly fifty years later, the model minority remains stubbornly lodged in the nation's racial landscape. It continues to obscure the severity of the dehumanization of people of color across the board, including those in the armed forces. In 2012, *New York* magazine reported on the nearly invisible "plight of the Asian-American soldier" (i.e., racism and hazing) by recounting the devastating demise of nineteen-year-old Danny Chen, the son of Chinese immigrants. The army private committed suicide after repeatedly enduring extreme physical and mental cruelty inflicted by eight of his comrades while deployed to Afghanistan. His last message to his parents was scrawled on his forearm in black ink: "Tell my parents I'm sorry."[43]

The Japanese American Citizens League mourned Private Chen's death as a "tragedy in every respect." The League joined with other Asian American advocacy groups to insist not only on bringing Chen's abusers to trial, but also on the necessity of the Army to confront the attitudes, behaviors, and rules that "fostered and led to [Chen's] racially abusive environment." Nodding to its own past, the JACL lamented the loss as a "tragedy for the United States Army" while simultaneously and fittingly acknowledging its potential as "an institution that draws great pride in serving as a model of tolerance and diversity."[44]

Danny Chen is the updated face of the Asian American soldier for the twenty-first century. But in contrast to Inouye and the rank and file of the 442nd, Chen is more antihero than hero; a symbol of miscarriage rather than triumph. His family and community soberly honored his memory by persuading the city of New York to rename a stretch of Elizabeth Street at Canal Street in Chinatown as "Pvt. Danny Chen Way." The Washington National Opera commissioned an original production based on his life; *An American Soldier*, with a libretto by celebrated playwright David Henry Hwang, premiered in June 2014 at the Kennedy Center.[45] "As a society, we need to come together to learn from it," said composer Huang Ruo. These highly public memorials openly acknowledge the tensions and contradictions that the iconization of GI Joe Nisei softened or even concealed. As Asian Americans and others continue to look to military service as an avenue for acceptance, equality, and justice, the life and death of Danny Chen obliges all of us to reflect on the myriad dimensions of martial patriotism: opportunities and drawbacks, promises and realities, anticipated outcomes and unintended consequences—heroic, tragic, and otherwise.[46]

NOTES

1. On the history of internment, see Roger Daniels, *Concentration Camps USA: Japanese Americans and World War II* (New York: Holt, Rinehart, and Winston, 1972); Michi Nishiura Weglyn, *Years of Infamy: The Untold Story of America's Concentration Camps* (Seattle: University of Washington Press, 1996); U.S. Commission on Wartime Evacuation and Relocation of Civilians (CWRIC), *Personal Justice Denied: Report of the Commission on Wartime Relocation and Internment of Civilians: Report for the Committee on Interior and Insular Affairs* (Washington, DC: U.S. Government Printing Office, 1983; repr., Seattle: University of Washington Press, 1997); Greg Robinson, *A Tragedy of Democracy: Japanese Confinement in North America* (New York: Columbia University Press, 2009). The total mainland population of Japanese Americans in 1940 was 126,947. U.S. Bureau of the Census, *Sixteenth Census of the United States, 1940* (Washington, DC: U.S. Government Printing Office, 1943).
2. In this chapter, *Nisei* refers to second-generation children of Japanese immigrants, born and raised on U.S. soil. *Issei* is the Japanese term for the immigrant cohort from Japan. *Nikkei* is the Japanese-language umbrella term for all persons of Japanese ancestry in the United States and elsewhere outside Japan, regardless of nativity.

3. CWRIC, *Personal Justice Denied*, 258–259.
4. I borrow the notion of "martial patriotism" from Cecilia Elizabeth O'Leary, *To Die For: The Paradox of American Patriotism* (Princeton, NJ: Princeton University Press, 1999); and Lucy E. Salyer, "Baptism by Fire: Race, Military Service, and U.S. Citizenship Policy, 1918–1935," *Journal of American History* 91, no. 3 (2004): 847–876.
5. On the history of the JACL, see Togo Tanaka, "History of the JACL," ch. 1, reel 84, Japanese American Evacuation and Resettlement Study collection (hereafter cited as JERS), Bancroft Library, University of California, Berkeley; Jere Takahashi, *Nisei/Sansei: Shifting Japanese American Identities and Politics* (Philadelphia: Temple University Press, 1997).
6. Paul R. Spickard, "The Nisei Assume Power: The Japanese [American] Citizens League, 1941–1942," *Pacific Historical Review* 52, no. 2 (1983): 147–174; Arthur A. Hansen and David A. Hacker, "The Manzanar Riot: An Ethnic Perspective," *Amerasia* 2, no. 2 (1974): 112–157; CWRIC, *Personal Justice Denied*, 174, 177–178, 187; Weglyn, *Years of Infamy*, 119–121, 135; Takahashi, *Nisei/Sansei*, 108–111; Brian Masaru Hayashi, *Democratizing the Enemy: The Japanese American Internment* (Princeton, NJ: Princeton University Press, 2004), 94, 100, 108, 111–112; Bill Hosokawa, *JACL in Quest of Justice: The History of the Japanese American Citizens League* (New York: William Morrow and Company, 1982), 190, 192, 197–201; Eric L. Muller, *Free to Die for Their Country: The Story of the Japanese American Draft Resisters in World War II* (Chicago: University of Chicago Press, 2001), 42–43; Masaoka to Milton S. Eisenhower, April 6, 1942, reel 83, JERS; Masaoka to Henry L. Stimson, January 15, 1943, file 400, box 846, RG 147, National Archives and Records Administration, Washington, D.C.
7. Salyer, "Baptism by Fire"; Gary Gerstle, *American Crucible: Race and Nation in the Twentieth Century* (Princeton, NJ: Princeton University Press, 2001), 203–237. On military service as an obligation of citizenship, see Linda K. Kerber, *No Constitutional Right to be Ladies: Women and the Obligations of Citizenship* (New York: Hill and Wang, 1998); James Sparrow, *Warfare State: World War II Americans and the Age of Big Government* (New York: Oxford University Press, 2011).
8. On World War II and post–World War II era racial liberalism, see Walter Jackson, *Gunnar Myrdal and America's Conscience: Social Engineering and Racial Liberalism, 1938–1997* (Chapel Hill: University of North Carolina Press, 1990); Gary Gerstle, "The Protean Character of American Liberalism," *American Historical Review* 99, no. 4 (1994): 1043–1073; Alan Brinkley, *The End of Reform: New Deal Liberalism in Recession and War* (New York: Vintage Books, 1995); Nikhil Pal Singh, "Culture/Wars: Recoding Empire in an Age of Democracy," *American Quarterly* 50, no. 3 (1998): 471–522; Ruth Feldstein, *Motherhood in Black and White: Race and Sex in American Liberalism, 1930–1965* (Ithaca, NY: Cornell University Press, 2000); Gerstle, *American Crucible*; Alice O'Connor, *Poverty Knowledge: Social Science, Social Policy, and the Poor in Twentieth-Century U.S. History* (Princeton, NJ: Princeton University Press, 2001); Nikhil Pal Singh, *Black Is a Country: Race and the Unfinished Struggle for Democracy* (Cambridge, MA: Harvard University Press, 2004); Carol A. Horton, *Race and the Making of American Liberalism* (New York: Oxford University Press, 2005); Thomas J. Sugrue, *Sweet Land of Liberty: The Forgotten Civil Rights Struggle in the North* (New York: Random House, 2008); Daniel Martinez HoSang, *Racial Propositions: Ballot Initiatives and the Making of Postwar California* (Berkeley: University of California Press, 2010); Mark Brilliant, *The Color of America Has Changed: How Racial Diversity Shaped Civil Rights Reform in California, 1941–1978* (New York: Oxford University Press, 2010); Ellen D. Wu, *The Color of Success: Asian Americans and the Origins of the Model Minority* (Princeton, NJ: Princeton University Press, 2014); Arissa H. Oh, *To Save the Children of Korea: The Cold War Origins of International Adoption* (Stanford, CA: Stanford

University Press, 2015). On racial liberalism and Japanese American internment, see Colleen Lye, *America's Asia: Racial Form and American Literature, 1893–1945* (Princeton, NJ: Princeton University Press, 2004); Mae M. Ngai, *Impossible Subjects: Illegal Aliens and the Making of Modern America* (Princeton, NJ: Princeton University Press, 2004); Wu, *The Color of Success*.

9. Arthur A. Hansen and David A. Hacker, "The Manzanar Riot: An Ethnic Perspective," *Amerasia* 2, no. 2 (1974): 112–157; Muller, *Free to Die*, 44–45; Lon Kurashige, *Japanese American Celebration and Conflict: A History of Ethnic Identity and Festival, 1934–1990* (Berkeley: University of California Press, 2002), 75, 85–89; Hayashi, *Democratizing the Enemy*, 134–135.

10. T. Fujitani, *Race for Empire: Koreans as Japanese and Japanese as Americans during World War II* (Berkeley: University of California Press, 2011), 220–223; CWRIC, *Personal Justice Denied*, 186–191; Muller, *Free to Die*, 45–47; Weglyn, *Years of Infamy*, 140–143; Hosokawa, *JACL in Quest of Justice*, 210–212; Mike Masaoka, with Bill Hosokawa, *They Call Me Moses Masaoka: An American Saga* (New York: William Morrow and Company, 1987), 123–159.

11. Weglyn, *Years of Infamy*, 143–151; Muller, *Free to Die*, 54–57.

12. Weglyn, *Years of Infamy*, 140–143; Muller, *Free to Die*, 60–63.

13. Muller, *Free to Die*, 62–63, 64–99.

14. See, for instance, "Sgt. Kuroki, Nisei War Hero, Returns to U.S.," *Pacific Citizen*, January 1, 1944, 1, 3; "Story of the Week: Sgt. Ben Kuroki Reveals Escape from Spaniards," *Pacific Citizen*, January 29, 1944, 1; "Japanese American War Hero," *Pacific Citizen*, February 5, 1944, 3.

15. JACL, "Official Convention Minutes, 1946," 8, 11, Japanese American Research Project (hereafter cited as JARP), Young Research Library, University of California, Los Angeles; CWRIC, *Personal Justice Denied*, 246, 256; Saburo Kido, "The President's Report: JACL Intensified Its Public Relations Activity in 1944," *Pacific Citizen*, December 23, 1944, 10; JACL, "PFC Thomas Higa's Lecture Tour Extended," (press release), September 6, 1944, reel 83, JERS.

16. Arthur A. Hansen, "Sergeant Ben Kuroki's Perilous 'Home Mission': Contested Loyalty and Patriotism in the Japanese American Detention Centers," in *Remembering Heart Mountain: Essays on Japanese American Internment in Wyoming*, ed. Mike Mackey (Sheridan, WY: Western History Publications, 1998), 153–175.

17. Saburo Kido, "JACL in Wartime," January 1, 1944, reel 83, JERS; JACL, "Official Convention Minutes, 1946," 11, 93; Hosokawa, *JACL*, 265; JACL, *Ben Kuroki's Story* (pamphlet), Salt Lake City, 1944; Saburo Kido, "The President's Report: JACL Intensified Its Public Relations Activity in 1944," *Pacific Citizen*, December 23, 1944, 10.

18. Masaoka, *They Call Me Moses*, 145, 178.

19. Ngai, *Impossible Subjects*, 177–182; U.S. Department of the Interior/War Relocation Authority, *Nisei in Uniform*, October 1944, folder "Minorities-Japanese-Pamphlets, 1943–1945," box 51, Philleo Nash Papers, Harry S. Truman Library, Independence, MO. See also U.S. Department of the Interior/War Relocation Authority, *What We're Fighting for: Statements by United States Servicemen about Americans of Japanese Descent* (Washington, DC: U.S. Government Printing Office, 1945).

20. "Blind Nisei," *Life*, February 7, 1944, 53; Lee Shippey, "Leeside," *Los Angeles Times*, February 2, 1944, A4; "Heroes: Ben Kuroki, American," *Time*, February 7, 1944; "Crapshooters, Jitterbugs," *Crisis*, November 1943, 327.

21. "American Fair Play?" *Time*, March 19, 1945; Linda Tamura, "'Wrong Face, Wrong Name': The Return of Japanese American Veterans to Hood River, Oregon, after World

War II," in *Remapping Asian American History*, ed. Sucheng Chan (Walnut Creek, CA: AltaMira Press, 2003), 107–125; U.S. Department of the Interior, *The Relocation Program* (Washington, DC: U.S. Government Printing Office, 1946), 65–66.

22. See, for instance, Sidney Carroll, "Purple Heart Battalion," *Coronet*, May 1945, 4–9.

23. Blake Clark and Oland D. Russell, "Japanese-American Soldiers Make Good," *American Mercury*, June 1945, 698–703, reprinted as "Hail Our Japanese-American GIs!" *Reader's Digest*, July 1945, 65–67. Russell served as a public relations officer with the 442nd during its training period at Camp Shelby, Mississippi.

24. JACL, "Official Convention Minutes, 1946," 87, folder 3, box 297, JARP; "Go for Broke," *Time*, July 22, 1946; Hodding Carter, "Go for Broke," *Delta Democrat-Times*, August 27, 1945; "Delta Prizewinner," *Time*, May 20, 1946.

25. Tetsuden Kashima, "Japanese American Internees Return, 1945 to 1955: Readjustment and Social Amnesia," *Phylon* 41, no. 2 (1980): 107–115; Charlotte Brooks, "In the Twilight Zone between Black and White: Japanese American Resettlement and Community in Chicago, 1942–1945," *Journal of American History* 86, no. 4 (2000): 1655–1687; Charlotte Brooks, *Alien Neighbors, Foreign Friends: Asian Americans, Housing, and the Transformation of Urban California* (Chicago: University of Chicago Press, 2009), 159–193; Scott Kurashige, *The Shifting Grounds of Race: Black and Japanese Americans in the Making of Multiethnic Los Angeles* Princeton, NJ: Princeton University Press, 2007), 158–204; Briliant, *The Color of America Has Changed*, 29–57; HoSang, *Racial Propositions*, 45–47.

26. JACL, "Official Convention Minutes, 1946," 87; JACL, official convention minutes, 1948, 33–36, folder 5, box 296, JARP; Hayashi to Satow, November 6, 1949, "Nisei Soldier Memorial Day," box 5, series 1, JACL History Collection, Japanese American National Library, San Francisco.

27. "Segregation to the Grave," *Pacific Citizen*, November 27, 1948, 4; "Cemetery Offers Desired Plot for Burial of Nisei GI," *Pacific Citizen*, November 27, 1948, 1. See also Brian Niiya, "Kazuo Masuda," *Densho Encyclopedia*, http://encyclopedia.densho.org/Kazuo_Masuda/ (accessed March 18, 2015).

28. "Report Japanese Americans Denied Burial Plots in Cemeteries in Chicago Area," *Pacific Citizen*, November 27, 1948, 1; "Chicago Cemeteries Restrict Burial Rights," *Chicago Shimpo*, December 1, 1948, 8; M. Tsutsumi, "Memorandum on Discriminatory Practices against People of Japanese Ancestry in the Cemeteries that Serve Chicago," January 4, 1949, Chicago Cemeteries—Survey and Memoranda, 1947–1949, folder 2.10, UIC-JASC Papers, Japanese American Service Committee Legacy Center, Chicago, IL; "Radio Talk Spurs Action: Discrimination in Cemeteries," *Chicago Shimpo*, January 7, 1949, 8; "Urge Follow Up Letters on Cemeteries Question," *Chicago Shimpo*, January 14, 1949, 8; "Three Cemeteries Drop Bar to Interment of Japanese," *Chicago Shimpo*, February 11, 1949, 8; Drew Pearson, "West Coast Embraces the Nisei," *Washington Post*, February 6, 1949, B5; "Non-discriminating Local Cemeteries on City List," *Chicago Shimpo*, February 18, 1949, 8; "Mutual Aid Society Buys Several Plots for Burial," *Chicago Shimpo*, March 4, 1949, 8. See also "Work of Mutual Aid Deserves Recognition," *Chicago Shimpo*, January 26, 1949, 8; Masako Osako, "Japanese Americans: Melting into the All-American Melting Pot," in *Ethnic Chicago: A Multicultural Portrait*, ed. Melvin G. Holli and Peter d'A. Jones (Grand Rapids, MI: William B. Eerdmans, 1995), 426; "Washington Cemetery Revokes Ban on Japanese Race Burials at Request of JACL Chapter," *Pacific Citizen*, September 29, 1951, 1. Special thanks to Karen Kanemoto, Brian Niiya, and Greg Robison for their assistance in locating sources and to Ryan Yokota for help with the *Chicago Shimpo*.

29. Muller, *Free to Die*, 42–43; Albert D. Cash, "Proclamation," City of Cincinnati, *City Bulletin*, May 29, 1951, folder 3, box 298, JARP; JACL, "Official Convention Minutes, 1950,"

6, folder 6, box 296, JARP; Masaoka, *They Call Me Moses Masaoka*, 215–216; JACL, "Official Convention Minutes, 1952," 12, 29–30, 41, folder 7, box 296, JARP; JACL, "National Headquarters to All JACL Chapters," March 1, 1951, folder 7, box 301, JARP; JACL, "Satow to All JACL Chapters," March 23, 1951, folder 7, box 301, JARP; JACL, "Official Convention Minutes, 1952," 29–30; Abbie Salyers Grubb, *"Go for Broke!"* (film), *Densho Encyclopedia*, http://encyclopedia.densho.org/Go%20for%20Broke!%20/ (accessed November 20, 2014); Larry Tajiri, "Epic of the 442nd: 'Go for Broke!,'" *Scene* 2, no. 10 (1951): 24–25, quoted in Grubb, *"Go For Broke!"* (film).

30. Mike Masaoka, statement before the President's Committee on Civil Rights, May 1, 1947, folder "JACL Anti-Discrimination Committee, Inc.," box 11, RG 220, Harry S. Truman Presidential Library, Independence, MO; Masaoka to the President's Committee on Civil Rights, April 23, 1947, folder "JACL Anti-Discrimination Committee, Inc.," box 11, RG 220, Harry S. Truman Presidential Library.

31. Robert M. Cullum, "Japanese American Audit—1948," *Common Ground* 9, no. 2 (1949): 87–89; Greg Robinson, *After Camp: Portraits in Midcentury Japanese American Life and Politics* (Berkeley: University of California Press, 2012), 195–216; Brooks, *Alien Neighbors, Foreign Friends*, 176–84. The JACL was virtually alone in pushing for the 1952 McCarran-Walter Act. Liberals and progressives, including President Harry Truman, declined to support the bill because of its reactionary agenda.

32. Senate Hearings Before the Committee on Interior and Insular Affairs, *Statehood for Hawaii*, 83rd Cong., 1st and 2nd sess., part 2, July 2, 1953, 256.

33. W.E.B. Du Bois, *The Souls of Black Folk* (New York: Vintage, 1990), 16.

34. Albert Q. Maisel, "The Japanese among Us," *Readers Digest*, January 1956, 182–184, 186, 189, 192, 194, 196; Demarre Bess, "California's Amazing Japanese," *Saturday Evening Post*, April 30, 1955, 38–39, 68, 72, 76, 80, 83; "Nisei: Disguised Blessing," *Newsweek*, December 29, 1958, 23. See also Gladwin Hill, "Japanese in U.S. Gaining Equality," *New York Times*, August 12, 1956, 38; Ted Le Berthon, "Vindication for the Nisei," *Commonweal*, January 16, 1959, 406–409; "20 Years After," *Time*, August 11, 1961.

35. On Cold War civil rights, see, for instance, Mary L. Dudziak, *Cold War Civil Rights: Race and the Image of American Democracy* (Princeton, NJ: Princeton University Press, 2000); Thomas Borstelmann, *The Cold War and the Color Line: American Race Relations in the Global Arena* (Cambridge, MA: Harvard University Press, 2001). On Japanese Americans in post–World War II discussions of racial integration, see Caroline Chung Simpson, *An Absent Presence: Japanese Americans in Postwar American Culture, 1945–1960* (Durham, NC: Duke University Press, 2002).

36. For an extended discussion of racialization of Japanese Americans as "definitively not-black," see Wu, *The Color of Success*.

37. Lawrence E. Davies, "A Nisei of Hawaii Aims for Senate," *New York Times*, March 17, 1959, 20; "War Hero Leads in Hawaii Vote," *Washington Post*, July 29, 1959, A1; "Oriental War Hero Is Champion Vote Getter," *Chicago Defender*, July 30, 1959, 3; "Daniel K. Inouye," *New York Times*, July 30, 1959, 14; Milton Viorst, "Rep.-Elect Inouye Arrives, Declares Hawaii Will Be Nation's Bridge to Asia," *Washington Post*, August 10, 1959, A2; "Japanese-American Lost Arm in World War II," *Chicago Defender*, August 15, 1959, 21; "Loss of Arm Makes Politician of Inouye," *Chicago Daily Tribune*, August 16, 1959, 43; John Ramsey, "All Capitol Eyes Will Be on Long, Fong, and Inouye" *Washington Post*, August 21, 1959, B2; Willard Edwards, "Nisei Hero Brings Battlefield Courage to Senate," *Chicago Daily Tribune*, February 17, 1963, 11.

38. "A Red Hot Hundred," *Life*, September 14, 1962, 5; "Eye-Catching Race," *Newsweek*, April 9, 1962, 39–40; "Big Ben and Young Danny," *Time*, October 5, 1962.

39. "Transcript of the Keynote Address by Senator Inouye Decrying Violent Protests," *New York Times,* August 27, 1968, 28. Notably, Inouye challenged this juxtaposition by dismissing the comparison as unsound. Unlike African Americans, Asians in the United States had never endured chattel slavery or been subjected to "systematic racist deprivation" comparable to Jim Crow. Therefore, the solution to what the social scientist Gunnar Myrdal had called the "American dilemma" could not be achieved by simply having blacks "be like" Asians.

40. I borrow this term from Karen M. Inouye, *The Long Afterlife of Nikkei Wartime Incarceration* (Stanford, CA: Stanford University Press, 2016).

41. "100% Americans," *60 Minutes* transcript, vol. 4, no. 12, January 9, 1972, Mike Wallace Collection, Bentley Historical Library, University of Michigan, Ann Arbor, MI.

42. Ibid.

43. Jennifer Gonnerman, "Pvt. Danny Chen, 1992–2011," *New York Magazine,* January 6, 2012, http://nymag.com/news/features/danny-chen-2012-1/; Hansi Lo Wang, "An Opera Remembers the Tragedy of an Asian-American Soldier," *National Public Radio,* June 14, 2014, http://www.npr.org/sections/codeswitch/2014/06/13/318906365/an-opera-remembers-the-tragedy-of-an-asian-american-soldier.

44. "JACL Statement on Pvt. Danny Chen," *Rafu Shimpo,* January 21, 2012, http://www.rafu.com/2012/01/jacl-statement-on-pvt-danny-chen/.

45. Tobias Salinger and Corrine Lestch, "'Private Danny Chen Way' Named in Honor of Chinatown Soldier Driven to Suicide from Hazing," *New York Daily News,* May 17, 2014, http://www.nydailynews.com/new-york/street-named-honor-danny-chen-chinatown-soldier-driven-suicide-hazing-article-1.1796590; Hansi Lo Wang, "An Opera Remembers the Tragedy of an Asian-American Soldier," *NPR,* June 13, 2014, http://www.npr.org/sections/codeswitch/2014/06/13/318906365/an-opera-remembers-the-tragedy-of-an-asian-american-soldier.

46. Tim Hsia, "An Asian-American Veteran Reflects on When Discipline Becomes Hazing," *At War* (blog), *New York Times,* January 6, 2012, http://atwar.blogs.nytimes.com/2012/01/06/an-asian-american-veteran-reflects-on-when-discipline-becomes-hazing/.

3 · INSTRUMENT OF SUBJUGATION OR AVENUE FOR LIBERATION?

Black Military Heroism from World War II to the Vietnam War

SIMON WENDT

Although there is no dearth of historical scholarship on African American soldiers, existing studies tend to reveal little about the complexities of black military heroism in the twentieth century. They either ignore the issue of heroism altogether or inadvertently replicate the efforts of black journalists, black scholars, and other commentators to demonstrate that soldiers of color have been no less heroic than their white comrades. Many historians thus merely shed light on the "unsung" heroic deeds of African American servicemen, rather than providing a thorough analysis of how black citizens interpreted and used acknowledgment of valor on the battlefield in their struggle against social and political marginalization. Neither do they explore how this struggle for recognition was interconnected with white notions of military heroism, U.S. nationalism, and the entrenched ideal of the masculine citizen-soldier that martial heroism entailed.[1]

This chapter intends to bridge this historiographical gap by examining how the U.S. military, the U.S. government, and African Americans constructed, construed, and utilized black military heroism between the late 1930s and the mid-1970s. World War II and the Vietnam War are particularly revealing in this regard, because the 1940s marked the simultaneous beginning of sustained civil rights activism and increasing visibility and acknowledgment of black soldiers' valor on the battlefield.[2] Military heroism helps in understanding the complex nexus of race, gender, and the nation because it constitutes a major discursive arena in which competing visions of racialized nationhood and nationalized masculinity are created, negotiated, challenged, and revised. In addition, the U.S. military, in the words of Holly Allen, continues to stand "as a repository and defender of U.S. national values," and of national identity.[3] The ideal of the heroic citizen-soldier encapsulates the seemingly egalitarian, but ultimately exclusionary ramifications of hero worship. According to R. Claire Snyder, "the Citizen-Soldier functions as a prescriptive ideal that calls for male individuals to engage in the civic and martial practices that constitute them as masculine republican citizens."[4] African Americans, however, tended to be excluded from this notion of masculine republican citizenship. Consequently, the acknowledgment of black military heroism took on tremendous social, cultural, and political significance.

The racially charged struggles that took place between the late 1930s and the mid-1970s over the meaning of black soldiers' heroism were a war of words fought primarily in black newspapers and magazines, although the U.S. military and the U.S. government also weighed in via means such as public award ceremonies, radio, and film. A thorough analysis of this discourse demonstrates that black military heroism became both an opportunity for African Americans to claim full membership in the American nation and an ambivalent means of social control that helped white authorities to ensure black citizens' national loyalty. Conceptually, William J. Goode's little-known study *The Celebration of Heroes: Prestige as a Control System* yields important insights into these ambivalences. Goode argues that social actors can utilize esteem or disapproval to control other groups when responding to their actions. Institutions that give prestigious awards such as the Medal of Honor, he writes, "remind people that the organization is a judge of achievement, possesses prestige to confer on others, and also deserves some prestige for its support of that activity."[5]

If Goode is used as a conceptual point of departure, we can see the discourse on black military heroism in a different light. Especially during World War II, white authorities used war heroes of color to soothe black discontent, suggesting to African American citizens that the U.S. military was willing to acknowledge their valor throughout American history. Revealingly, however, white audiences were rarely exposed to such official commendations, and awards for heroism did not affect the harsh reality of racial discrimination. White authorities thus deliberately intended their praise for black war heroes as a form of social control in the face of racial tensions and civil rights protest. As part of that protest, black journalists and pundits did use black military heroism as a political resource to argue that African Americans deserved to be treated as first-class American citizens because they loyally served the nation as manly citizen-soldiers who were willing to sacrifice their lives for the country. However, throughout the period 1941 to 1975, notwithstanding growing black militancy and antiwar activism, black journalists' comments on African American valor tended to reflect an abiding faith in official definitions and standards of military heroism, as well as in the masculine patriotism that was associated with it. The ways that white authorities and African Americans interpreted black military heroism thus testify to the enormous cultural power of the ideal of the heroic citizen-soldier and reveal that, paradoxically, heroism could be both an ideological instrument of subjugation and an avenue for liberation.

Theoretical insights from cultural studies and political science shed light on the intricate links between military heroism, nationalism, race, and gender. Nationalist movements generally claim that a unique and sovereign nation exists, that its members have a common destiny and a national "homeland," and that the nation trumps all other loyalties. Although the nation is an "imagined community," people come to believe in its existence because constant iterations of this construct permeate public discourse and their daily lives.[6] Convinced that the nation is real, its members constantly debate the question of who should belong to it. Scholars have long differentiated between civic and ethnic nationalism to analyze the inclusionary and exclusionary functions of nationalist ideologies. In the case of civic nationalism, people are accepted as members of the nation because they pledge allegiance to its political institutions and values, regardless of their "race" or ancestry. In the case of ethnic nationalism, membership qualifications are tied to a specific racialized ancestry and notions of national culture that are purportedly shared by all citizens. These two forms frequently exist in tandem and in tension, reflecting power struggles over who belongs to the nation and who does not.[7]

If nationalism is a relational construct that is intertwined with race, it is just as connected to notions of gender, which can be defined as a fluctuating process through which dichotomous views of masculinity and femininity are performatively produced, practiced, and naturalized as stable and fixed.[8] The nation tends to be imagined as a brotherhood of heterosexual men who readily incorporate women into national ideologies as patriotic symbols, but tend to restrict their active participation in nation building. In general, nationalism depends on and perpetuates gender difference. Not only is national membership frequently limited to persons who embody "appropriate" notions of femininity and masculinity, but strengthening the idea of fixed gender identities also helps nationalism to be perceived as natural and unchanging. In nationalist ideologies of the nineteenth and twentieth centuries, the manly warrior was probably the most important archetype that contributed to this reciprocal process of naturalization. Manly warrior heroes had long been hailed as embodiments of strong masculinity, but by the early nineteenth century, their heroism was increasingly linked to their willingness to sacrifice their lives for the nation. A soldier's death on the battlefield came to be seen as the highest form of patriotic loyalty—an idea that strengthened what Raewyn Connell has called hegemonic masculinity.[9]

For the analysis of black military heroism, historical memory serves as a crucial analytical tool, since memory plays an important role in the construction and naturalization of racialized and gendered interpretations of the nation. Memory can be understood as selective interpretations of the past that shape and frame individual and collective identities, norms, and values in the present. Nationalists generally use it to create unity and solidarity, claiming that the nation's populace has a common past, as well as a common destiny. However, despite efforts to downplay difference and conflict, there are multiple memories that are constantly debated, contested, and reinterpreted. Such contests over memory reflect power struggles among various groups and institutions that vie for political and cultural power. Yet, nationalist elites cannot simply expect the masses to accept their particular interpretations. Instead, they need to incorporate competing collective memories to succeed in their efforts to strengthen people's allegiance to the nation.[10]

When looking at the general history of military heroism in the United States, these theoretical insights provide a useful analytical lens through which to view the meanings and uses of martial valor on the battlefield. In nineteenth-century Europe and North America, military heroism was gradually democratized as official recognition of martial valor was increasingly extended to ordinary soldiers for their willingness to die for the nation. During the War of 1812 and the Mexican-American War, more and more common servicemen received praise for successfully defending the United States. This process of transforming ordinary warrior heroes into icons of the nation received a boost during the Civil War, when the Medal of Honor was introduced as part of the Union's efforts to boost soldiers' morale, and was complete after the Spanish-American War.[11]

Despite its egalitarian tendencies, however, heroism remained a form of acclaim that was largely confined to white men, who remained the most cherished paragons of masculine valor, physical strength, and patriotism. African Americans were largely absent from national hero narratives, a consequence of the general belief that people of color were "unheroic" by nature. Black soldiers repeatedly proved their valor on the battlefield and were awarded coveted prizes such as the Medal of Honor by white authorities, but neither the almost 200,000 black soldiers who fought for the Union during the Civil War nor the thousands of African American men who saw action during the Spanish-American War were acknowledged as heroic citizen-soldiers in public discourse. Black pundits and journalists tried to counter this deliberate neglect. For example, renowned scholar and civil rights activist W.E.B. Du Bois unearthed past heroic deeds by African Americans and praised their manly exploits in his writings, and black editors similarly called attention to the daring deeds of soldiers of color. But this was all to no avail, because around 1900, white Anglo-Saxon heroism reigned supreme and reinforced pseudoscientific theories on the alleged inferiority of nonwhite people in general and African American soldiers in particular.[12] Consequently, as Jim Crow segregation, disfranchisement, and racial violence became ubiquitous in the American South in the early twentieth century, the acknowledgment of black servicemen's military heroism became crucially important in the African American freedom struggle.

Black citizens' martial valor, or the alleged lack thereof, continued to be debated during World War I and the 1920s, but took on renewed significance between the late 1930s and the end of World War II, as more and more African Americans refused to accept their subordinate status in U.S. society.[13] Black soldiers especially resented segregation and racial discrimination in an army that was supposed to save the world from Nazi Germany's white supremacist ideology. During their training at segregated military facilities in the American South, many of the more than 900,000 black draftees clashed with white officers and local whites over racial discrimination. Between 1941 and 1943, more confrontations occurred on army bases, as well as in numerous U.S. cities. In September 1941, the black magazine *Opportunity* warned the War Department that few "Negro soldiers who are being trained to kill Germans, or perhaps Japanese" would "endure being shoved around and insulted by Americans" without fighting back.[14]

As gun battles between African American GIs and white military police became common during the first years of the war, black civilians, too, were no longer willing to tolerate racist insults, and frequently resorted to violence if attacked by whites. In 1943 alone, 242 racial clashes erupted in 47 cities across the United States.[15] Meanwhile, and just as disconcerting to white authorities, nonviolent African American activists tried to pressure local, state, and federal authorities into living up to the democratic ideals that were invoked in America's war propaganda. In early 1941, labor and civil rights leader A. Philip Randolph organized an all-black March on Washington Movement (MOWM), which threatened to bring 100,000 African Americans to the White House to protest against racial discrimination in the defense industry. Faced with a potentially embarrassing demonstration in the nation's capital, President Franklin D. Roosevelt relented, issuing an executive order that ended discrimination in the defense industry.[16] In the following two years, moreover, members of the newly founded Congress of Racial Equality launched a series of nonviolent sit-ins in Chicago, Detroit, and other cities outside the South to challenge the custom of racial segregation in restaurants, movie theaters, and other public places. Meanwhile, the black newspaper *Pittsburgh Courier* launched a "Double-V" campaign, which demanded victory over Adolf Hitler abroad and racial discrimination and disfranchisement at home.[17]

In the face of this mounting discontent, official praise of black valor on and off the battlefield assumed enormous symbolic value for both white authorities and African American commentators. With regard to the depictions of black World War II soldiers in the U.S. media, mainstream newspapers and magazines tended to ignore or minimize the achievements of servicemen of color, even though their coverage reflected a general desire to portray the American military as diverse, pluralistic, and unified in the face of Germany's white supremacist ideology.[18] The U.S. military, by contrast, acknowledged black heroism far more often and far more enthusiastically than was suggested by the scarcity of stories about black soldiers in white publications. During World War II, the War Department spared neither expense nor effort to praise African American servicemen's valor in America's past wars in radio shows, feature films, and press releases. In August 1941, for example, Under Secretary of War Robert P. Patterson spoke on "The Negro and the Army" on national public radio, highlighting black soldiers' loyalty and heroism. "No one dare question the Negro citizen's loyalty," he said on the program, "and none dare question his courage—such courage as in 1918 took Private John Baker, with two fingers of his right hand shot off, through three hundred yards of heavy machinegun fire to deliver an urgent message to his commanding officer." According to Patterson, there were "less spectacular, but just as genuine examples of courage today."[19] Four months later, the U.S. Office of Education financed a radio program on the heroism of black World War I hero Henry Johnson. "The Battle of Henry Johnson" was part of the *Freedom People* program, which was arranged for the purpose of informing the world of African Americans' contributions to American life.[20] And in September 1942, the U.S. Army aired its own radio tribute to black troops. The program was called "Judgment Day," and revolved around the heroism of America's black soldiers from the American Revolution to World War II. Professionally produced, it featured the music of well-known composer Allie Wrubel and a renowned African American singer to make the show more appealing.[21] The War Department's Bureau of Public Relations also issued numerous press releases that informed black journalists and civil rights organizations about the official citations for valor that soldiers of color had received during the war, and frequently echoed the words of praise that were uttered in radio tributes to black war heroes.[22]

In late 1943 and early 1944, the press branch of the War Department's Bureau of Public Relations had one of its most visible tributes to black heroism published in various African American newspapers, including the *New Journal and Guide*, the *Cleveland Call and Post*, and the *Philadelphia Tribune*. The press branch's staff had written and designed an entire page on black war heroes. In the center of the page was a banner emblazoned with the word *Valor*. Underneath the banner was an image of the Medal of Honor and a description of the types of exploits for which it was awarded, as well as a photograph of George H. Wanton, a black soldier who had received the coveted decoration during the Spanish-American War. Grouped around the conspicuous banner and Wanton's image were descriptions of the military's lesser awards, including the Soldier's Medal, the Purple Heart, and the Distinguished Service Cross, all of which were also accompanied by photographs of soldiers of color who had won these awards in past wars and in World War II.[23] Just as they had done in their radio programs and press releases, U.S. military authorities deliberately evoked the memory of black war heroes and the official awards they had been granted, suggesting that the nation was grateful for African American soldiers' heroic service and therefore deserved continued loyalty in the present conflict.

However, all of these efforts targeted primarily black audiences, which was also true of the U.S. military's most ambitious, and certainly most expensive attempt to celebrate African American military heroism during World War II: the feature film *The Negro Soldier*. The U.S. Army commissioned famous Hollywood director Frank Capra to create a propaganda film that would instill in black soldiers patriotism and a will to fight for the American nation. The forty-three-minute film was approved in early 1944 and was produced like a typical Hollywood movie, with a pleasing narrative style, professional lighting, and impressive visual effects. Strikingly different than previous movies, *The Negro Soldier* highlighted the heroism of black soldiers who had fought for the United States in the nineteenth and twentieth centuries, acknowledging their contributions to American nation building and depicting blacks as equals in America's efforts to defeat Nazi Germany. Racial segregation and the mistreatment of black soldiers and African American civilians, however, were completely ignored. Initially, the film was intended primarily for black troops, and since new recruits of color were required to watch it, almost every black member of the Army and Air Corps had seen it by the end of the war. After intense lobbying by African American civil rights organizations, the film was also released for commercial distribution. When it did poorly at the box office, a shortened version was quickly approved, but similarly failed to attract large audiences. In the end, only black audiences saw *The Negro Soldier* at screenings that took place at black civic institutions, churches, and schools.[24] While the *New York Times* mentioned the discrepancy between the film's depictions of heroic black soldiers and its silence on racism, many African Americans lauded "their" film. The National Association for the Advancement of Colored People (NAACP), a powerful civil rights organization that had lobbied tirelessly for its commercial distribution, praised the film, as did some black editors. In May 1944, for instance, the *Philadelphia Tribune* called *The Negro Soldier* "a stirring movie story of our fighting heroes," which its editors regarded as "a great tribute to our boys."[25] White media, by contrast, generally ignored the film.[26]

Ultimately, the War Department's various efforts to assure African Americans that white America was aware of and admired war heroes of color and their manly contributions to the nation's military victories were a thinly veiled attempt to diminish the risk of racial unrest during a period that was rife with tensions among black and white citizens. In addition, and perhaps even more importantly, the War Department's tributes implied that the U.S. military was the sole and infallible judge of who was a hero, and what behavior was to be considered heroic. Since white citizens tended to be unaware of the U.S. military's lavish praise for black martial valor, such unprecedented tributes to African American heroism can be regarded as a sophisticated form of social control that aimed to assuage disaffected citizens of color while trying to strengthen their loyalty to the nation.

The African American print media's coverage of black military heroism during World War II has to be analyzed against the backdrop of this state-sponsored propaganda campaign. African American heroism certainly offered black journalists a crucial opportunity to affirm black men's masculinity and their loyalty to the United States. But their tributes to soldiers of color also reflected a general acceptance of the U.S. military's definitions and standards of what constituted heroism—even if journalists and editors of color called upon white America to honor its rhetorical commitment to civic nationalism as a reward for black soldiers' patriotism. In general, black newspapers reported almost weekly about black soldiers who had received official awards for heroic conduct. Every citation for heroism—regardless of whether it was the Air Medal or the Distinguished Service Cross—was worth an article.[27] Many of these articles—which often appeared on the publications' front pages—were accompanied by photographs of the award ceremonies that evoked the symbolism of martial masculinity. The awardees were generally shown standing at attention as their superior officers pinned the awards on their uniforms.[28]

In light of the fact that so many black soldiers were regularly cited for valor, African American editors insisted that servicemen of color were just as heroic as their white counterparts, refuting centuries of taunts that men of color were cowards. In 1943, for example, the *Chicago Defender* wrote on the record of the black soldier in World War II: "In the current global war, the Negro has definitely established himself in the hierarchy of distinguished soldiers."[29] Such articles mattered greatly to African American institutions fighting for racial change, including the National Urban League, a civil rights organization that collected dozens of clippings on black military heroism that appeared in the black press.[30]

With regard to African Americans' alleged cowardice, black sailor Dorie Miller became one of the war's most visible heroes of color after firing at attacking enemy planes during the Japanese attack on Pearl Harbor in 1941—despite the fact that he was barred from joining combat units. As Paul Alkebulan has shown, African American journalists and editors used the example of Miller to exhort other black soldiers, sailors, and Marines to measure up to Miller's heroism. Early on, the NAACP called upon President Franklin D. Roosevelt to award a Distinguished Service Cross to the intrepid sailor. Miller's heroism was seen as irrefutable evidence that black men could fight.[31] Even before detailed reports on the story emerged, the *Chicago Defender* editorialized in early 1942: "We do not know whether Navy officials at Washington will give appropriate recognition of this act of bravery performed by a loyal, fearless and obscure messman. But we do know that the story will serve to open up the eyes of those in authority who have been discounting the Negro's ability to discharge the obligations of higher naval ranks."[32] And once the courageous sailor had been identified and widely praised, George W. Blount of the *New Journal and Guide* opined: "Dorie Miller's Heroism at Pearl Harbor and the heroism of many other Negroes have fully exemplified the first class fighting qualities of the American Negro in America's armed forces from the Civil War on."[33]

Occasionally, African Americans protested against what they perceived as deliberate slights toward black servicemen who were believed to have performed heroically in battle. A medical corpsman named Waverly Woodson, for instance, was recommended by a superior officer for the Medal of Honor for performing important medical work while wounded and under fire during the Allied invasion of Normandy on D-Day in 1944. The *Philadelphia Tribune* wrote about black reactions when he did not receive the award: "The feeling is prevalent among Negroes that had Woodson been of another race the highest honor would have been granted him."[34]

Significantly, World War II and the debates surrounding black military service prompted numerous black authors to keep alive the historical memory of black military heroism. In fact, the memory of black war heroes' past exploits might have been even more important than current reports of martial valor for their argument that African American servicemen conformed to the dominant ideal of the manly citizen-soldier hero. Most African American commentators used stories of black soldiers' past deeds to explicitly criticize white authors who tended to ignore their heroic accomplishments. In February 1942, for example, Cliff Mackay of the *Atlanta Daily World* wrote: "One of the most disheartening things that is developing in World War II and for which there was a precedent in World War I, is the apparently adamant determination of America's white press to conceal the exploits of black men serving their country both at home and on foreign battlefields."[35] That same year, the *New Journal and Guide* published an article on the heroism of black World War I soldiers, similarly lamenting that black heroes did not get the publicity they deserved.[36] To rectify this neglect, and to underscore that African Americans were loyal citizens who were entitled to full equality, journalists penned numerous articles that detailed the heroic deeds of black men in the wars the United States had fought since American independence. In March 1942, for instance, the *Philadelphia Tribune* published a long article on the black soldiers of the American Revolution. An editor's note that accompanied the article was explicit about what this neglected aspect of U.S. history meant for African American citizens: "Here is the proof of the bravery and courage and loyalty of Colored Americans; here is the proof that they have been cogs in every American victory. And with that proof goes the firm conviction that no power under heaven will stop them from defending their country from foreign foes and receiving equality of citizenship at home."[37]

Although some journalists stressed the importance of this heroic memory for race consciousness and race pride, regardless of official white recognition, the black press generally accepted white authorities' definitions of what constituted military heroism, since they repeatedly recounted the history of the U.S. military's awards for heroism and reported on how many African Americans had won which awards.[38] Numerous journalists recounted the history of the Medal of Honor in their articles on the memory of black martial valor, providing details on the black men who had won the sought-after prize, and musing about white authorities' reasons for refusing to bestow it on black soldiers after the end of the Spanish-American War. In December 1943, the *Philadelphia Tribune* used the example of the heroism of Private George Watson during World War II to recount how many black soldiers had won military awards for valor in the past. Between 1862 and 1926, its editors wrote, "soldiers serving in all colored outfits were awarded 31 Congressional Medals of Honor and 57 Distinguished Service Crosses."[39] Such detailed accounts of the U.S. military's awards for heroism call attention to white authorities' success in trying to convince African Americans that the U.S. military was the final arbiter of what constituted "true" valor on the battlefield, and that striving to win awards that honored heroism might help them win acceptance as full members of the American nation.

Of course, the discourse on black military service reflected an important truth about heroism—namely, that it is subject to constant negotiation and revision. After World War II, for instance, many African Americans continued to be dissatisfied with what they perceived as a lack of appreciation for black soldiers in general and black war heroes in particular.[40] In November 1950, for example, the *Pittsburgh Courier* published a scathing critique by journalist Joseph D. Bibb, who vented his anger about *Life* magazine's pictorial history of World War II, which suggested that virtually no blacks had participated in the war.[41] In this context, Bibb and others probably appreciated the fact that a few white allies tried to counter such omissions. For instance, liberal white politician Helen Gahagan Douglas, a congresswoman from California's 14th District, prepared a seventy-page article on black valor during the war years, reading it into the *Congressional Record* in early 1946.[42] However, despite their criticism of white neglect, African Americans neither questioned the U.S. military's authority in evaluating black heroism, nor challenged the idea of the heroic citizen-soldier and his patriotic duty to risk his life for his country. Consequently, even African Americans' calls for full inclusion in the nation in the context of black military heroism attest to the powerful role of America's citizen-soldier ideology in the state's efforts to ensure citizens' loyalty to the nation.

Black newspaper coverage of the Korean War reflected the same ambiguities. Black journalists once more sang the praises of black war heroes, who—because of Executive Order 9981, which in 1948 ordered the U.S. military to desegregate—fought mostly in integrated combat units. Similarly important, the period 1950 to 1953 saw the first black Medal of Honor awardees since the late nineteenth century. Historian Christine Knauer has provided a superb analysis of the ways in which the Korean War reflected and shaped debates on citizenship, heroism, civil rights, and gender in the 1950s. As Knauer has shown, decorated soldiers like Jesse L. Brown, the first black naval officer to be killed in Korea, and Courtney L. Stanley, a combat soldier who valiantly defended a bunker against approaching enemy troops, became symbols of manly black courage and the patriotic citizen-soldier.[43] "Numerous stories of black soldiers' heroism," Knauer concludes, "overtly or covertly countered decades of belittling assessments of black war performance, manhood, and racial and national identity. The successful black soldier embodied and bestowed black male agency."[44] The fact that black servicemen such as Cornelius H. Charlton finally received the Medal of Honor for their valorous service—in the case of Charlton, for leading an assault and killing several enemies before being mortally wounded—satisfied many commentators who had long lamented the fact that the U.S. military appeared to deliberately ignore black soldiers' exploits. It also allowed black journalists to further push the argument that African Americans deserved full equality for their patriotic sacrifices.[45] At the same time, such reports reflected a steadfast commitment to the nation and its symbols, since the U.S. military's awards and its authority to bestow them were seen as legitimate and more evenhanded than in the past. Even the emerging civil rights movement did not appear to shake that commitment.

While the nonviolent freedom struggle managed to pressure the U.S. government into passing pathbreaking civil rights legislation, America's growing military involvement in Southeast Asia rekindled the discourse on black military heroism. In fact, the Vietnam War may have provided African American commentators with the largest pool of black war heroes to choose from, since soldiers of color were drafted in disproportionately large numbers, served in more combat units than had been the case in previous wars, were killed at a disproportionate rate, and, in contrast to white soldiers, frequently chose to reenlist after their first tour in Vietnam because of the economic security and the prospect of promotion that their military service offered. In 1967, in response to public concerns about racial bias in troop assignments, the U.S. Army began assigning more blacks to noncombat units. However, by 1969, African Americans still made up approximately 20 percent of combat troops and accounted for 14 percent of battlefield casualties.[46] In addition, eligible African Americans continued to be drafted in disproportionate numbers. Prior to 1968, much of the increase in black recruits was due to the U.S. Defense Department's Project 100,000, which aimed to reduce the high rejection rate of African Americans and was promoted as a form of economic support for poor black communities. The program enabled recruitment officers to accept applicants whom they otherwise would have rejected because of criminal records or lack of skills. Ultimately, it supplied more than 340,000 new recruits for Vietnam, 40 percent of whom were black.[47]

These numbers and the racial bias that appeared to produce them, as well as the ongoing civil rights struggle, led many African Americans to oppose the war. In 1969, nearly 70 percent of the black population opposed U.S. military operations in Vietnam, because many disagreed with America's war objectives, believed that young black men were unfairly called upon to fight, or felt that the war took federal funds away from direly needed domestic programs. In addition, the emerging Black Power movement not only opposed the Vietnam War, but also regarded it as part of white supremacists' efforts to subdue people of color across the globe.[48]

Despite African Americans' widespread opposition to the war and the radicalization of the black freedom movement, numerous black soldiers reenlisted during the Vietnam era, but their decision tended to have little to do with ambitions to conform to the idea of the heroic citizen-soldier. "Black GIs and Marines," the historian Kimberley Phillips concludes, "patiently explained to the national press that they found the additional pay and the higher promotion rates important incentives. Men with children considered the extra combat pay critical." Faced with the prospect of economic hardship upon their return, even those young black men who had not planned on pursuing a military career frequently chose combat pay in Vietnam over unemployment at home. Just as importantly, the threat of being jailed for refusing to go to Vietnam prompted many African Americans to voluntarily enlist in order to have at least some agency in deciding their fate.[49] Similarly, for many of those soldiers who received awards for heroism, such forms of recognition had little meaning. Anecdotal evidence suggests that this was due to not just disillusionment with what was increasingly viewed as a senseless war that did little to help African Americans at home, but also what could be regarded as a deliberate devaluation of heroism.[50] Colin Powell, for instance, who rose to prominence in the post-Vietnam era—first as a four-star general and later as secretary of state in the administration of President George W. Bush—expressed his frustration over the award inflation he had witnessed during his service in Southeast Asia. "The Legion of Merit I received?," he asked in his memoirs. "It might have meant more to me in a war where medals were not distributed indiscriminately. . . . Awards were piled on to a point where writing the justifying citations became a minor art form."[51] While black World War II and Korean War veterans might have harbored ill feelings as well, African American Vietnam War veterans became utterly disillusioned, a sentiment that found expression in a general disregard for the ideal of the citizen-soldier hero and the values it stood for.[52]

Yet, as during the 1945 to 1965 period, white authorities and African American journalists and pundits continued to uphold this ideal and use it in their efforts to strengthen black citizens' loyalty to the nation, and, in the case of the black press, to demand a type of civic nationalism that ensured true equality for all citizens. Breaking with much of the prejudiced tradition of the past, the white mainstream press and public television generally acknowledged the heroism of black soldiers, reporting about them and their role in the integrated military of the 1960s and 1970s in much the same manner that they covered news about white servicemen. Reflecting this tendency toward egalitarian reporting, numerous news reports and print media images showed integrated combat units without commenting on their racial implications.[53]

With regard to the U.S. government's reactions to black military heroism, the White House staged widely publicized ceremonies to honor decorated servicemen of color that would have been unthinkable in the World War II era. During the second half of the 1960s, one black war hero was selected for particularly lavish praise: Milton Lee Olive, a young man who in 1965 had thrown himself on a grenade to save the members of his platoon, and had posthumously received the Medal of Honor for this ultimate sacrifice. Olive, and the official White House ceremony during which President Lyndon B. Johnson presented the dead hero's parents with his award, were the subject of numerous articles that appeared in black and white newspapers—in many cases, on the front pages. Even the *New York Times* and *Los Angeles Times* reported extensively about the White House ceremony, with large accompanying images showing President Johnson, Olive's father, and some of the members of his platoon who also attended the ceremony.[54]

President Johnson, who had invited Olive's parents and numerous other relatives, used the ceremony to justify America's military involvement in Southeast Asia, and described heroism as a manly virtue that reflected admirable loyalty to the nation. Stressing that America was in Vietnam to resist Communist aggression and to defend democracy, Johnson suggested that Olive's heroic death spoke to the importance of "national honor." He said, "Men like Milton Olive die for honor. Nations that are without honor die, too, but without purpose and without cause."[55] He thus portrayed Olive as a paragon of the citizen-soldier who affirmed his own masculinity, as well as the masculine strength of the nation, by willingly sacrificing his life for the nation's cause. Johnson's praise was not the end of it. In 1966, there followed a number of other awards for and tributes to the fallen black hero. Chicago's mayor Richard Daley awarded the Chicago native the Medal of Merit, the city's highest award. Chicago authorities also named a lakefront park after him and dedicated a monument to the Medal of Honor recipient.[56] That same year, the U.S. Army named a training field at Fort Polk, Louisiana, after him, since it was the place where Olive had been trained as a paratrooper. During the dedication ceremony, which was also attended by Olive's parents, a temporary sign with a portrait of Olive was unveiled, with plans to replace it with a permanent bronze plaque bearing the soldier's likeness.[57] In the eyes of white journalists and the White House, Olive—the first of twenty soldiers of color who received the Medal of Honor during the Vietnam War—seemed to symbolize the possibility of interracial brotherhood, racial reconciliation, and race-neutral patriotism.

Black journalists, echoing the mainstream media's assessments of black heroism, continued to endorse the idea of the heroic citizen-soldier and the affirmations of hegemonic masculinity this ideal entailed, though their coverage of black war heroes during the Vietnam era was interspersed with more critical comments than had been the case before 1965. For example, the black publications that reported about Milton Olive's exploits and the White House award ceremony hinted at the possibility of racial reconciliation, but they also viewed his award as yet more proof that racist stereotypes about "cowardly" black soldiers were untrue. Writing in May 1966 in the *New Journal and Guide*, African American sociologist and minister Gordon Hancock said, "I wept with joy that young Olive's supreme sacrifice helped refute the cooked-up rumor and monumental lie that prejudiced whites so cheerfully pass along to the effect that Negroes are cowards on the battlefield."[58] One month later, the middle-class magazine *Ebony* used the case of Olive to once more remind readers of the many deeds of heroism that black soldiers had performed in the past, chiding President Johnson for misstating the number of African Americans who had been granted the Medal of Honor. "Negro American troops have performed with valor in every war in American history from the Revolution to the present conflict," *Ebony* emphasized, accusing Pentagon officials of having "done a great injustice to at least 39 other Negroes who have received their country's highest award since it was created in the beginning years of the Civil War."[59] While some black journalists linked Olive's heroic sacrifice to the black civil rights struggle, most of them concentrated on setting the record straight with regard to white arguments about African Americans' alleged "unheroic" nature.[60] What this and similar articles in black middle-class and working-class publications suggest is that officially acknowledged heroism continued to be regarded as evidence that black citizens were "true" men and full members of the American nation. However, they also indicate that most black journalists continued to accept white definitions and standards of heroism.

Initially, this general acceptance of the U.S. military's perspective on valor on the battlefield could also be seen in the coverage of black war heroes after Olive's death. As in the past, many black newspapers dutifully reported about every official award that black soldiers received for heroic service during the Vietnam War, and many of their articles once more were accompanied by images of the award ceremonies that showed the recipients in uniform and standing at attention.[61] As the war wore on, however, an increasing number of commentators combined their praise for heroic black soldiers with calls for the federal government to reward African Americans for their sacrifices on the battlefield. As more and more reports highlighted the discrimination that black soldiers were confronted with in Vietnam, journalists moved away from supporting the idea of interracial brotherhood and highlighted the prejudices and hardships that even decorated war heroes faced upon their return home.[62] In April 1967, for instance, Whitney Young, the head of the National Urban League, entered the debate on heroism with an editorial that appeared in the *New Journal and Guide*. "The role of our Negro fighting men is perhaps best typified by Specialist 6 Lawrence Joel, who recently received the nation's highest military honor, the Medal of Honor," Young wrote. "The nation is in the debt of men like Specialist Joel who undergo such hardship and danger." According to Young, the nation had to ponder the question of whether it could "ask so much from these men without doing something about the discrimination which [limited] their opportunities" back home. Young believed that there was "a bill to be paid, in the form of open housing, better educational and job opportunities, and the end of discrimination, and it must be paid soon."[63] While increasingly critical of the treatment of African Americans in Vietnam, as well as of the slow pace of change in the United States, black commentators still refrained from questioning the idea of the heroic citizen-soldier itself.

In addition, black journalists continued the prewar tradition of proudly preserving the memory of black heroism, and of emphasizing it even in the face of looming military defeat and the country's ultimate withdrawal from Vietnam. In 1968, for example, *Ebony* published a lengthy article on black soldiers' service in America's wars. "Always, from the first days of the Republic," its editors wrote, "the black soldier has fought away from home for the freedoms denied him at home. At the back of his mind always has been the vain hope that America would recognize his bravery away from home by recognizing him as a man at home. And in pursuing that hope, the black soldier has written in blood a testament of generosity and gallantry which is a standing reproach and invitation to the Republic."[64] Such attempts to affirm the heroic memory of soldiers of color could also be seen in some political debates, as in 1969 in the Illinois legislature, when a black politician named Corneal A. Davis countered a white legislator's claim that the country owed nothing to African Americans. An agitated Davis asserted that Americans "wouldn't have a country if it [hadn't been] for the black man." He then proceeded to remind fellow legislators of black soldiers' heroism in America's wars, and asserted that the Civil War would have been lost without their valorous service.[65] Echoing Davis's passionate comments, African American civil rights activists managed to convince several cities to organize Crispus Attucks Day celebrations in the late 1960s to celebrate the first black martyr of the American Revolution. Similarly, in 1968 the NAACP issued a series of press releases titled "Black Heroes of the American Revolution" to remind young African Americans of the valor of soldiers of color in the past.[66] While the Vietnam War sullied the history of heroism in the eyes of many, African American journalists, pundits, and politicians still endorsed the memory of black martial valor and linked it to their vision of egalitarian civic nationalism and strong black manhood.

This triumphant narrative of African American exploits on the battlefield could still be observed in the face of military defeat, at least in the black working-class magazine *Jet*. In 1975, when the last U.S. troops left Southeast Asia, *Jet* devoted an entire issue to the Vietnam War's black soldiers, in which journalists lamented the fact that so little had been published about "the heroism of the inner-city and rural Blacks who became some of the great jungle fighters."[67] While criticizing the injustices that many black veterans faced after their return to the United States, *Jet* proudly presented the twenty African Americans who had won the Medal of Honor during the war, and concluded: "At no time in the history of U.S. warfare has the Black American distinguished himself more as a valorous and intrepid fighter than he did in the Vietnam War."[68] Although the war left a bitter aftertaste among black journalists because it reminded them of the reality of racism, commentators of color tended to revel in black servicemen's heroic accomplishments, which were deemed noteworthy because they had been validated by white authorities.

After Vietnam, as the draft was abolished and the all-volunteer army became a reality, African Americans continued to enlist and frequently distinguished themselves on the battlefield. However, for many African Americans, echoing the sentiments of black soldiers who had fought in Vietnam, notions of national loyalty or proving one's masculinity were not necessarily among the most important motivations to join the military. As Kimberley Phillips explains, "African Americans have historically enlisted and reenlisted at high rates, not because of any oversized sense of nationalism or patriotism, but because the military remains a steady job. Since the Vietnam War, the armed forces have served as a de facto job program for black Americans and a symbol of a gain in their long struggle for full citizenship. In a postindustrial economy of the late twentieth century, the military has provided steady work and important benefits, including health care, child care, and education."[69] In the minds of many citizens of color, however, the idea that black military heroism proved black soldiers' worth as masculine citizens-soldiers and therefore entitled them to full membership in the American nation remained powerful. Tireless lobbying on the part of black activists for Medals of Honor for black World War II veterans who had been denied this award despite their heroic exploits reflect this long tradition of using the memory of black military heroism to express faith in and lay claim to the civic nationalism that the United States tends to present as the nation's ideological foundation.[70]

While additional research will be necessary to fully understand the various strands of martial heroism that converged during the period from World War II through the Vietnam War, this chapter has demonstrated that the nationalized and gendered meanings of black heroism have to be viewed as the result of a dialectical process that involved both white authorities and African American commentators, pundits, activists, and politicians. Although the Vietnam War led many people to question the validity of the cherished ideal of the citizen-soldier hero, the period 1941 to 1975 was characterized by much continuity with regard to white and African American interpretations of black valor on the battlefield. Especially during World War II, white authorities used black heroism to soothe black discontent, suggesting to African Americans that the U.S. military readily acknowledged their valor, while continuing to discriminate against them. On occasion, the U.S. government also publicly honored decorated black soldiers, similarly hoping that such official acknowledgments would strengthen African American citizens' national loyalty. White authorities thus deliberately used black heroism as a means of social control in the face of black discontent and civil rights protest.

For black journalists, pundits, and other commentators, black heroism—especially, the memory of martial valor—certainly became an important political resource, which fueled their argument that African Americans were "true" men and patriotic citizen-soldiers who deserved full membership in the American nation. However, throughout the period 1941 to 1975, the comments of black reporters, editors, and pundits revealed an abiding faith in white definitions and standards of military heroism, as well as in the patriotic values that were associated with them, since they continually argued that black soldiers conformed to or even exceeded these standards. Neither the black freedom struggle of the 1960s nor the anti–Vietnam War movement seemed to negatively affect the black press's faith in these definitions. This proved to be true for almost all black newspapers and magazines that were analyzed, regardless of their editors' political leanings or the different sections of the black community the publications tried to reach. Ironically, then, black calls for the acknowledgment of African American heroism became both a means of empowerment and a testament to the cultural power of America's citizen-soldier ideology, which revolved around masculine loyalty to the nation and the professed ideal of civic nationalism. For African Americans, then, military heroism was a double-edged sword—both an avenue for liberation and an instrument of subjugation.

NOTES

1. See, for example, Linda Hervieux, *Forgotten: The Untold Story of D-Day's Black Heroes, at Home and at War* (New York: Harper, 2015); J. Todd Moye, *Freedom Flyers: The Tuskegee Airmen of World War II* (New York: Oxford University Press, 2010); Robert F. Jefferson, *Fighting for Hope: African American Troops of the 93rd Infantry Division in World War II and Postwar America* (Baltimore: Johns Hopkins University Press, 2008); Stephen L. Harris, *Harlem's Hell Fighters: The African-American 369th Infantry in World War I* (Washington, DC: Potomac Books, 2003); Gail Buckley, *American Patriots: The Story of Blacks in the Military from the Revolution to Desert Storm* (New York: Random House, 2002); Catherine Clinton, *The Black Soldier: 1492 to the Present* (Boston: Houghton Mifflin, 2000); Lawrence P. Scott and William M. Womack Sr., *Double V: The Civil Rights Struggle of the Tuskegee Airmen* (East Lansing: Michigan State University Press, 1998); Gerald Astor, *The Right to Fight: A History of African Americans in the Military* (Novato, CA: Presidio Press, 1998); Bernard C. Nalty, *Strength for the Fight: A History of Black Americans in the Military* (New York: Free Press, 1986).

2. See, for example, Adriane Lentz-Smith, *Freedom Struggles: African Americans and World War I* (Cambridge, MA: Harvard University Press, 2009); Chad L. Williams, *Torchbearers of Democracy: African American Soldiers in the World War I Era* (Chapel Hill: University of North Carolina Press, 2010).

3. Holly Allen, "Gender, Sexuality and the Military Model of U.S. National Community," in *Gender Ironies of Nationalism: Sexing the Nation*, ed. Tamar Mayer (New York: Routledge, 2000), 309.

4. R. Claire Snyder, *Citizen-Soldiers and Manly Warriors: Military Service and Gender in the Civic Republican Tradition* (Lanham, MD: Rowman and Littlefield, 1999), 2.

5. William J. Goode, *The Celebration of Heroes: Prestige as a Control System* (Berkeley: University of California Press, 1978), 152.

6. John Breuilly, *Nationalism and the State* (Chicago: University of Chicago Press, 1993), 2; Craig Calhoun, *Nationalism* (Buckingham, UK: Open University Press, 1997), 4–5; Nira Yuval-Davis, *Gender & Nation* (Thousand Oaks, CA: Sage, 1997), 21; Michael Billig, *Banal Nationalism* (London: Sage, 1995).

7. Benedict Anderson, *Imagined Communities: Reflections on the Origin and Spread of Nationalism*, rev. ed. (New York: Verso, 1991); David Brown, "Are There Good and Bad Nationalisms?," *Nations and Nationalisms* 5, no. 2 (1999): 281–302; Andreas Fahrmeir, *Citizenship: The Rise and Fall of a Modern Concept* (New Haven, CT: Yale University Press, 2007), 2–4.

8. Judith Butler, *Undoing Gender* (New York: Routledge, 2004); Judith Butler, *Bodies that Matter: On the Discursive Limits of "Sex"* (New York: Routledge, 1993); Judith Butler, *Gender Trouble: Feminism and the Subversion of Identity* (New York: Routledge, 1990).

9. John Pettegrew, "'The Soldier's Faith': Turn-of-the-Century Memory of the Civil War and the Emergence of Modern American Nationalism," *Journal of Contemporary History* 31, no. 1 (1996): 49–73; Edward Tabor Linenthal, *Changing Images of the Warrior Hero in*

America: A History of Popular Symbolism (New York: Edwin Mellen Press, 1982), 27; Kevin Alexander Boon, "Heroes, Metanarratives, and the Paradox of Masculinity in Contemporary Western Culture," *Journal of Men's Studies* 13, no. 3 (2005): 303–304; Laura C. Prividera and John W. Howard III, "Masculinity, Whiteness, and the Warrior Hero: Perpetuating the Strategic Rhetoric of U.S. Nationalism and the Marginalization of Women," *Women and Language* 29, no. 2 (2006): 29, 31; Joshua S. Goldstein, *War and Gender: How Gender Shapes the War System and Vice Versa* (Cambridge, UK: Cambridge University Press, 2001), 265–272, 274–279; R. W. Connell, *Masculinities* (Cambridge, UK: Polity Press, 1995), 37–38, 78, 213.

10. Eviatar Zerubavel, "From 'Social Memories: Steps towards a Sociology of the Past,'" in *The Collective Memory Reader*, ed. Jeffrey K. Olick, Vered Vinitzky-Seroussi, and Daniel Levy (New York: Oxford University Press, 2011), 223; Alon Confino, "Collective Memory and Cultural History: Problems of Method," *American Historical Review* 102, no. 5 (1997): 1398–1400; Nancy Wood, "Memory's Remains: Les Lieux de mémoire," *History & Memory* 6, no. 1 (1994): 144; David Lowenthal, *The Past Is a Foreign Country* (Cambridge, UK: Cambridge University Press, 1985); Barry Schwartz, *Abraham Lincoln and the Forge of National Memory* (Chicago: University of Chicago Press, 2000), 18; W. Fitzhugh Brundage, "Introduction: No Deed but Memory," in *Where These Memories Grow: History, Memory, and Southern Identity*, ed. W. Fitzhugh Brundage (Chapel Hill: University of North Carolina Press 2000), 3–5; "The Nation: Real or Imagined? The Warwick Debates on Nationalism," *Nations and Nationalism* 2, no. 3 (1996): 362; Confino, "Collective Memory and Cultural History," 1402.

11. Karen Hagemann, "Of 'Manly Valor' and 'German Honor': Nation, War, and Masculinity in the Age of the Prussian Uprising against Napoleon," *Central European History* 30, no. 2 (1997): 219; Pettegrew, "'The Soldier's Faith,'" 49–73; Editors of Boston Publishing Company, *The Medal of Honor: A History of Service Above and Beyond* (Minneapolis, MN: Zenith Press, 2014), 12–15.

12. Connell, *Masculinities*, 37–38, 78, 213; Boon, "Heroes, Metanarratives, and the Paradox of Masculinity in Contemporary Western Culture," 303–304; Goldstein, *War and Gender*, 265–272, 274–279; William L. Van Deburg, *Black Camelot: African-American Culture Heroes in Their Times, 1960–1980* (Chicago: University of Chicago Press, 1997), 24–37; Nathan I. Huggins, "W.E.B. Du Bois and Heroes," *Amerikastudien* 34, no. 2 (1989): 167–174; Pettegrew, "'The Soldier's Faith,'" 64–68; Christine Bold, "Where Did the Black Rough Riders Go?," *Canadian Review of American Studies* 39, no. 3 (2009): 274.

13. Williams, *Torchbearers of Democracy*, 30, 126.

14. Elmer A. Carter, "Trouble in the South," *Opportunity*, September 1941, 258.

15. Harvard Sitkoff, "Racial Militancy and Interracial Violence in the Second World War," *Journal of American History* 58, no. 3 (1971): 661–681; Herbert Shapiro, *White Violence and Black Response: From Reconstruction to Montgomery* (Amherst: University of Massachusetts Press, 1988), 305.

16. On Randolph and the MOWM, see David Lucander, *Winning the War for Democracy: The March on Washington Movement, 1941–1946* (Champaign: University of Illinois Press, 2014); Cornelius L. Bynum, *A. Philip Randolph and the Struggle for Civil Rights* (Champaign: University of Illinois Press, 2010); Paula F. Pfeffer, *A. Philip Randolph, Pioneer of the Civil Rights Movement* (Baton Rouge: Louisiana State University Press, 1996).

17. See August Meier and Elliott M. Rudwick, *CORE: A Study in the Civil Rights Movement, 1942–1968* (New York: Oxford University Press, 1973); Rawn James Jr., *The Double V: How Wars, Protest, and Harry Truman Desegregated America's Military* (New York: Bloomsbury, 2013), 141–143.

18. Christina S. Jarvis, *The Male Body at War: American Masculinity during World War II* (DeKalb: Northern Illinois University Press, 2004), 122, 148–149; Andrew J. Huebner, *The Warrior Image: Soldiers in American Culture from the Second World War to the Vietnam Era* (Chapel Hill: University of North Carolina Press, 2008), 43.
19. "The Negro and the Army" (radio program), NBC, August 12, 1941, address by Honorable Robert P. Patterson, Under Secretary of War, War Department, Bureau of Public Relations, "Future Release," National Urban League Papers, part 1, F17, folder "War Department, 1941–1942," Library of Congress (hereafter cited as LOC), Washington, D.C.
20. "Heroism of Negro Soldiers to Be Dramatized on Air," *Atlanta Daily World*, December 21, 1941, 5.
21. "Negro Soldier Heroes Honored on Network Broadcast," *New Journal and Guide*, October 3, 1942, 17.
22. War Department, Bureau of Public Relations, "Legion of Merit to 4 Negro Soldiers for Outstanding Service at Guadalcanal" (press release); War Department, Bureau of Public Relations, "Negro Personnel in Army Total More than 450,000," February 27, 1943, 2, both in National Urban League Papers, part 1, F17, folder "War Department, 1943–1945"; "273 Army Heroes Listed," *Chicago Defender*, October 13, 1945, 18.
23. This page appeared in almost identical designs in at least three black newspapers. See "Distinguished Soldiers," *New Journal and Guide*, January 8, 1944, B20; "Valor," *Cleveland Call and Post*, November 27, 1943, 11A; "Distinguished Soldiers," *Philadelphia Tribune*, December 11, 1943, 9.
24. Thomas Cripps and David Culbert, "The Negro Soldier (1944): Film Propaganda in Black and White," *American Quarterly* 31, no. 5 (1979): 616–640.
25. Ibid., 631, 635; "4 Film Houses Show 'The Negro Soldier,'" *New York Times*, April 22, 1944, NAACP Papers, group 2, box A278, folder 2, LOC; "Royal Premieres 'Negro Soldier,'" *Philadelphia Tribune*, May 6, 1944, 2.
26. Huebner, *The Warrior Image*, 46–47.
27. See, for example, Gertrude B. Rivers, "Negro Heroes in the Present War," *Negro History Bulletin*, May 1944, 173–174, 176, 188–189; "Three Illinois Soldiers Decorated for Heroism," *Chicago Defender*, December 9, 1944, 11; "'Extraordinary Heroism' Wins DS Cross," *Philadelphia Tribune*, December 4, 1943, 11; "Southerner Given Medal for Heroism," *Chicago Defender*, February 27, 1943, 10; "Two Soldiers Rewarded for Their Heroism," *Atlanta Daily World*, June 18, 1943, 1.
28. See, for example, "Award for Heroism," *Philadelphia Tribune*, March 4, 1944, 1; "Heroism Rewarded," *Philadelphia Tribune*, November 4, 1944, 1; George Coleman Moore, "Heroism Wins Bronze Medal," *Atlanta Daily World*, February 24, 1945, 1; "Hero Gets Soldier's Medal," *Atlanta Daily World*, November 21, 1943, 5.
29. "War Records Show Negro Soldiers Have Earned Big Share of Honors," *Chicago Defender*, December 4, 1943, 7.
30. See National Urban League Papers, part 1, F17, folder "Heroism of Negro Soldiers and Sailors in World War II."
31. Paul Alkebulan, *The African American Press in World War II: Toward Victory at Home and Abroad* (Lanham, MD: Lexington Books, 2014), 41–50.
32. "Negro Heroism at Pearl Harbor," *Chicago Defender*, January 10, 1942, 14.
33. George W. Blount, "Blount—Speaks Softly," *New Journal and Guide*, June 6, 1942, A10.
34. "Slighting of Heroic GI Arouses Citizens' Ire," *Philadelphia Tribune*, December 1, 1945, 1.
35. Cliff Mackay, "The Globe Trotter: Black Heroes Unsung!," *Atlanta Daily World*, February 8, 1942, 4.

36. A. M. Rivera Jr., "Add: Heroes of World War No. 1—Robert Lee Campbell, D.S.C.," *New Journal and Guide*, January 10, 1942, A9.
37. "Colored American Can Save America," *Philadelphia Tribune*, March 14, 1942, 5. See also Lucius C. Harper, "Should Arm for Freedom: Black Heroes Play Historic Role in Every Single War from Revolution to 1942," *Chicago Defender*, September 26, 1942, B2.
38. William Walker, "Shall Our Glorious History Be a Forgotten Past?," *Cleveland Call and Post*, August 10, 1939, 6. See also "Heroism of Race Soldiers Recounted in New Book," *Chicago Defender*, August 24, 1940, 12.
39. "Extraordinary Heroism Wins DS Cross," *Philadelphia Tribune*, December 4, 1943, 11. For a similar assessment, see Luther P. Jackson, "Sergeant William H. Carney—Hero of the Civil War," *New Journal and Guide*, November 18, 1944, C10.
40. Nat Brandt, *Harlem at War: The Black Experience in World War II* (Syracuse, NY: Syracuse University Press, 1996), 225.
41. Joseph D. Bibb, "Our GIs Slighted," *Courier* (formerly *Pittsburgh Courier*), November 4, 1950, 21. See also John H. Young III, "Negroes Have Received Fewer Top Decorations in This War," *Pittsburgh Courier*, June 2, 1945, 15.
42. Helen Gahagan Douglas, "The Story of the Negro Soldier in World War II," *Los Angeles Sentinel*, February 21, 1946, 21.
43. Christine Knauer, *Let Us Fight as Free Men: Black Soldiers and Civil Rights* (Philadelphia: University of Pennsylvania Press, 2014), 64, 220–222.
44. Ibid., 176.
45. See Venice T. Spraggs, "Second Hero of Korea Gets Medal of Honor," *Chicago Defender*, February 23, 1952, 1, 2; "Receives U.S. Highest Award for Heroism," *Atlanta Daily World*, February 17, 1952, 1.
46. James E. Westheider, *The African American Experience in Vietnam: Brothers in Arms* (Lanham, MD: Rowman and Littlefield, 2008), 17–62.
47. Kimberley L. Phillips, *War! What Is It Good For? Black Freedom Struggles and the U.S. Military: From World War II to Iraq* (Chapel Hill: University of North Carolina Press, 2012), 203–204.
48. Ibid., 223–227; Simon Hall, *Peace and Freedom: The Civil Rights and Antiwar Movements in the 1960s* (Philadelphia: University of Pennsylvania Press, 2005), 39–71. On the Black Power movement's history and multilayered agenda, see, for example, Peniel E. Joseph, *Waiting 'til the Midnight Hour: A Narrative History of Black Power in America* (New York: Henry Holt, 2006); Peniel E. Joseph, ed., *The Black Power Movement: Rethinking the Civil Rights–Black Power Era* (New York: Routledge, 2006); Jeffrey O. G. Ogbar, *Black Power: Radical Politics and African American Identity* (Baltimore: Johns Hopkins University Press, 2004); William L. Van Deburg, *New Day in Babylon: The Black Power Movement and American Culture, 1965–1975* (Chicago: University of Chicago Press, 1992).
49. Phillips, *War! What Is It Good For?*, 207.
50. See, for example, "Vietnam: Consensus at Large," *Jet*, May 22, 1975, 52–53; James E. Westheider, *Fighting on Two Fronts: African Americans and the Vietnam War* (New York: New York University Press, 1997), 169.
51. Colin Powell, with Joseph E. Persico, *My American Journey*, rev. ed. (New York: Ballantine Books, 2003), 145–146.
52. Westheider, *The African American Experience in Vietnam*, 63–79.
53. Huebner, *The Warrior Image*, 184–185.
54. "Negro Is Top Viet Nam Hero," *Chicago Daily Defender*, October 27, 1965, 1; "LBJ Gives Youth Highest Award: Honor for Dead Soldier," *Chicago Defender*, April 23, 1966, 1; "Negro GI Wins Medal of Honor Posthumously," *Los Angeles Times*, April 21, 1966, 18; James

Goodrich, "Nation Honors Negro GI Who Gave Life for Mates," *Los Angeles Sentinel*, April 28, 1966, A1; Laurence Burd, "Heroism of Slain GI Told at Rites," *Los Angeles Times*, April 22, 1966, 1; John W. Finney, "Johnson Extols a Soldier's Valor in Vietnam," *New York Times*, April 22, 1966, 1.

55. Quoted in Finney, "Johnson Extols a Soldier's Valor in Vietnam," 1.

56. "Heroes and History," *Ebony*, June 1966, 10; "Park Named for Hero Olive Pictured on City Book," *Jet*, December 8, 1966, 9.

57. "Training Field to Be Named for Milton Lee Olive," *Chicago Defender*, July 23, 1966, 6.

58. Gordon Hancock, "Highest Award to Hero and Tears for America," *New Journal and Guide*, May 7, 1966, B14.

59. "Heroes and History," 10.

60. Lawrence Allen Eldridge, *Chronicles of a Two-Front War: Civil Rights and Vietnam in the African American Press* (Columbia: University of Missouri Press, 2011), 189.

61. See, for example, "Vietnam Heroism Nets 25 GI's Bronze Stars," *New Journal and Guide*, February 25, 1967, A5; "Bronze Star for Vietnam Heroism," *Afro-American*, October 1, 1966, 14.

62. Eldridge, *Chronicles of a Two-Front War*, 209.

63. Whitney M. Young Jr., "To Be Equal," *New Journal and Guide*, April 1, 1967, 6.

64. "These Truly Are the Brave . . . ," *Ebony*, August 1968, 164. For a similar assessment from the pre-1968 period, see Betty Washington, "Negro Soldiers Did Their Part in the Civil War," *Chicago Defender*, May 28, 1966, 1.

65. Simeon B. Osby, "Rep. Davis Lashes Legislators. Cites Black Heroism," *Chicago Daily Defender*, February 22, 1969, 1.

66. "Crispus Attucks Day Recognized," *Jet*, March 20, 1969, 28–29; "Press Release—March 20," "Press Release—April 10," "Press Release—April 24," "Press Release—May 22," all in NAACP Papers, group 3, box A252, folder 3.

67. Simeon Booker, "What the Vietnam War Did to Blacks," *Jet*, May 22, 1975, 14–17.

68. "Blacks Made Heroic Efforts in Vietnam," *Jet*, May 22, 1975, 22–23, 51.

69. Phillips, *War! What Is It Good For?*, 277.

70. Buckley, *American Patriots*, 480–483.

4 • "WARRIORS IN UNIFORM"

Race, Masculinity, and Martial Valor among Native American Veterans from the Great War to Vietnam and Beyond

MATTHIAS VOIGT

Each year on July 4, Native American veterans and their families join in a huge display of patriotism by flying the Stars and Stripes, offering their pledge of allegiance, and proudly parading at traditional powwows before their tribal communities. Native American veterans frequently adorn their service uniforms with eagle feathers, war bonnets, and other items of high significance in what is a syncretic blending of various cultural elements. Indian Country represents a highly militarized space.[1] Native Americans have the highest per capita enlistment of any racial group in the United States, yet they account for the smallest of such groups.[2] An overwhelming number of Native veterans have also seen combat, and during the course of it, distinguished themselves through martial valor.

Native American notions of traditional warriorhood constitute a powerful counternarrative to the dominant Western ideal of the white warrior hero. While other marginalized minorities have utilized martial valor on the battlefield to prove their loyalty to the United States and to gain legitimacy and equal U.S. citizenship rights, Native Americans have utilized the U.S. military for different purposes. Native Americans continue to join the U.S. military as members of both their tribal nations and the United States, and as such, seek to maintain both their treaty rights and their civil rights. As dual citizens, Native Americans have an ambiguous and hybrid status on the boundaries of the American settler nation as well as within the democratic settler state.[3] First, Native Americans have never sought to completely adhere to Western norms, values, and beliefs, but rather sought to maintain their own cultural identities. Scholarship suggests that military service has allowed Native veterans to maintain their cultural identity as Indigenous people vis-à-vis dominant society.[4] Second, at the same time—and to a much lesser extent—Native veterans have also utilized their veteran status to challenge their subaltern position within the American settler state, in particular after World War II and during the Vietnam War era. They have done so less by trying to emulate the Western ideal of the patriotic white warrior hero than by pointing to their military service in general or their battlefield valor in particular to gain civil rights.[5]

NATIVE AMERICAN MILITARY SERVICE FROM WORLD WAR I TO THE PRESENT

Native Americans have fought in every conflict in U.S. history—first as auxiliaries, then as scouts, and finally as soldiers in the various branches of the U.S. armed forces. During World War I, an estimated 12,000 of them served at a time when they were not officially American citizens. During World War II, another 44,000 wore U.S. uniforms. In the Korean conflict there were an estimated 10,000. During the Vietnam War era, 42,000 served in Southeast Asia, and about 90 percent of them were volunteers—simultaneous with the military draft that was in place until 1973.[6] During the Vietnam War, one in four eligible Native Americans served in the military, as opposed to one in twelve of the general American population.[7] In the post-Vietnam era, Native men and women took part in high numbers in combat actions across the world—in Grenada, Panama, Somalia, Iraq, and Afghanistan.[8]

Despite this service record, the nation at large has only recently begun to recognize the contributions made by Native Americans. The Medal of Honor Society counts thirty-two Native recipients.[9] The code talkers, perhaps the best-known group of World War I and World War II Native veterans, gained belated national recognition in 2013 with the bestowment of congressional medals.[10] The United States has also honored its Native veterans through two national memorials, one in Phoenix, Arizona, and another in Riverside, California. On December 26, 2013, President Barack Obama signed into law a bill authorizing the erection of a veteran statue at the National Museum of the American Indian (NMAI) on the National Mall in Washington, D.C. There has also been a proliferation of Native memorials, veteran parks, cemeteries, and Veteran Administration–administered veterans facilities.

The exemplary military service record of Native Americans can be understood as an attempt to maintain their cultural distinctiveness and tribal traditions, rather than validate themselves as U.S. citizens.[11] Throughout American history, Native Americans have utilized the U.S. military for reasons of their own, rather than those expected of them by the dominant society. In doing so, they have maintained a strong sense of their own cultural identity and perpetuated their own cultural construct of martial manliness. Sometimes, that cultural construct runs counter to the norms, values, and beliefs of mainstream American society (e.g., by attaching different meanings to military service and by utilizing alternative customs and practices to recognize and honor war veterans). On other occasions, it reaffirmed hegemonic masculine qualities and national loyalty, for example by recognizing and honoring non-Native veterans as warriors.

Studies on masculinity have frequently focused on white Western masculinities—the world's most salient form of masculinity—as well as the intricate relationship between nation and gender. Lately, scholars have also turned their attention to various racial groups to better understand their relationships to the American nation. Until recently, Native subaltern masculinities—those with a natural land base, and that have been impacted by the oppressive forces of colonialism—have largely been ignored.[12] New trends in masculinities studies suggest a turning away from Eurocentric paradigms, and instead favor the study of masculinities within their own, culturally specific contexts and in their respective local settings.[13]

The U.S. military not only produces and reproduces masculinities (and more recently, femininities); it also constitutes a site where hegemonic notions of military valor and heroic soldiering exist side by side with traditional Native American understandings of warriorhood, military service, and martial valor. In general, Western notions of military valor have resonated with Native notions of martial valor. Native recipients of the Medal of Honor, for example, are highly respected across Indian Country. However, the way tribal communities continue to recognize and honor their veterans (who are also called warriors) provides a powerful counternarrative to the white warrior hero ideal and to the norms and values of the white settler nation this ideal entails. Native notions of traditional warriorhood differ significantly from what Anglo-Americans commonly associate with military heroism, and tend to undermine the narratives that dominate American hero-making processes.

WARRIORS IN UNIFORM: ANGLO-AMERICAN AND NATIVE AMERICAN PERSPECTIVES

Anglo-American motivations to recruit Native men into the U.S. military were largely inspired by certain cultural notions and stereotypical imagery. The most pervasive of these was the perception of Indigenous people as a "martial race" of fierce warriors naturally belonging to the battlefield.[14] Many of these hypermasculine images were forged in the white popular perception during centuries of fighting Native tribes. Anglo-Americans' high regard for

Native people as superior warriors tapped into their own, white notions of martial heroism. As a result, Native Americans became subjected to two inherently conflicting agendas: first, white citizens' high regard for the supposedly superior fighting abilities of warriors and second, white efforts to assimilate this worthy "martial race," with its propensity for soldiering, into American society (e.g., through boarding schools and the U.S. military recruitment from reservations).[15] Situated at the intersections of colonial domination and cultural resiliency (or assimilation and cultural renewal), Native Americans' service in the white man's army has become highly ambiguous. Native warriors-turned-soldiers have come to be seen either as (passive) pawns in upholding the very colonial regime that keeps them the subaltern, or, alternatively, as (active) agents in shaping their own destiny, and cultural navigators. The latter view has recently gained widespread recognition through the scholarly works of Holm, Meadows, and Carroll.

Throughout the twentieth century, a hypermasculine warrior imagery has guided popular perceptions about Native men in uniform. The "scout syndrome," deeply embedded in the national consciousness, was most salient during World War I and World War II, but frequently resurfaced during subsequent wars. It was also something that many Native servicepersons experienced firsthand while serving in one or another capacity in the U.S. armed forces. Native veterans' accounts abound with stories that revealed prevailing stereotypes. Frequently, they were called "chief," and found themselves assigned to scouting duties or were made to walk point—because of their supposedly superior martial abilities.[16] During World War I, Anglo-American perceptions of Native men's suitability for service were partially confirmed in 1919 when the American Expeditionary Forces circulated a questionnaire about the suitability of Native men for scouting service. Apparently, the army officer conducting the survey was convinced of their innate predisposition to make outstanding scouts, since, according to Al Carroll, he designed the questionnaire to elicit a desired outcome.[17] World War II echoed and affirmed these racial stereotypes about Native men's superior fighting abilities.[18] During subsequent wars, most notably the Korean and Vietnam conflicts, hypermasculine notions of Native manliness were largely gone from the public media, but popular preconceptions frequently resurfaced in unexpected places. While little is known about scout imagery during the Korean War, the Vietnam War saw warrior imagery from the Indian Wars: enemy-held territory was called "Indian Country," U.S. bases turned into "Fort Apaches," and Vietnamese defectors were named "Kit Carson scouts."[19]

Native Americans' subaltern status vis-à-vis a colonialist government, as well as popular misconceptions of prevailing warrior imagery, have made the processes of Native militarization highly complex and ambivalent. Non-Native persons frequently assume that Native service in the colonizer's army, the very instrument used to keep them oppressed and subaltern, testifies to their own dependency on hegemonic society. Adherents of dependency theory have interpreted Native entrance into the U.S. military as an effort to legitimize themselves in the eyes of the American nation as loyal citizens.[20] However, Native motives for enlistment continue to be fundamentally different from those of Anglo-Americans, and they cannot be easily compared with those of other marginalized groups.

Recent scholarship has reinterpreted Native military service as largely based in culture and less a result of assimilationist and acculturative motivations. Native motivations for military service are often interrelated, and too complex to reduce to a single cause. These motivations center around (1) a hybrid patriotism that is both Native and American; (2) cultural issues related to warrior-based themes (e.g., the continuation of tribal and family traditions, being honored by tribal members and communities, etc.); (3) economic considerations (e.g., employment opportunities); and (4) acculturative and assimilationist influences (e.g., boarding schools).[21]

Apparently, Native veterans have enlisted in the U.S. military for reasons of their own, and their motives are largely culturally motivated.[22] Most Native veterans regard themselves as members of sovereign tribal nations first and members of the American nation second. Paul Rosier has called the dual allegiance to these different entities "hybrid patriotism."[23] Native veterans' reasons for military service are intertwined, be they political, cultural, or economic. Most importantly, many veterans feel that by joining the U.S. military they can defend their ancestral homeland(s) and their tribal peoples, as well as the United States, or that joining up is necessary to uphold treaty obligations. Others feel they are continuing a cultural tradition of being warriors (in uniform), and/or they are continuing a family tradition of military service. Joining the military is also a way to escape the poverty and remoteness of reservation life and see the world and experience adventures. Whatever their motives, Native veterans have utilized the U.S. military, an essentially foreign institution, for their own benefit.[24]

TRADITIONAL NOTIONS OF MARTIAL VALOR AMONG PLAINS INDIAN TRIBAL SOCIETIES

Native notions of martial valor can best be understood by giving consideration to Native people's cross-cultural situatedness between their own cultural traditions and the larger forces of U.S. colonialism and modernity. Pre-reservation perspectives on Native manhood/warriorhood and aspects of war and warfare offer important insights into the cultural context of tribal societies and their understandings of martial valor. They also shed light on how Native veterans carried on, modified, and invented warrior traditions in the form of veteran traditions under U.S. colonialism—all in an effort to preserve their own cultural identity in which martial valor played a significant role.

When talking about their motives for military service and their understanding of traditional valor, Native veterans frequently refer to the old ways. In Plains Indian[25] tribal societies, notions of martial valor were closely connected with a series of interrelated aspects, with culture playing a major role: an ancient perspective that regarded war and warfare as essentially honorable; a set of tribal virtues that encouraged participation in war and warfare; a close interrelationship between manhood and warriorhood; and a particular, reciprocal relationship between the individual and the tribal community.[26]

Prior to U.S. colonialism, Native communities lived in what Donald Fixico has called a "natural democracy," a cultural concept in which human and nonhuman relationships combined in a metaphysical and physical relationship.[27] Native tribes constituted holistic societies and regarded culture, religion, economy, and war and warfare as inherently related to all other spheres of life. This culturally infused perspective also explains the fundamentally different understanding (as opposed to Western societies) that Plains tribal communities attached (and still attach) to war and warfare, manhood, and martial valor.

During the nineteenth century, Plains tribes adhered to a concept of honorable warfare, a predominantly nonlethal way of testing their physical and mental skills and abilities. Honor could be gained by counting coup on an enemy—by touching an enemy with a stick, by hand, or something else—and then making a safe escape. Counting coup was a male way of demonstrating one's bravery and gaining honor. Intertribal warfare often resembled a rough game rather than a bloody battle, because honor was gained not by killing someone, but by demonstrating one's physical and spiritual superiority over an enemy. Those who successfully counted coup were given eagle feathers, the highest awards that could be bestowed upon a warrior. Notched and decorated in certain ways, these eagle feathers signified a carrier's coups and social status. In Plains Indian cultures, warriors and hunters were responsible for the well-being and the protection of the entire tribe. For their actions and deeds, they were honored publicly, thereby gaining social recognition and status. Killing and scalping did not warrant any particular honors. Warfare was also conducted for revenge, to gain spiritual power and spiritual objects, and for economic gains (e.g., horses). Warfare was essentially ritualized and waged against traditional enemies to maintain tribal identity.[28] When settler encroachments upon their lands intensified during the latter half of the nineteenth century, Plains tribes adopted a more lethal approach to warfare in order to defend what was theirs. The battles of the Rosebud and the Little Bighorn were both clear victories of Native warriors over the U.S. military—first, by outmaneuvering them and gaining a nonlethal victory; and second, by showing their lethality when forced to take a stand, and completely wiping out Custer's command.[29]

In Plains tribal societies, notions of manhood and warriorhood were closely tied together, while also connecting to the concept of honorable warfare and nonlethal martial valor. Among the Lakota Sioux, the four cardinal male virtues were bravery, fortitude, generosity, and wisdom—all of which connected to the concept of honorable warfare.[30] A man could seek to master these virtues through his various life stages by counting coup; by showing reserve during periods of stress and endurance; by sharing food or property; and by mastering a deep understanding of the culture's spiritual beliefs, which could be achieved only with experience and age, thus gradually gaining rank and status in the tribal community. Warrior societies were associated with a wide range of duties and responsibilities, such as the validation of veterans and the maintenance of a martial spirit—all of which enhanced tribal integration.[31]

Traditional Native notions of martial valor, encapsulated in the concept of honorable warfare, were decidedly different from Western notions of military heroism and warfare. Western societies waged war for largely economic and/or political reasons. Western warfare involved territorial conquest and/or political subjugation, and ended either when the enemy was forced into submission, or when both sides had exhausted all available means and were too exhausted to carry on fighting. Native people went to war for entirely different reasons—such as sustenance, prestige, or revenge—but rarely to force their will upon another people, to conquer territory, or for purely economic reasons.[32]

The way of the Plains Indian warrior was fundamentally determined by his relationship to the tribal community. This reciprocal and interactive relationship between individual and community has defined Native manhood and warriorhood to the present day. Tom Holm writes that "in most tribal societies, warriorhood was not as much a social role as it was a relationship with the rest of the community. . . . By comparison, soldiers in modern western-style armies are servants of the state. . . . Those outside the military service relate to soldiers as being the functionaries of a larger, very impersonal institution rather than as contributors to the contiguous community. Soldiering is playing a role; warriorhood is a relationship."[33] Essentially, tribal communities and veterans have maintained this particular relationship between masculine responsibility and communal relationship as a remnant of an older tradition. The dependent interrelationship has also led to a natural affinity for service and duty among service-age tribal members.[34]

REINVENTING THE WARRIOR: NATIVE AMERICAN VETERAN TRADITIONS AND MARTIAL VALOR FROM WORLD WAR I TO VIETNAM

Throughout the twentieth century, Native veterans have utilized U.S. military service to reinvent warrior traditions by preserving, revitalizing, and modifying some, while inventing others. The continual process of reinvention was consistent with a fundamental Native mindset of adapting to changing circumstances and incorporating foreign elements into their way of life; this cultural fluidity is a key tool to ensure tribal survival.

Military service has offered Native men a way to access traditional masculine roles of the past. Significantly, according to Tom Holm, Native men enlisted "because they were patriots in the tribal sense of the world. To them, military service was part of an honorable family and/or tribal tradition. They wanted to be warriors—to protect their land and their people. And, in the tribal tradition of reciprocity, they wanted to gain respect from other Native Americans."[35]

Native veterans have continually utilized their military service to reinvent themselves as warriors in a much older tradition. For them, military service offered another avenue to revitalize and reinvent various cultural and spiritual practices and beliefs, songs, and ceremonies. Each war, too, can be understood as an opportunity to reinvent cultural traditions, while perpetuating established notions of warriorhood and masculinity (as well as femininity). Each generation of Native veterans has instigated a need in tribal communities to ritually send off and welcome back Native soldiers in a traditional way. Each conflict of the twentieth century triggered a cultural renaissance in tribal communities through the need to revitalize songs, dances, ceremonies, and languages. No other racial or ethnic group in the United States shares Native people's cultural and martial traditions, a central element that explains their unique war experience.[36] This cultural distinctiveness finds expression in a hybrid patriotism that is Native first and American second.[37]

Servicepersons' send-offs to and homecomings from various wars and conflicts were fundamental in continuing past warrior traditions in the reinvented form of veteran traditions. Soldiers leaving for war were given farewell ceremonies and protection rites, and upon their return were given purification and honoring ceremonies. These cultural and spiritual practices involved fasting, purification rites, prayers, dances, and feats—as was typical during pre-reservation times. Like their ancestors before them, Plains tribal societies honored their warriors in their own culturally specific ways. Similar to the days of old, they also helped them to make the transition from peace to war and back again. Today, not just Native veterans utilize traditional ceremonies to cope with post-traumatic stress syndrome; so, too, do veterans from other racial/ethnic groups.[38]

Natives' participation in World War I, World War II, the Korean War, and the Vietnam War led to a widespread cultural revitalization. Each war produced a generation of veterans who were once again regarded as warriors by their tribal elders, and each generation of veterans continued warrior and veteran traditions in syncretic form, akin to earlier pre-reservation times. The regained status as veterans required a traditional honoring by others—either by warrior/veteran societies or by women societies. Generations of veterans responded by reinventing military societies—key elements were veteran status and the honoring of veterans.[39] Women societies frequently assumed the role of an auxiliary society and, according to tribal traditions, honored their warriors through dances, songs, and ceremonies. Thus, military service was directly linked to cultural revitalization.[40]

For Native veterans, then, U.S. military service was not necessarily a means to validate themselves in the eyes of white America and gain entry into U.S. society; instead, it was a way to maintain their cultural identities as members of tribal nations vis-à-vis the American settler nation, and to do so in a syncretic fashion.[41] In that sense, Native military valor on the battlefield has served Native men partly to embody their own cultural norms, values, and beliefs, allowing them to reinvent themselves and become role models that subsequent generations of veterans seek to emulate—thus passing on and perpetuating their own cultural constructs of martial manliness.

TRIBAL RECOGNITION AND PUBLIC HONORING OF NATIVE AMERICAN VETERANS

Susan J. Drucker and Robert S. Cathcart have emphasized the significance of the relationship between the hero and his community for hero-making processes.[42] The primary public forum for the honoring of non-Native veterans' heroic deeds is the American public—through parades, speeches, medals, and the like. Similar to their non-Native counterparts, Native veterans are also honored, but the most significant place where they receive public recognition is in their own tribal communities.[43]

Powwows represent *the* place most commonly associated with the honoring of Native veterans—who are also called warriors in an older tradition—in front of the entire tribal community. As Kathleen Roberts observed, powwows have emerged from a tradition of Plains Indian war dances.[44] In tribal communities, the relationship between the individual and the community is highly significant. According to tribal beliefs, each individual is in a symbiotic, reciprocal relationship with the entire tribal community—thus, each single warrior/veteran is in a particular relationship with his/her respective tribal community.[45]

Powwows involve a number of practices that reflect the "hybrid patriotism" of Native people: American flag raisings; the singing of flag songs (that is, songs with warrior/veteran-related themes) and honor songs to praise a person's valor; and parades and public honoring of Native veterans. Powwows are initiated by the raising of one American flag in the center of the powwow ground, and one flag for each deceased veteran on flagpoles around the arena. The Grand Entry precedes the dancing. At the Grand Entry, a particularly distinguished veteran carries the eagle staff. The veteran is followed by a row of flag carriers who carry the U.S. flag on one side and the flag of the respective tribal nation on the other; in between is the POW-MIA flag, and often also a service flag or the flag of a veteran's organization. Often, more flags are carried, such as other service flags (Army, Marines, Navy, Air Force, and Coast Guard) or those of other participating veteran groups. Dancers—men, women, and children—follow the veterans into the arena. Powwows officially start and end with a flag ceremony and the singing of flag songs/honor songs. Occasionally, powwows include a veteran's retelling of his or her war experiences, and the singing of honor songs for a group of veterans, a certain service branch, or individuals; powwows also involve giveaways to honor an individual.[46]

The public honoring of homecoming/outgoing Native warriors/veterans involves several cultural elements that signify martial valor, much in line with older traditions. As of today, outgoing or homecoming servicepersons are honored for their military service with eagle feathers. However, what is honored by tribal communities is not so much a special deed, but rather military service as such. While there are rare accounts in which Native veterans gained recognition by adhering to elements of honorable warfare, the changing nature of warfare in the twentieth century has made it virtually impossible for Native veterans to gain honors and recognition through martial valor in the ways of their warrior ancestors.[47] Modern warfare has fundamentally reshaped how tribal communities recognize and honor martial valor and military service. Tribal communities honor all those who went into the service—whether they served during peace time or wartime, whether they saw combat or not, and whether they are male or female. In honoring both combat and noncombat veterans, tribal communities highlight the communal nature of their warriors to protect their people and homeland, since modern warfare has made the old code of honorable warfare obsolete. "United States military service," William Meadows writes about the post–World War I period, "became a modern and obtainable substitute for past means of gaining prestige through individual valor," setting a precedent for subsequent generations of Native men to gain recognition in their tribal communities.[48]

Traditionally, Native veterans are highly revered in their tribal communities and across Indian Country, and frequently take on leadership roles in their communities. Today, many Native Americans regard military service as another means to protect their people and their homeland. Native veterans see themselves in line with that old tradition of being warriors and defenders of their tribe. Against this cultural backdrop, the American flag encapsulates an entirely different meaning for Native peoples than for non-Native people.[49] For their military service, a male veteran is given an eagle feather; a female veteran receives an eagle plume.[50] At powwows, individual martial valor is recognized through the public recitation of someone's war experience. The Red Feather Society honors wounded Native veterans with an eagle feather with a red-tipped end, symbolizing the bloodshed in combat. During the Red Feather ceremony, new inductees recite their record of valor and service and are recognized by the community on the powwow grounds and are then acknowledged by other members of the Red Feather Society.[51]

Warrior traditions apply not only to men, but also to women. During the Plains Wars, women occasionally took to the warpath; they were honored in essentially the same way as their male counterparts. However, while it was not uncommon for Native women to temporarily take on a warrior role, there is only sketchy evidence of Native women who took to the warpath. During the wars of the twentieth century, Native American women joined the U.S. military as auxiliaries such as mechanics, ambulance drivers, pilots, administrators, and nurses in noncombat roles. During the gradual opening of the U.S. military to women, they later served in service academies (1976), in noncombat roles (1978), on combat planes (1991), on combat ships (1993), and finally in all military combat positions (2015). Regardless of gender, Indigenous cultural traditions continue to influence the ways in which Native soldiers interpret their military service. For example, Native veterans—male and female alike—frequently state that the feathers they received from their tribal communities carry a much higher significance for them than any Anglo-American awards for military valor—a tribute to the strong relationship between veterans and their tribal communities.[52]

Native cultural constructs of warriorhood and martial valor provide a strong alternative to hegemonic ideals of military heroism. Just as the white warrior hero is a key representative of the white, masculine nation, so do Indigenous cultural performances of Native veterans at powwows symbolize tribal sovereignty. Similar to the white warrior hero who embodies the norms and ideals of dominant society, Native veterans are role models to be emulated by the next generation of warriors. As a consequence, Western notions of heroic manliness hold little appeal for Native veterans, who see little use in emulating dominant heroic ideals. For generations of Native veterans, martial valor on the battlefield first and foremost has been a Native cultural and political expression that inherently challenged the American settler nation. However, occasionally, Native veterans also utilized their military service to demand full citizenship rights from that same settler nation.

U.S. MILITARY SERVICE, CIVIL RIGHTS/TREATY RIGHTS, AND THE TRIBAL/AMERICAN NATION

Native Americans occupy a distinct space in the American nation; a space that is both transcultural and transnational. All racial minorities in the United States have a relationship to the American nation that is characterized by civil rights and U.S. citizenship. Native Americans, however, have a special relationship to the nation, which is determined not only by civil rights, but also by treaty rights. Whereas civil rights determine their status in the American nation, treaty rights determine their distinct status vis-à-vis the American nation. Treaty rights describe the relationship between the federal government and tribes as federal guardianship on the one hand, and Native wardship on the other. Therefore, Native people have considered themselves entities different from mainstream America. Native Americans' ambiguous and hybrid status in U.S. society explains the two ways that they resist colonization: first, Indigenous people continue to struggle against colonial domination of the settler nation for their (tribal) sovereignty; and second, Indigenous people continue to struggle within dominant settler society for their own political identity as dual citizens.[53] Native political actors have demanded political rights and resources from the American settler state while simultaneously challenging colonial domination over their lives. Kevin Bruyneel has fittingly termed this special relationship—in which Native Americans neither reside inside nor outside the American nation-state—a "third space of sovereignty."[54] Native people's patriotism is inherently hybrid, and their allegiance is divided between their tribal nation and the American nation.[55]

During each war, Native people served as a model minority, fully throwing themselves into the war effort. In a way, Native Americans acted similarly to other racial/ethnic minorities who unequivocally supported the war. In a society in which citizenship and national belonging went hand in hand, military heroism offered racial minorities such as Japanese Americans, African Americans, and others an avenue to prove their loyalty in order to become fully-fledged U.S. citizens. However, Native motivations were different from those of other racial and ethnic minorities. Instead of gaining integration into the dominant society, they have struggled to maintain both their distinct cultural identity as an Indigenous people and their distinct political status as tribal nations.[56]

Gaining one right could mean curtailing another. For example, in 1924, as reward for their wartime service, the U.S. extended its citizenship rights to Native Americans. While a minority of progressive, college-educated Native people welcomed U.S. citizenship, others saw it as a further erosion of sovereignty and their distinct position as tribal nations. In order to maintain their distinct political status and not be subjected to U.S. selective service or conscription laws, several tribal nations made their own declarations of war against hostile nations during World War I and World War II, in an attempt to circumvent issues that could inhibit their own sovereignty rights vis-à-vis the American nation. When faced with a draft that violated their treaty rights and infringed upon their sovereignty, draft-eligible men enlisted before they could be drafted. Native enlistment not only circumvented sovereignty issues, but also was an attempt to (re-)masculinize their tribal nations for war.

Native veterans have utilized their military service primarily to protect their tribal communities from the imposition of colonial rule and to defend their tribal sovereignty. Their demand for civil rights from within the settler state was connected to their military service, but remained secondary. Essentially, after each war of the twentieth century, Native veterans returned to a situation of domestic colonialism characterized by government indifference, subalternity, and reservation (or urban) squalor; in many regards, this paralleled the return of black veterans into segregation, discrimination, and poverty. In the postwar era, Native World War I veterans set a precedent of organizing and lobbying for their rights.[57] In 1944, Native World War II veterans founded the National Congress of American Indians (NCAI), an organization that lobbied for both civil rights and treaty rights.[58] In addition, the war experience empowered Native veterans in their struggle for postwar civil rights (e.g., against the ban of alcohol on reservations, and for voting rights), leading to a reassertion of their cultural identity and claims for self-determination—in this regard, they foreshadowed the Red Power movement.[59] During the Vietnam War, Native soldiers increasingly questioned their military service and were at odds as to why they should put their lives on the line for a government that continued to impose its colonial policies and practices on the "Other" in Southeast Asia and its own people at home in America. They joined a movement for social change—the Red Power movement (1969–1978)—in an effort to preserve their cultural identity, to insist on social justice and civil rights, to uphold the recognition of treaty rights, and to put forward their demands for self-determination.[60] While the World War II generation utilized more established political procedures, the Vietnam War generation tended to utilize social protest to secure redress for political disadvantages.

Up to the present day, cultural constructs of warriorhood and manliness are deeply ingrained in Native tribal cultures. Native veterans have utilized the U.S. military, an essentially foreign institution, as a way to carry on, revive, defend, and protect traditional cultural and spiritual practices, institutions, and beliefs.[61] Frequently, these cultural traditions take precedence over Western ideals of heroic soldiering. However, occasionally, Native veterans have utilized their military service to push for civil rights. Their notions of martial manliness ultimately became a powerful alternative to white hegemonic notions of military heroism.

NOTES

1. Tom Holm, "The Militarization of Native America: Historical Process and Cultural Perception," *Social Science Journal* 34, no. 4 (1997): 461–474.
2. Tom Holm, "Patriots and Pawns, State Use of American Indians in the Military and the Process of Nativization in the United States," in *The State of Native America: Genocide, Colonization, and Resistance*, ed. M. Annette Jaimes (Boston: South End Press, 1992), 345.
3. Kevin Bruyneel, *The Third Space of Sovereignty: The Postcolonial Politics of U.S.-Indigenous Relations* (Minneapolis: University of Minnesota Press, 2007), 20–21.
4. Tom Holm, *Strong Hearts, Wounded Souls: Native American Veterans of the Vietnam War* (Austin: University of Texas Press, 1996), 22–25, 117–123; William Meadows, *The Comanche Code Talkers of World War II* (Austin: University of Texas Press, 2002), xiv, 9–14; Al Carroll, *Medicine Bags and Dog Tags: American Indian Veterans from Colonial Times to the Second Iraq War* (Lincoln: University of Nebraska Press, 2008), 2.
5. Jeré Franco, "Empowering the World War II Native American Veteran: Postwar Civil Rights," *Wicazo Sa Review* 9, no. 1 (1993): 32–37; Holm, *Strong Hearts*, 171–183.
6. Department of Veterans Affairs, *American Indian and Alaska Native Service Members and Veterans*, September 2012, 4–5, http://www.va.gov/TRIBALGOVERNMENT/docs/AIAN_Report_FINAL_v2_7.pdf (hereafter cited as AIAN report). There are only a handful of accounts on Native people's participation in each war. For World War I, see Susan Applegate Krouse, *North American Indians in the Great War* (Lincoln: University of Nebraska Press, 2007); Thomas A. Britten, *American Indians in World War I: At Home and at War* (Albuquerque: University of New Mexico Press, 1997). For World War II, see Kenneth William Townsend, *World War II and the American Indian* (Albuquerque: University of New Mexico Press, 2000); Jeré Bishop Franco, *Crossing the Pond: The Native American Effort in World War II* (Denton: University of North Texas Press, 1999); Alison R. Bernstein, *American Indians and World War II: Toward a New Era in Indian Affairs* (Norman: University of Oklahoma Press, 1991). On Native Americans' experiences in Vietnam, see Holm, *Strong Hearts*. For a general account of Native military heroism, see Herman J. Viola, *Warriors in Uniform: The Legacy of American Indian Heroism* (Washington, DC: National Geographic, 2008). The participation of the Native American code talkers during World War I and World War II has inspired its own strand of historiography. Most scholarly accounts and autobiographical writings focus on the Navajo code talkers of World War II. The Comanche code talkers of World War II have also been covered.
7. Holm, *Strong Hearts*, 123.
8. AIAN report, 5.
9. The cross-cultural heritage of some recipients might have led to contradictory counts. The U.S. Army and U.S. Navy websites differ in their lists of Native MoH recipients. See https://history.army.mil/moh/; www.navy.mil/ah_online/moh/index.html (both accessed January 9, 2018).
10. The most meticulous research on the code talkers has been conducted by William Meadows, who also testified before Congress on his findings. William C. Meadows, "Honoring Native American Code Talkers," *American Indian Culture and Research Journal* 35, no. 3 (2011): 10.

11. Holm, *Strong Hearts,* 19–25; William C. Meadows, *Kiowa, Apache, and Comanche Military Societies: Enduring Veterans, 1800 to the Present* (Austin: University of Texas Press, 1999), 28; Meadows, *Comanche Code Talkers,* xiv, 9; Carroll, *Medicine Bags,* 2; Paul C. Rosier, *Serving Their Country: American Indian Politics and Patriotism in the Twentieth Century* (Cambridge, MA: Harvard University Press, 2009), 9.

12. For fresh perspectives on this flourishing field, see Simon Wendt and Pablo Dominguez Andersen, eds., *Masculinities and the Nation in the Modern World: Between Hegemony and Marginalization* (New York: Palgrave Macmillan, 2015); Ronald L. Jackson and Muali Balaji, eds., *Global Masculinities and Manhood* (Urbana: University of Illinois Press, 2011). Scholarly studies on Indigenous masculinities are rare. Exceptions are Ty P. Kawika Tengan, *Native Men Remade: Gender and Nation in Contemporary Hawai'i* (Durham, NC: Duke University Press, 2008); Kathleen Glenister Roberts, "War, Masculinity, and Native Americans," in Jackson and Balaji, *Global Masculinities and Manhood,* 141–160; Robert Alexander Innes and Kim Anderson, eds., *Indigenous Men and Masculinities: Legacies, Identities, Regeneration* (Winnipeg: University of Manitoba Press, 2015); Sam McKegney, ed., *Masculindians: Conversations about Indigenous Manhood* (East Lansing: Michigan State University Press, 2014).

13. Jackson and Balaji, *Global Masculinities and Manhood,* 20–24.

14. Holm, *Strong Hearts,* 83–90.

15. Michael L. Tate, "From Scout to Doughboy: The National Debate over Integrating American Indians into the Military, 1891–1918," *Western Historical Quarterly* 17, no. 4 (1986): 417–437; Thomas W. Dunlay, *Wolves for the Blue Soldiers: Indian Scouts and Auxiliaries with the United States Army, 1860–90* (Lincoln: University of Nebraska Press, 1982), 199–209; Bruce White, "The American Army and the Indian," in *Ethnic Armies, Polyethnic Armed Forces from the Time of the Habsburgs to the Age of Superpowers,* ed. N. F. Dreisziger (Waterloo, ON: Wilfrid Laurier University Press, 1990), 72, 85–86; Holm, "Patriots and Pawns," 350–354; Holm, "The Militarization of Native America," 462–464, 470–473; Meadows, *Comanche Code Talkers,* xiv; Britten, *American Indians in World War I,* 13–17; Carroll, *Medicine Bags,* 5.

16. Author's interviews with Native American veterans in summer of 2013. See also Holm, *Strong Hearts,* 88–90.

17. Carroll, *Medicine Bags,* 112.

18. Frank Usbeck, "Fighting like Indians: The 'Indian Scout Syndrome' in U.S. and German War Reports during World War II," in *Visual Representations of Native Americans: Transnational Contexts and Perspectives,* ed. Karsten Fitz (Heidelberg: Winter, 2012), 125–144.

19. Carroll, *Medicine Bags,* 161.

20. On World War I, see James S. Olson and Raymond Wilson, *Native Americans in the Twentieth Century* (Urbana: University of Illinois Press, 1986), 84–86. On World War II, see Bernstein, *American Indians and World War II,* 22–42; James R. Rawls, *Chief Red Fox Is Dead: A History of Native Americans since 1945* (New York: Harcourt Brace 1996), 5.

21. Holm, *Strong Hearts,* 18–25, 117–123; Meadows, *Comanche Code Talkers,* xiv, 9–14.

22. Holm, *Strong Hearts,* 18–25; Meadows, *Comanche Code Talkers,* xiv, 9–14; Carroll, *Medicine Bags,* 2. These findings corroborate my own findings during a 2013 field trip to South Dakota, North Dakota, and Montana, where I conducted extensive interviews with Native American veterans who fought in World War II, the Korean War, the Vietnam War, and subsequent wars.

23. Rosier, *Serving Their Country,* 3.

24. Holm, *Strong Hearts,* 18–25; Meadows, *Military Societies,* 28; Meadows, *Comanche Code Talkers,* xiv, 9–14; Carroll, *Medicine Bags,* 2.

25. Indian tribes share relatively homogeneous cultural patterns in otherwise diverse and distinct Native cultures. Plains tribes—the Lakota (Sioux), Cheyenne, Arapahoe, Crow, and others—originally occupied the vast area bounded by Canada (north), Mexico (south), the Rocky Mountains (west), and the Mississippi River (east).

26. Tom Holm, "The National Survey of Vietnam Era American Indian Veterans, A Preliminary Reconnaissance," *Wicazo Sa Review* 1, no. 1 (1985): 36–37; Holm, "Culture, Ceremonialism, and Stress: American Indian Veterans and the Vietnam War," *Armed Forces & Society* 12, no. 2 (1986): 237–251; Holm, "PTSD in Native American Veterans: A Reassessment," *Wicazo Sa Review* 11, no. 2 (1995): 83–86; Holm, *Strong Hearts*, 183–197.

27. Donald Lee Fixico, *Call for Change: The Medicine Way of American Indian History, Ethos and Reality* (Lincoln: University of Nebraska Press, 2013).

28. Holm, *Strong Hearts*, 22.

29. Holm, "Patriots and Pawns," 357.

30. Royal B. Hassrick, *The Sioux: Life and Customs of a Warrior Society* (Norman: University of Oklahoma Press, 1964), 32.

31. Meadows, *Military Societies*, 10.

32. Holm, *Strong Hearts*, 22.

33. Holm, "PTSD in Native American Vietnam Veterans," 84.

34. Roberts, "War, Masculinity, and Native Americans," 148.

35. Holm, *Strong Hearts*, 118.

36. Holm, *Strong Hearts*, 19–25; Meadows, *Comanche Code Talkers*, 11–13; Carroll, *Medicine Bags*, 8.

37. Rosier, *Serving Their Country*, 9.

38. National Center for PTSD, ed., *Wounded Spirits, Ailing Hearts: PTSD and Legacy of War among American Indian and Alaska Native American Veterans*, October 2000, https://hsdl.org/?abstract&did=13651; Holm, "Culture, Ceremonialism, and Stress," 242–251; John P. Wilson, "Culture-Specific Pathways to Healing and Transformation for War Veterans Suffering PTSD," in *Healing War Trauma: A Handbook of Creative Approaches*, ed. Raymond Monsour Scurfield and Katherine Theresa Platoni (New York: Routledge, 2013), 47–67; John P. Wilson, "Culture and Trauma: The Sacred Pipe Revisited," in *Trauma, Transformation, and Healing: An Integrative Approach to Theory, Research, and Post-Traumatic Therapy*, ed. John P. Wilson (New York: Brunner/Mazel Publishers, 1989), 38–71; Steven Silver and John P. Wilson, "Native American Healing and Purification Rituals for War Stress," in *Human Adaptation to Extreme Stress: From the Holocaust to Vietnam*, ed. John P. Wilson, Zev Harel, and Boaz Kahana (New York: Plenum Press, 1988), 337–355.

39. Meadows, *Military Societies*, 385–398.

40. Accounts of a cultural renaissance in Indian Country during the wars of the twentieth century are manifold. On World War I, see Britten, *American Indians in World War I*, 149–153; William K. Powers, *War Dance: Plains Indian Musical Performance* (Tucson: University of Arizona Press, 1990), 50–51. On World War II, see Townsend, *World War II*, 140–142, 170–171. On the Vietnam War, see Holm, *Strong Hearts*, 183–197. On war mothers, see Meadows, *Military Societies*, 391. See also Carroll, *Medicine Bags*, 106–111, 118–130, 140–145, 151–160; Meadows, *Comanche Code Talkers*, 9–14.

41. Holm, *Strong Hearts*, 18–25; Meadows, *Comanche Code Talkers*, xiv–xv, 9–14; Carroll, *Medicine Bags*, 3, 8–13, 87–88.

42. Susan J. Drucker and Robert S. Cathcart, "The Hero as a Communication Phenomenon," in *American Heroes in a Media Age*, ed. Susan J. Drucker and Robert S. Cathcart (Cresskill, NJ: Hampton Press, 1994), 5–6.

43. Holm, "PTSD in Native American Vietnam Veterans," 84–85; Holm, *Strong Hearts*, 39–40.

44. Roberts, "War, Masculinity, and Native Americans," 145–149.

45. Holm, *Strong Hearts*, 44–46.

46. Author's observations during a powwow in Sisseton-Wahpeton in North Dakota, July 4–7, 2013.

47. For exceptions, see Viola, *Warriors in Uniform*, 9–11, 103–108.

48. Meadows, *Comanche Code Talkers*, 12.

49. Douglas A. Schmittou and Michael H. Logan, "Fluidity of Meaning: Flag Imagery in Plains Indian Art," *American Indian Quarterly* 26, no. 4 (2002): 559–604.

50. This is a cultural practice that can often be observed at powwows, during which male and female veterans are honored by their respective tribal communities.

51. Wilson, "Culture-Specific Pathways," 56–57.

52. Author's interviews with Native American veterans in 2013.

53. Bruyneel, *The Third Space of Sovereignty*, 20–21.

54. Ibid., xvii–xix.

55. Carroll, *Medicine Bags*, 3; Rosier, *Serving Their Country*, 9–10; Meadows, *Comanche Code Talkers*, xiv, 11; Holm, *Strong Hearts*, 24–25.

56. Carroll, *Medicine Bags*, 2–5.

57. Britten, *American Indians in World War I*, 159–187.

58. Thomas W. Cowger, *The National Congress of American Indians: The Founding Years* (Lincoln: University of Nebraska Press, 2001), 30–48.

59. Franco, *Crossing the Pond*, 190–204; Franco, "Empowering the World War II Native American Veteran," 32–37; Townsend, *World War II*, 215–228.

60. Holm, *Strong Hearts*, 169–183.

61. Carroll, *Medicine Bags*, 1–5; Meadows, *Comanche Code Talkers*, xiv, 10–14; Meadows, *Military Societies*.

5 • MY LAI

The Crisis of American Military Heroism in the Vietnam War

STEVE ESTES

As Lieutenant William Calley got on the chopper early in the morning of March 16, 1968, he steeled himself for a fearsome firefight in the cluster of My Lai hamlets on the coast of South Vietnam. In the prebattle briefing, Captain Ernest Medina had warned Calley and the other men of Charlie Company that about 250 members of the 48th Viet Cong Battalion were hiding out in the village. "Our job," Calley recalled Medina saying, "is to go in rapidly and to neutralize everything. To kill everything."[1]

Lieutenant Calley's platoon jumped off the chopper into what they were told was a "hot" landing zone, meaning someone had reported enemy fire. By the time Calley and his men entered the village, however, the Viet Cong who had been there overnight had retreated into the jungle nearby. Calley's platoon rounded up Vietnamese villagers and lined them up for questioning. "Push all those people in the ditch," Calley ordered, referring to a group of villagers—mostly women, children, and old men. Calley opened fire and ordered his men to do the same, saying, "Waste them."[2]

Flying above My Lai that morning in a small scout helicopter, Chief Warrant Officer Hugh Thompson and his crew were shocked by what they saw. The helicopter had received no enemy fire, so the amount of shooting in the village surprised them. In a drainage ditch near the village, Thompson and his crew saw the bodies of what looked like Vietnamese civilians. Setting down his helicopter, Thompson approached a sergeant guarding the ditch. Some of the villagers were wounded, but still alive. "Those people need help," Thompson said. "Any way y'all could help 'em out?" "We can help put 'em out of their misery," the sergeant replied.[3]

Thompson found Calley and asked, "What's going on here, lieutenant?" Calley responded that he was "just following orders." When Thompson questioned Calley further, the lieutenant replied angrily, "I'm in charge here. . . . You better get back in your chopper and mind your own business." As Thompson took off, Calley's men once again began shooting into the ditch. The scout helicopter landed twice more, helping to evacuate nearly a dozen villagers from My Lai. Thompson would later testify against the men of Charlie Company in subsequent investigations into what became known as the My Lai massacre.[4]

My Lai catalyzed both antiwar sentiment and support for American soldiers in an increasingly difficult war. Examining the public's response to William Calley, Hugh Thompson, and the other men at My Lai, we see a crisis of American military heroism and masculinity during the Vietnam War. For some Americans who supported the war, Calley's willingness to fight, follow his superior officers' orders, and stoically defend himself in the face of a court-martial made him an American hero. For opponents of the war, Calley was a villain, a bad man fighting a bad war. Similarly, Americans were divided on Hugh Thompson's role in My Lai. To war supporters, Thompson had fought against his brothers-in-arms and later "snitched" on them. After the trials, Thompson retreated into obscurity, adopting a nickname to shield his identity for the rest of his military career. It was thirty years after My Lai that the military finally honored Thompson and his crew. Belatedly calling Thompson and his helicopter crewmates the true American heroes of My Lai, the United States in the 1990s was both repairing relations with its former enemies in Vietnam and becoming a global peacekeeper in the post–Cold War era. In this chapter, I analyze the reactions to Calley, Thompson, and the other American soldiers at My Lai to show how American military heroism evolved during and after the Vietnam War. The debate in the early 1970s about whether Calley was a hero or war criminal reflected the crisis of martial manhood and heroism at the conclusion of Vietnam, caused by the division on the home front over the war's aims and the ultimate retreat of U.S. forces. The subsequent lionization of Thompson as a hero in the 1990s illustrated changes in American military heroism and masculinity in the thirty years after Vietnam, but also the new role of the United States in the increasingly globalized economy that emerged after the Cold War.

More than almost any other single event in the Vietnam War, the My Lai massacre has received intense media coverage and scholarly scrutiny. From 1969 to 1971, the Army undertook three investigations, and the House Armed Services Committee held hearings on the My Lai assault. American journalists, led by Seymour Hersh, interviewed many of the participants for their own investigative reports. Legal and military historians have further analyzed the massacre. Much of this research tried to determine what happened, why it happened, and how the American public and political establishment responded. There is near unanimity that this was an illegal massacre of approximately 500 Vietnamese civilians, but why the massacre took place remains a subject of some debate. The three most likely causes are: (1) the mental breakdown of American soldiers and units fighting a guerilla enemy embedded in civilian communities; (2) the failure of leadership to control American soldiers' interactions with civilians; and (3) U.S. military policy that measured success by "body counts" of casualties among Vietnamese communist forces. As German scholar Bernd Greiner argues, these factors led to more violence against civilians in Vietnam than in earlier American wars—violence that was epitomized by, but not limited to, My Lai.[5]

Many of the journalists and scholars who have covered My Lai have noted that men such as Calley and Thompson were portrayed as heroes by different segments of the American public, but few have analyzed the effect of the massacre on the concept of military heroism. During and immediately after Calley's court-martial trial, public support for Calley bordered on hero worship, stunning many of the journalists who covered the story. Richard Hammer, the *New York Times* reporter covering the trial, bemoaned the tragedy that Calley had become "a hero for our time." Hammer found it "impossible to think of him as a hero or to consider his acts of heroic stature." Legal scholar Michael Belknap called Calley an "unlikely hero" in his account of the lieutenant's conviction and the popular backlash to it. The men who investigated My Lai for the Army also scratched their heads over the popular support for Calley. Lieutenant General Peers concluded that Calley "is certainly no hero as far as I am concerned." Decades after My Lai, in the wake of the terrorist attacks of September 11, 2001, Peter Gibbon tried to understand the deeper impact of Vietnam on American military heroism in his call for a renewed appreciation of American heroes. "Vietnam did more than tarnish the military in our culture and our schools," Gibbon argued. "It contributed to a value shift harmful to heroism." Although I do not share Gibbon's uncritical admiration for traditional military heroism, I do agree that Vietnam altered—at least, temporarily—older conceptions of American heroism. My Lai and other atrocities called into question the image of the heroic American soldier, who had defended freedom in "good wars" like the Civil War, World War I, and World War II.[6]

American troops who served in Vietnam were weaned on the heroic tales of soldiers who fought in World War II. As Vietnam veteran Ron Kovic explained in his memoir *Born on the Fourth of July*, World War II movies such as *Sands of Iwo Jima* defined heroism and patriotism for his generation. Similarly, journalist Richard Hammer reminisced: "When we were young, it was a time of heroes . . . a more innocent time perhaps, when we believed in heroes, believed we needed them and believed they symbolized the best of their times, and because above all, they were men, the possibilities of heroism were open to all of us." Hammer believed Lieutenant William Calley's conviction of murder for his role at My Lai led to a crisis of American heroism. Yet, many Americans had the opposite reaction to Calley's conviction. He was, in their eyes, a hero.[7]

Growing up in a middle-class Florida family in the 1950s, William Calley had dreamed of heroes. Calley was typical of the baby boomers who filled the ranks during the Vietnam War, but compared to many in his generation, he was an underachiever. By his own estimation, he was not a good student. He failed the seventh grade and later dropped out of junior college. Rejected once by the military because of a minor medical condition, Calley successfully signed up on his second attempt in 1966, when the military lowered recruitment standards during Vietnam. As a result of his brief stint in college, Calley was tapped to become an officer. He would lead a combat infantry unit—the 1st platoon of C (Charlie) Company, 1st Battalion, 20th Infantry.[8]

Scholars have offered harsh assessments of the young lieutenant. "If a Hollywood director were going to cast a cold-blooded wartime villain," historians James Olson and Randy Roberts suggested, "the short, nondescript Calley would not get a second glance." Olson and Roberts described the lieutenant's "soft face . . . weak chin, nervous gerbil-like eyes, and pasty skin" in arguing that he failed even at being a "good" bad guy. Another scholar and veteran, Philip Beidler, characterized Calley as the "laughing stock of Charlie Company," a "pariah" whose bluster was "characteristic of the little man in the military, the proverbial short-round."[9]

Interviews with Calley and his men bear out some of these negative character assessments, playing into the depiction of him as inept and even cowardly. Roy Wood, a rifleman in Calley's platoon, told Seymour Hersh that his commanding officer "couldn't read no darn map, and a compass would confuse his ass." Another of Calley's men, Robert Maples, said that Calley worked too hard to impress superiors, doing "things that would make him out to be a hero" and making "something out of himself that he wasn't." Calley was also critical of himself. He admitted that his own stupidity cost the life of his radioman on one mission when he ordered his platoon to march single file atop an embankment. Journalists and scholars have repeated these statements in building a case against Calley, without fully acknowledging that the lieutenant was trying to diminish his culpability for the massacre. By downplaying his own abilities, Calley could argue that he was a simple man, only following the orders of his superior officer.[10]

In fact, everyone in Charlie Company who killed civilians said that they were following orders. Captain Medina was ordered to "neutralize" the My Lai hamlets where Viet Cong (VC) had been hiding and receiving civilian support for years. On March 15, 1968, Medina briefed Charlie Company on the next day's mission in My Lai. Intelligence suggested that most civilians would be away at a market, and that the 48th VC Battalion was hiding in the area. Passing along orders of his superiors, Medina told the men to neutralize the villages, burn huts, shoot livestock, capture weapons, and kill VC. When asked about civilians, the captain said that the men should "use common sense," firing if the villagers attacked first. Still, many soldiers got the impression that civilian casualties were acceptable and anticipated. "People were talking about killing everything that moved," recalled Robert Pendleton. Medina "said to level the village," testified Robert Carter. A South Vietnamese interpreter testified that Charlie Company soldiers told him the night before the mission that "they would kill women, children, cattle, and everything."[11]

Two infantry companies and several air assault teams participated in the My Lai massacre, but most narratives focus on two platoons of Charlie Company: the 1st, led by Calley, and the 2nd, led by Lieutenant Stephen Brooks, who was killed in action months after My Lai. These two platoons moved through the southern and northern sectors of the hamlet known as My Lai 4 on the morning of March 16, 1968. When the 1st Platoon got off the helicopter just west of the village, an old man came up to them waving his arms. Calley's men immediately shot him and the livestock he was tending. Making their way through the village, Calley's men received no enemy fire. They shot some villagers and rounded up others into two groups. Paul Meadlo and Dennis Conti guarded several dozen villagers taken to a rice paddy south of the hamlet. Calley told Meadlo and Conti to "take care" of these villagers. According to Calley, he then spoke to Captain Medina, who asked why it was taking so long to get through the village. Calley testified that Medina told him to "waste" the civilians and get moving, although Medina denied this. Calley returned to the rice paddy where he castigated Meadlo and Conti: "I thought I told you to take care of them." When the two enlisted men said that they were "taking care" of the villagers, Calley said, "I meant kill them. Come on, we'll line them up here, and we'll kill them." Conti begged off, saying that he would watch the tree line. Together, Meadlo and Calley "burned through" seven or eight magazines of bullets (twenty bullets per magazine), killing the villagers. "The people were pretty messed up," Conti later testified. "Lots of heads was shot off, pieces of hands and pieces of flesh flew off the sides and arms." While shooting, Meadlo started to cry. Prosecutors later contrasted his remorse with Calley's callousness. Conti testified that the lieutenant looked like he was "enjoying it."[12]

As 1st Platoon worked its way through the southern part of the village, Charlie Company's 2nd Platoon searched the northern sector. Lieutenant Brooks's men did not kill as many villagers as Calley and his men, but 2nd Platoon raped several of the girls and women that they encountered. One of the men in 2nd Platoon, Varnado Simpson, admitted to Army CID that he killed about eight people, including a woman and a baby. "I shot the baby in the face," he said. Then he saw four of his buddies "go into a hut and rape a seventeen- or eighteen-year-old girl." Simpson "watched from the door. When they all got done, they all took their weapons, M-60s, M16s, and caliber .45 pistols and fired into the girl until she was dead." Despite his apparently cavalier attitude toward murder, Calley tried to stop his men from raping villagers. All told, however, American soldiers raped twenty of the villagers in My Lai, ranging in age from ten to forty-five.[13]

"We've got another job to do, Meadlo," ordered Calley after they killed the villagers in the rice paddy. Other members of 1st Platoon were guarding a group of sixty to seventy villagers near an irrigation ditch west of the hamlet, and Calley took Meadlo and several other members of his platoon to the ditch. Five of the soldiers fired on the elderly men, women, and children in the ditch, killing most but not all of them. At least one soldier testified that Calley shot a Vietnamese toddler who was trying to crawl out of the ditch. One Vietnamese villager who survived the massacre later told investigators, "In the ditch, I pushed my daughter down under my stomach and told her not to cry. . . . I pretended to be dead and dared not move. The Americans were waiting to see if anyone moved, and then they shot them."[14]

Among the air support helicopters flying above My Lai was a small scout ship piloted by Warrant Officer Hugh Thompson. Thompson and his two crewmates had arrived at the hamlet early in the morning, firing on one fleeing Vietnamese man who appeared to be carrying a weapon, but missing him. After refueling, Thompson and his crew saw what appeared to be a number of civilian casualties in and around My Lai (4). He reported his concerns about "unnecessary killing" to headquarters and then flew over to the ditch, where he saw more dead and wounded civilians. Thompson set down his helicopter three times during the morning of the My Lai assault. First, he confronted members of Charlie Company's 1st Platoon about the civilian casualties in the ditch. After Calley told him to mind his own business, Thompson got back in his helicopter and flew to another area of My Lai (4), where he saw civilians run into a bunker to hide. He landed his helicopter between the bunker and advancing soldiers who were in Charlie Company's 2nd Platoon. As he exited the helicopter, he told his crew to cover him in case any of the American soldiers started shooting. He coaxed two women, five children, and two elderly men from the bunker and called in a larger helicopter to ferry them a safe distance from the village. Before leaving My Lai, Thompson's crewmate saw movement in the ditch west of the village. They landed a third time, pulled a young boy covered with blood from the ditch, and flew him to a nearby hospital.[15]

Thompson's story is included in most of the chronicles of the My Lai massacre, but before the 1990s, the helicopter pilot was rarely given the same detailed attention given to the men in Charlie Company. Like William Calley,

Thompson was from the South, raised near Atlanta, Georgia. He learned to fly helicopters after enlisting in the Army in 1966. He arrived in Vietnam in December 1967, just as Calley did. One Army investigator lauded Thompson's actions at My Lai, arguing in 1979, "If there was a hero of My Lai, he was it," but this was far from the majority view in the decade after the massacre. In fact, Thompson's challenge to Charlie Company's actions earned him persecution, not accolades, for three decades after the massacre.[16]

When Thompson returned to his base from My Lai, he told his chaplain and superior officer what he had seen, threatening never to fly again unless something was done. Military brass responded to Thompson's complaints by covering up what had happened and challenging the pilot's story. Officers claimed that Thompson was too distraught to articulate what he had seen. For instance, one investigator questioned the helicopter pilot's initial report. "I think I presented the best I could at that time. I'd say I was upset, or, you know, disturbed," Thompson explained. The investigator asked Thompson if he was crying, "Oh, no. I wasn't crying, sir." If Thompson had cried, this seemed to call into question his testimony and character—perhaps he was too weak to face the realities of war. Thompson was no hero, investigators implied. He might just be a coward.[17]

The initial Army accounts of My Lai manufactured a battle to justify the Vietnamese casualties. Only one American soldier was wounded at My Lai—a self-inflicted gunshot to the foot. Yet, a press release authored by an eyewitness touted the "killing [of] 128 [enemies] in a running battle." A combat action report a few weeks later concluded: "This operation was well-planned, well-executed, and successful." It was so successful—at least, on paper—that General William Westmoreland, commander of U.S. forces in Vietnam, congratulated the troops who dealt the enemy a "heavy blow" at My Lai. Although Army brass did not investigate his complaints, they awarded Hugh Thompson and his crewmates the Distinguished Flying Cross for heroic action "without regard for the Viet Cong fire" to rescue My Lai villagers. As Thompson had told his superiors, however, he never received enemy fire at My Lai. He was rescuing the villagers from Americans.[18]

Vietnamese accounts of My Lai told a very different story than initial American reports. One local village leader claimed that Americans killed 570 civilians and destroyed 90 percent of the homes in My Lai. A few weeks later, Lieutenant Tran Ngoc Tan of the Army of the Republic of Vietnam (ARVN) reported nearly 500 civilians killed in "an act of insane violence," and requested an immediate investigation of the incident. Viet Cong propaganda castigated the "fierce American devils" for killing "innocent civilian people . . . some just born babies and pregnant women," as they drank "our people's blood with all their animal barbarity." The Viet Cong accounts depicted Vietnamese civilians as the heroes and American military personnel as the villains of the day.[19]

The Vietnamese were not the only ones horrified by My Lai; rumors of the massacre roiled the Army's ranks, eventually reaching the American public. In March 1969, one year after My Lai, Vietnam veteran Ron Ridenhour wrote a letter to his congressman and other Washington officials, including President Richard Nixon. Ridenhour informally investigated rumors of the massacre while stationed in Vietnam. After chronicling what he had heard, Ridenhour admitted that he did not know all of what had happened, but he was "convinced that it was something very black indeed." He demanded a "widespread and public investigation."[20]

Ridenhour's letter inspired the first real investigation of the My Lai assault by the Army, an investigation that would bring William Calley and Hugh Thompson face-to-face once more. Staffers from the Office of the Inspector General called several men in for questioning to explain what had happened at My Lai. Hugh Thompson once again told his version of the My Lai massacre, and picked Calley out of a lineup in June 1969. In August, the Army charged Calley with several counts of murder. By November 1969, journalist Seymour Hersh had published an article on the massacre, and former Army photographer Ronald Haeberle published shocking images taken with his private camera on the day of the assault. The ensuing media firestorm ensured that William Calley and the members of Charlie Company would forever be associated with debates about the aims, strategies, and tactics of the Vietnam War.[21]

Although most investigators valued Hugh Thompson's testimony, he experienced a backlash for his role in uncovering My Lai. Thompson was largely vilified in a special investigation by the House Armed Services Committee, led by staunchly prowar congressmen Mendel Rivers (D-SC) and Edward Hébert (D-LA). When Thompson and his door gunner Lawrence Colburn testified before the congressional committee, the questioning became an interrogation. Congressional investigators insinuated that Thompson and Colburn had lied about their roles in My Lai to get the Distinguished Flying Cross. "If medals are to retain their significance as a reward for heroic action," one investigator concluded, "they should not be dispensed under such questionable circumstances." More dramatically, they accused the helicopter crew of aiming weapons at fellow American soldiers in a potentially treasonable offense. "Let's get the cards on the table," Rep. Hébert said, trying to determine if the helicopter crew had pointed their guns at American troops. Ultimately, Thompson was so cowed that he used his Fifth Amendment rights to avoid answering further questions. Satisfied that he had defended the good name of the U.S. Army by debunking Thompson's story, Congressman Rivers told the press, "From his testimony, nobody can be charged, in my opinion, with having massacred anybody."[22]

Congressional denigration of Thompson and his role as a key witness against members of Charlie Company earned him public enmity. In the early 1970s,

Thompson received death threats, and dead animals were left on his front porch. "You should be stripped of your stripes, you chicken-livered traitor," wrote one anonymous critic from Atlanta. "Your kind is the worst enemy, the rat commie within our country. . . . You are a disgrace to the South (which is a producer of patriots), a disgrace to the nation." After being wounded in a helicopter crash, Thompson had been transferred back to the States to train other Army pilots. When other soldiers dubbed him a "snitch," he started introducing himself by the nickname "Buck." One soldier asked the pilot if he was related to "that s.o.b. Hugh Thompson," and he responded cagily, "Never heard of him."[23]

As Calley's court-martial trial progressed, the lieutenant found himself more and more alone in facing the repercussions of My Lai. Since most of the enlisted men in the assault had left the Army by the time the massacre was revealed, they were seen as immune from military prosecution. Trials of others who were still in the service ended in acquittals, as officers in court-martial trials refused to convict enlisted personnel for following orders to "neutralize" the village. The few officers besides Calley who were tried by the military were acquitted for lack of evidence. While some high-ranking officers were demoted, censured, or forced to resign, none were convicted of committing a crime. Calley's court-martial came to symbolize the debate over accountability, justice, and the conduct of the Vietnam War itself. No single man or trial could bear this weight, and Calley's conviction of "at least twenty-two premeditated murders" in My Lai elicited a fearsome public outcry.[24]

At the same time Americans were sending hate mail to Hugh Thompson, thousands of letters, telegrams, editorials, and speeches offered support for Calley. One month after the verdict, the White House had received 260,000 letters and 75,000 telegrams, the vast majority condemning the court-martial verdict. Liberals who opposed the war argued that the court-martial was unjust because military and government policies were ultimately responsible for the atrocities at My Lai. "We are all of us in this country guilty for having allowed the war to go on," Vietnam veteran and future secretary of state John Kerry argued. "We only want this country to realize that it cannot try a Calley for something which generals and Presidents and our way of life encouraged him to do." Conservatives who supported the war lauded Calley as a patriot who volunteered to serve his country and followed orders when others of his generation evaded the draft and shirked their duty. "The silent majority is beginning to speak and we beg the officials to listen," beseeched one letter writer. Calley's "one of the few real men left in this country," argued a supporter from Atlanta. Rallies for Calley were held across the country. "There was a crucifixion 2000 years ago of a man named Jesus Christ," intoned a minister at one rally. "I don't think we need another crucifixion of a man named Rusty Calley." Southerners, in particular, supported Calley. Georgia governor

Jimmy Carter declared "American Fighting Man's Day," asking his state's residents to "honor the flag as 'Rusty' had done." Soldiers at Fort Benning (where Calley was confined by house arrest) marched to the cadence "Calley, Calley, he's our man. If he can't do it, Medina can." A group of men from Alabama telegrammed the secretary of defense: "Calley is not only innocent, in our opinion, but a hero, and should be decorated merely for risking his life for the country all Americans are supposed to love."[25]

Further evidence of the depth of support for Calley can be found in the number of songs penned and recorded about him, and about My Lai more generally. Songs have long been a means to laud the deeds of military heroes. More than sixty-five American songs addressed My Lai, and most were pro-Calley. The most famous of these was "The Battle Hymn of Lt. Calley," which sold two million copies, becoming a top forty hit in the spring of 1971. "Battle Hymn" chronicles the life of a boy who grew into a soldier to fight bravely for his flag and country, despite the fact that protestors at home undermined the American cause. Supporting Calley equated to supporting the war. Yet, the song took poetic license in making My Lai out to be a battle rather than massacre. "We took the jungle village exactly like they said / We responded to their rifle fire with everything we had / And when the smoke had cleared away a hundred souls lay dead." Most of the pro-Calley songs extolled his patriotism and bravery, but only one of them explicitly called Calley a hero. In "The Voice from Beyond the Grave," Carlyle Hughey sings, "In other wars this country has had, this kid would have had it made. / They would have made a big hero out of him, even given him a big parade." Carlyle admits that he is ambivalent about the killing Calley did, but he argues that this is part of war, and not for civilians to judge. At the end of the song, he concludes that if Calley is to be judged, we need to rethink previous wars and heroes. "If we are going to play the almighty let's go back and do things up-round. / Let's make heroes out of the guys at Nuremberg and tear the Unknown Soldier's tomb down."[26]

Lionization of Calley astonished critics of the war. Soul singer Sylvia Robinson recorded a song titled "Lieutenant (Had Any Lately?)," which calls Calley "inhuman" and reminds him of the mothers and children he killed, before concluding with disgust, "Now, they call you a hero." Addressing the morality of My Lai for the Jesuit magazine *America*, Thomas Gannon critiqued "the misguided campaign to admit Lieutenant Calley to the pantheon of our national heroes." Senator Jacob Javits (R-NY) echoed these concerns: "If the nation really is encouraged to believe that he [Calley] did nothing wrong—indeed, he is a hero—then we have changed as a people during the course of this tragic war even more disastrously than I had imagined."[27]

In 1971 these liberal critics were in the minority as the groundswell of support for Calley and opposition to his guilty verdict convinced President Richard Nixon to intervene in the case. Facing a life of hard labor, Calley found his sentence reduced to house arrest while the case was on appeal. Nixon's intervention in the case was a popular move in 1971. With the president's approval, the United States Secretary of the Army Howard H. Callaway paroled Calley in 1974. He married and moved to Columbus, Georgia, where he managed a jewelry store.[28]

As Calley retreated from the spotlight, refusing requests for interviews, his popularity declined in a parallel trajectory to opinions of the war that he had, in part, come to represent. By the late 1970s, President Nixon and General William Westmoreland refused to defend Calley's actions in their memoirs, even as they chastised liberals who had used My Lai to score political points against the war. Calley's silence appeared to be one factor in the increasingly critical tone taken by My Lai chroniclers. Michael Belknap, who offered a relatively balanced view of Calley in his legal study of My Lai, bitterly noted Calley's refusal to respond to interview requests, explaining that if his book contained an unfair appraisal of the former lieutenant's motivations, "the responsibility for that rests with Calley himself." As oral historians have long known, the relationship between interviewees and interviewers complicates (and often softens) critical analysis of historical actors. Although heroes are expected not to laud themselves, Calley's silence enabled writers to depict him as the primary villain of My Lai.[29]

After Calley drifted into ignominious obscurity, in the 1990s Americans rediscovered Hugh Thompson as a hero of My Lai. A dogged effort by a few Vietnam veterans led the military to consider Thompson for the Soldier's Medal, but top Pentagon brass were reluctant to honor the former helicopter pilot for fear of reopening the wounds of My Lai. General Colin Powell rebuffed one such request, arguing, "Soldiers perform many acts of bravery during wartime, many of which pass unrecorded. Also, it is very difficult to distinguish between a soldier's duty and an exemplary act of heroism during the demands and chaos of battle." Finally, in 1998 the Army awarded the Soldier's Medal to Thompson and his crewmates (one posthumously) at the Vietnam War Memorial in Washington, D.C. "We are here to recognize the heroic actions of three former soldiers," said Major General Michael Ackerman in his opening remarks. Nearly everyone who spoke that day lauded the heroism of Thompson and his crew for risking their lives to defend civilians.[30]

As important as self-sacrifice and courage are to the definition of heroism in modern America, so too is the attribute of humility, which Thompson displayed at the Soldier's Medal ceremony and in the years to come. "I proudly and humbly accept [this award], not only for myself, but for all the men who served their country with honor on the battlefields of Southeast Asia." Thompson, who had demanded that his crewmates be awarded the medal, extended the honor to all Vietnam veterans. He hoped that their heroism, which had been tarnished by My Lai and the divisiveness of the war, could also be acknowledged. When the television news show *60 Minutes* did a feature on the increasingly famous helicopter crew, the cameras captured a debate between Thompson and his former door gunner Lawrence Colburn. "I don't classify myself as a hero, and I don't think Larry does either," said Thompson, responding to a question from interviewer Mike Wallace. Colburn interjected, "*I* classify *you* as a hero!"[31]

Thompson's rediscovery as a hero was long overdue, but it also said something about the way American heroism had changed over the decades since Vietnam. A spate of movies about the Vietnam War in the 1970s and 1980s allowed Americans to wrestle with the demons of that war on the silver screen, offering no-holds-barred (sometimes cartoonish) depictions of the war's violence. Many of the films portrayed soldier protagonists as antiheroes struggling with the morality of their individual actions and the larger policies of the U.S. military. *Apocalypse Now* (1979), *Full Metal Jacket* (1987), and *Born on the Fourth of July* (1989) all fit this mold, but *Platoon* (1986), which deals most explicitly with the issues raised by the My Lai massacre, is perhaps the best treatment of the American soldier as antihero. Peter Gibbon argues that these films depicting American soldiers in Vietnam as antiheroes contributed to the "fall of the warrior/hero" at the very same time that the women's and men's movements challenged macho war film heroes like John Wayne. As American filmmakers and historians moved away from traditional military heroism and history, Gibbon worried that they had substituted antiwar literature for real military heroes. Perhaps Gibbon's concerns were overblown, as other Vietnam War films of this period could easily by categorized as heroic epics. This was particularly true of the series starring Sylvester Stallone as John Rambo (1982, 1985, 1988, and 2008) that saw an antihero protagonist morph into a traditional war hero who turns the tables not only on the Vietnamese, but also on inept, immoral American military superiors. Similarly, Mel Gibson's *We Were Soldiers* (2002) offered a heroic narrative of the average American soldier in Vietnam, even if the American military and public rarely gave these heroes the support they needed to win the war. In the context of Hollywood's cinematic schizophrenia regarding Vietnam, Hugh Thompson made a perfect American hero—a soldier who fought against the excesses of the Vietnam War, without necessarily challenging the war itself. As a result, Thompson could be seen simultaneously as both a hero and antihero.[32]

Thompson's rediscovery was also well timed in another way—it came just as the United States was reopening diplomatic and trade relations with Vietnam. In 1995, three years before Thompson was finally awarded the Soldier's Medal, Presidents Bill Clinton and Lê Đức Anh (a former Viet Cong officer) normalized relations between the United States and Vietnam. Before the end of the decade, Vietnam would grant "most favored status" to American companies such as Nike that constructed large manufacturing centers in the country.

As a result of improved diplomatic and economic relations, American tourists began traveling to Vietnam in larger numbers. Some of these tourists were American veterans returning to a country they had not seen in three decades. Hugh Thompson and Lawrence Colburn flew back to Vietnam with cameras in tow as part of the *60 Minutes* story on their service. Because Thompson's picture had been in the local paper, a few Vietnamese people recognized him. "It's an honor to meet an American war hero," one said. Choking up, she continued, "And you are a hero to my people too." "Oh, no ma'am," Thompson protested. "Don't think of me as a hero, but as a friend of the people of Vietnam." According to his biographer, Thompson then explained, "You see, to me, heroes are people who do something above and beyond the call of duty. We didn't do anything besides our duty that day—nothing the average American soldier wouldn't have done. I'm just an average guy, no better than anyone else who fought honorably in Vietnam, and worse than some." While this encounter seems too perfectly scripted for a biography called *The Forgotten Hero of My Lai*, Thompson and Colburn seemed to be genuinely embraced by the Vietnamese people. Yet, photographs of the two men surrounded by Vietnamese schoolchildren were eerily reminiscent of an infamous 1970 cover photo for *Esquire* magazine that depicted a smiling William Calley surrounded by Asian children. American heroism in both eras rested on personal humility and a protective, almost paternalistic relationship with Vietnamese people.[33]

Thompson's rediscovery as a hero paralleled one final geopolitical trend of the 1990s, as the United States took on a new role of global peacekeeper in the post–Cold War era. During the administrations of George H. W. Bush and Bill Clinton, the United States deployed troops not only to protect American interests, but also to defend the human rights of innocent civilians. Major operations in Kuwait, Somalia, Haiti, and Kosovo all reflected this shift in American military policy. Given this new role for the U.S. military, Hugh Thompson's courageous actions to save the lives of Vietnamese civilians (albeit from the weapons of other American troops) suggested that American heroism was not based primarily on defeating or killing an enemy, but on defense of the defenseless. In this context, Thompson's return trip to Vietnam in the late 1990s and the U.S. government's acknowledgement of him as a hero for saving Vietnamese civilians in My Lai must be understood as part of the United States' shifting diplomatic and economic priorities after the end of the Cold War. As admirable as Thompson's actions had been at My Lai, one wonders if he was as much a "hero for our time" as Calley had been in the early 1970s.

Calley and Thompson will be forever linked as the antagonist and protagonist of the My Lai massacre. I have argued that these historical constructions of heroism are comparable in that they reveal much about the eras in which the two men were lionized and vilified. But I would not equate their actions at My

Lai. Calley was a murderer, regardless of how he was later depicted, and Thompson served honorably, saving the lives of civilians who would almost surely have perished at the hands of Charlie Company. Does that make Thompson a hero for all time? Perhaps not. It simply means that on one spring day during the Vietnam War, he was the far better soldier and, in fact, the better man.[34]

NOTES

1. Seymour M. Hersh, *My Lai 4: A Report on the Massacre and Its Aftermath* (New York: Random House, 1970), 39–43; John Sack, *Lieutenant Calley: His Own Story* (New York: Viking Press, 1970), 88–89, 99–101.
2. Sack, *Lieutenant Calley*, 101–106; Hersh, *My Lai 4*, 62–64; Richard Hammer, *The Court-Martial of Lt. Calley* (New York: Coward, McCann, and Geoghegan, 1971), 129–132.
3. Trent Angers, *The Forgotten Hero of My Lai: The Hugh Thompson Story* (Lafayette, LA: Acadian House, 1999), 101–106, 116–118.
4. Angers, *The Forgotten Hero of My Lai*, 119–121, 124–34; Sack, *Lieutenant Calley*, 114–116; Hersh, *My Lai 4*, 64–66; W. R. Peers, *The My Lai Inquiry* (New York: W. W. Norton and Company, 1979), 70. Calley remembers this differently, arguing that when it came to evacuating the civilians, he "helped him [Thompson] carry them on" to waiting helicopters. Thompson himself did not have verbatim recollection of his conversation with Calley when he testified before the Army inquiry board in 1970. This version of the conversation comes from Thompson's authorized biography.
5. Army CID investigation excerpted in James S. Olson and Randy Roberts, eds., *My Lai: A Brief History with Documents* (Boston: Bedford Books, 1998). The inspector general's investigation is covered in William Wilson, "I Had Prayed to God that This Thing Was Fiction," *American Heritage* 41, no. 1 (1990): 44–53. The Peers Inquiry produced the *Report of the Department of the Army Review of the Preliminary Investigations into the My Lai Incident*, March 14, 1970, http://www.loc.gov/rr/frd/Military_Law/Peers_inquiry.html (hereafter cited as Peers Inquiry). For the three theories explaining My Lai, see David L. Anderson, ed., *Facing My Lai: Moving beyond the Massacre* (Lawrence: University of Kansas Press, 1998), 6–7; Bernd Greiner, *War without Fronts: The USA in Vietnam*, trans. Anne Wyburd (New Haven, CT: Yale University Press, 2009), 12–22.
6. Hammer, *The Court-Martial of Lt. Calley*, 4–5; Michael R. Belknap, *The Vietnam War on Trial: The My Lai Massacre and the Court-Martial of Lieutenant William Calley* (Lawrence: University Press of Kansas, 2002), 191; Peers, *The My Lai Inquiry*, 227–228; Peter Gibbon, "Military Heroism Denied," *Veterans of Foreign Wars Magazine* 90, no. 5 (2003): 12–18; Petter H. Gibbon, *A Call to Heroism* (New York: Grove Press, 2002).
7. Ron Kovic, *Born on the Fourth of July* (New York: McGraw-Hill, 1976), 65; Anderson, ed., *Facing My Lai*, 14; Hammer, *The Court-Martial of Lt. Calley*, 1.
8. Hammer, *The Court-Martial of Lt. Calley*, 55–59; Sack, *Lieutenant Calley*, 24–25; Hersh, *My Lai 4*, 16–20.
9. Olson and Roberts, *My Lai*, 12; Philip Beidler, "Calley's Ghost," *Virginia Quarterly Review* 79, no. 1 (2003): 37; Belknap, *The Vietnam War on Trial*, 23.
10. Hersh, *My Lai 4*, 20–21; Olson and Roberts, *My Lai*, 15; Drew Lindsay, "'Something Dark and Bloody': What Happened at My Lai?," *MHQ: Quarterly Journal of Military History* 25, no. 1 (2012): 53.
11. Peers Inquiry, vol. 1, sec. 5-12 to 5-14; Olson and Roberts, *My Lai*, 19, 63, 67, 70–71.

12. Dennis Conti testimony in Olsen and Roberts, *My Lai*, 77–78; Dennis Conti, Charles Sledge, Paul Meadlo, and Calley testimony in Hammer, *The Court-Martial of Lt. Calley*, 122–124, 129–132, 154–155, 250.

13. Varnado Simpson testimony and CID report on My Lai rapes in Olsen and Roberts, *My Lai*, 88–89, 99–102; Calley testimony in Hammer, *The Court-Martial of Lt. Calley*, 250, 257.

14. Meadlo, Conti, and James Dursi testimony in Hammer, *The Court-Martial of Lt. Calley*, 123–124, 142–143, 154–155; Lindsay, "'Something Dark and Bloody,'" 56.

15. Angers, *The Forgotten Hero of My Lai*, 117–132.

16. For background on Thompson, see Angers, *The Forgotten Hero of My Lai*; Peers, *The My Lai Inquiry*, 243.

17. Thompson testimony included in Olson and Roberts, *My Lai*, 116.

18. Press release and combat action report in Olson and Roberts, *My Lai*, 27, 30–31; Hammer, *The Court-Martial of Lt. Calley*, 18; Committee on Armed Services, House of Representatives, *Investigation of the My Lai Incident*, 213.

19. "Report from Son My Village Chief" (March 22, 1968); "Lt. Tran's Letter to Province Chief" (April 11, 1968); "VC Propaganda Broadcast, 'American Evil Appears'" (1968), in Peers, *The My Lai Inquiry*, 277, 279, 280–281.

20. Ridenhour letter in Peers, *The My Lai Inquiry*, 4–7.

21. Account of the IG investigation in Wilson, "I Had Prayed to God that This Thing Was Fiction," 44–53; chronology of early My Lai investigation reporting in Belknap, *The Vietnam War on Trial*, 260–261.

22. Committee on Armed Services, *Investigation of the My Lai Incident*, 208, 213, 217–218, 231–232; Hammer, *The Court-Martial of Lt. Calley*, 107; Greiner, *War without Fronts*, 336.

23. Angers, *The Forgotten Hero of My Lai*, 177–178; Nell Boyce, "Hugh Thompson: Reviled, Then Honored for His Actions at My Lai," *U. S. News & World Reports*, August 20, 2001.

24. For charges and evidence against both enlisted personnel and officers in regards to My Lai, see Peers Inquiry, vol. 1, sec. 12. For more on the handling of other court-martial trials related to My Lai, see Hammer, *The Court-Martial of Lt. Calley*, 33–45; Belknap, *The Vietnam War on Trial*, 216–235. Peers was particularly incensed that the Army was unable to bring formal charges against officers superior to Calley after he had gathered so much evidence of the massacre's cover-up. See Peers, *The My Lai Inquiry*, 221–227. Calley's verdict is explained in Belknap, *The Vietnam War on Trial*, 188–189.

25. Immediately after the verdict, a *Newsweek* poll found that 79 percent of those surveyed disapproved of it, and only 9 percent approved. More detailed surveys revealed a nearly even three-way split in war attitudes among those who disapproved (28% hawks, 28% doves, and 29% middle-of-the road). Polling and public reaction analysis in Belknap, *The Vietnam War on Trial*, 191–215; "The Hero Calley," *Time*, February 15, 1971; Greiner, *War without Fronts*, 341–343, 348; Lindsay, "'Something Dark and Bloody,'" 57; Angers, *The Forgotten Hero of My Lai*, 181–182.

26. For a list of recorded songs related to My Lai and William Calley, see http://rateyourmusic.com/list/JBrummer/vietnam_war__my_lai_and_lt__william_calley_songs/ (accessed January 15, 2015). Julian Wilson and James Smith, "Battle Hymn of Lt. Calley," Plantation Records #PL-73 (1971); Carlyle Hughey, "The Voice from Beyond the Grave," Chart Records #5127 (1971).

27. Mother of Three (Sylvia Robinson), "Lieutenant (Had Any Lately?)" Stang Records, #ST-5027 (1971); "The Hero Calley," *Time*, February 15, 1971; Thomas Gannon, *America*, April 17, 1971; "Calley Conviction," *Congressional Quarterly Almanac* 27, no. 6 (1971): 744.

28. For more on Nixon's decision to intervene in the Calley case, see Belknap, *The Vietnam War on Trial*, 197–215, 245–256.

29. Olson and Roberts, *My Lai*, 192–193, 196–198; Belknap, *The Vietnam War on Trial*, xiv.

30. Angers, *The Forgotten Hero of My Lai*, 16, 39, 44–46.

31. Ibid., 70–71.

32. Gibbon, "Military Heroism Denied," 12–14.

33. Angers, *The Forgotten Hero of My Lai*, 90–91; "The Confessions of William Calley," *Esquire*, November 1970.

34. James Zumwalt, "Hidden Heroics: Negative Press Should Not Make Us Forget Model Warriors," *Navy Times*, July 31, 2006.

6 • LEONARD MATLOVICH

From Military Hero to Gay Rights Poster Boy*

SIMON HALL

On March 6, 1975, Leonard P. Matlovich, a technical sergeant in the U.S. Air Force, wrote to his commanding officer at Langley Air Force Base to explain that "after some years of uncertainty," he had "arrived at the conclusion that my sexual preferences are homosexual, as opposed to heterosexual." He also added that this fact would "in no way interfere with my Air Force duties, as my preferences are now open."[1] Writing the letter, a move that Matlovich had been mulling over for several months, was intended as a deliberate challenge to the military's blanket ban on homosexuals—when his "stunned" captain asked, "What the hell does this mean?," Matlovich replied, "It means *Brown* v. *Board of Education*."[2] After an Air Force board of inquiry decided to discharge him from service, Matlovich contested the decision all the way to the U.S. Court of Appeals before accepting a substantial out-of-court settlement in 1980.[3] But within months, his case had become a cause célèbre: Matlovich was interviewed by the *New York Times* and the major television networks, became the first openly gay man to feature on the front cover of *Time* magazine, and was hailed as a "hero" by the gay rights movement. In the words of his friend and fellow gay rights activist Michael Bedwell, he "became a poster boy for gay rights.... He became a hero particularly to [gays] in the military. I remember where I was when Kennedy was assassinated and I remember where I was when I saw when Matlovich was on *Time* magazine."[4]

By any reckoning, Leonard Matlovich was a military hero. A self-proclaimed "Air Force brat" (his father was a career Air Force sergeant), he had joined the service in 1963, aged just nineteen, determined to prove his manhood (and, he hoped, to overcome the strong homosexual feelings that he had experienced from an early age), before going on to win a clutch of medals during three tours of duty in Vietnam.[5] On February 8, 1966, during his first tour, Matlovich (then merely an airman first class) ventured to the perimeter of his base, braving enemy mortar fire, to strengthen the defenses and search for possible casualties; his courage earned him the Air Force Commendation Medal.[6] That same year, he was awarded the Bronze Star for "meritorious service while serving with friendly foreign forces engaged in military operations against an opposing armed force" (on one occasion, he reportedly killed two Viet Cong guerrillas while on sentry duty). He also won praise for his "exemplary leadership, personal endeavor, and devotion to duty." Then, in November 1970, Matlovich was awarded the Purple Heart for wounds received in action (he had suffered serious shrapnel injuries on August 17, 1969, after stepping on a Viet Cong land mine in Da Nang).[7]

Remarkably, Matlovich's response to nearly losing his life was to volunteer for a third tour of duty. On returning to the United States in late 1971, he worked as a race-relations instructor in a pioneering Air Force program designed to "promote awareness and understanding of our multi-racial ethnic society, the causes of social unrest, prejudice, racism, and discriminatory practices." Matlovich, who had abandoned the racist views of his youth, earned a Meritorious Service Medal for his much-admired efforts.[8] In his 1973 to 1974 performance review, he was described by Major Donald D. Baines as "one of the most outstanding NCOs I have had the pleasure of working with during my Air Force career." Matlovich, Baines declared, had a "dynamic personality with an exceptional command of the communicative skills. He is a dedicated, sincere, and responsible NCO who applies his total ability to any task. . . . TSgt Matlovich is an absolutely superior NCO in every respect and should be promoted to Master Sergeant well ahead of his contemporaries."[9] It was clear to everyone that Matlovich had, as his defense lawyers put it, "rendered long and exceptionally meritorious, courageous, and unusual service to the United States Air Force."[10]

Matlovich's exemplary military record featured prominently in the gay rights campaign that enveloped him, and it formed part of a wider appeal that was rooted in his respectability and love of country. Indeed, leading gay rights strategists viewed Matlovich as the "ideal" candidate to challenge the blanket ban.[11] Here was a "tall and trim" sergeant, six feet, two inches and 165 pounds, with short reddish-brown hair, "a thin line moustache, brown eyes" and—particularly significant considering popular stereotypes—a "firm handshake" and no known psychological problems.[12] In fact, aside from his sexual orientation, Matlovich embodied conservative values and traditional masculinity (he had, after all, fought and killed for his country). He was a lifelong Republican (he had campaigned for Barry Goldwater in 1964) who expressed his desire to settle down in a stable, loving, monogamous relationship. He dressed smartly (notwithstanding a brief experiment with flowered shirts after his public coming out), foreswore cigarettes and alcohol, and extolled the virtues of individual effort and hard work.[13] Matlovich also challenged the widely held view of gay men as weak, effeminate, and perverted (prejudices that, to some extent, he had internalized), explaining that "[I] thought that to be gay I had to wear women's clothes, to go into the bathroom and watch people, to molest little children, all the stereotypes. Well, I'm gay and I never wanted to do any of those things."[14] He described how, when he finally plucked up the courage to enter a gay bar for the first time, rather than being met with scenes of wild depravity, he "only saw ordinary-looking men and women sitting at tables."[15] Matlovich was also at pains to distance himself from the more controversial or provocative aspects of gay sexuality, emphasizing that his partners had included white-collar professionals—doctors, dentists, and lawyers—who were, in his words, "without exception respectable average citizens."[16] As one Associated Press report put it, "He could be your next-door neighbor, a mechanic, accountant or the family doctor. He wants what you want: a decent job, a comfortable home, love."[17]

For Bruce Voeller, the founder of the National Gay Task Force (NGTF), which had been founded in 1973 to lobby for gay rights, Matlovich was "a godsend in that he did not fit the public perception of what gays are like. There he was, a very proud war hero with his ribbons, having been wounded and having worked his way up through the ranks. He was myth- and stereotype-defeating. It was quite wonderful to have that.... He could serve as a dynamite role model.... With Lenny's example, there was no way that people in the Armed Forces could maintain that homosexuals were automatically unfit for military service."[18] Matlovich's attorney, the ACLU's David Addlestone, concurred: the Air Force sergeant was "a patriotic, conservative middle-class war hero. He destroyed the popular myth of homosexuality."[19]

In challenging his discharge, Matlovich continually emphasized both his distinguished service record and his strong desire to serve his country: "I love the military," he explained, "I want to stay in the Air Force."[20] He simply wanted the opportunity to remain in the job for which he had been trained, and at which he excelled. The NGTF, which promptly set up a Gay Veterans Committee to fight for the rights of gay military service personnel, drew attention to Matlovich's bravery, describing him as a "courageous man, winner of the Purple Heart and many other medals, [who] gives hope and pride to countless lesbians and gay men through his fight to integrate the armed forces and society."[21] The invocation of Matlovich's military record complemented the wider effort to challenge the military ban on explicitly patriotic grounds. In Matlovich's first major press interview—with the *New York Times*—which was deliberately timed to appear on Memorial Day (the federal holiday honoring those killed while on military service), he claimed that his military oath to uphold the Constitution obligated him to challenge the ban, because it violated his right to the equal protection of the laws.[22] Like countless dissenters before (and since), Matlovich claimed his right to protest as an *American*, pointing out that he would not be able to undertake such a challenge if he lived behind the Iron Curtain.[23] Recalling his speech at New York's gay pride parade in June 1975, Matlovich explained how "it was just great pride to be an American, to know I'm oppressed but able to stand up there and say so."[24] At a news conference held Friday, September 19, 1975, shortly after the Air Force review board had recommended that he be given a general (i.e., less than honorable) discharge, a "smiling" and "determined" Matlovich "held up a bicentennial half-dollar and said, 'It says 200 years of freedom. Not yet... but it will be some day.'"[25] The following month, at a fund-raising party held at a gay disco in Washington, D.C., he told a cheering crowd of supporters that "one day, we, too, will be able to say, 'My country, 'tis of thee, sweet land of liberty.'"[26]

The fusion of the "patriotic military hero" and the "gay rights campaigner" would continue to characterize Matlovich's public persona. On June 7, 1977, Anita Bryant and her conservative supporters were savoring their success in repealing a gay civil rights ordinance in Miami-Dade County, Florida, following a nasty campaign that had seen homosexual men portrayed as amoral "fiends" (akin to thieves and murderers) and child molesters. Matlovich had played a prominent role in the effort to defend the antidiscrimination measure, with his war record, patriotism, and particular brand of masculinity all used to challenge the stereotypes about gay men that were being promoted so aggressively by the religious Right. Now he sought to rally dispirited supporters in a ballroom across town by holding aloft a large American flag, and invoking the principles of liberty and justice for which the republic stood.[27] Ten years later, Matlovich—wearing his Air Force jacket, replete with Bronze Star and Purple Heart, and carrying a small American flag—was arrested while leading protests outside the White House against the Reagan administration's woeful response to the AIDS crisis. Matlovich's status as both a military and a gay rights hero also shaped the commemorations that followed his own death from an AIDS-related illness. On June 24, 1988, just two days after Matlovich's passing, the Christopher Street West pride parade in Los Angeles hosted a moving tribute: a riderless horse preceded by a man carrying a red, white, and blue banner bearing the words, "Sgt. Leonard Matlovich Hero."[28] Matlovich was buried with full military honors at the Congressional Cemetery in Washington, D.C., on July 4, 1988; his coffin was taken through the streets of the capital on a gun carriage, accompanied by an Air Force honor guard, while mourners carried both American and rainbow flags.[29] His headstone bears the inscription, "When I was in the military they gave me a medal for killing two men, and a discharge for loving one." He had chosen this epitaph himself, he explained, "because the military can honor death and heroism, but discharge for love. It just doesn't make any sense."[30]

Matlovich continued to influence the campaign to end the ban on gays in the military from beyond the grave. In 1993, Vince Patton III, a master chief petty officer in the U.S. Coast Guard, resigned from the Presidential Commission for the Study of Gays in the Military after it recommended a policy of "Don't Ask, Don't Tell." Patton, a (heterosexual) African American who supported repealing the ban, believed that the "compromise" proposal "was ridiculous; we came up with a policy that allowed you to lie, but then every service's core value says, 'Don't lie.'" Patton, who drew a parallel between racial discrimination and homophobia, explained that "one of my biggest military heroes is Leonard Matlovich. . . . I was impressed that here was a man who laid his life on the line, earned a Bronze Star, did all kinds of things and then, all of a sudden, after he comes out, he's no good. What about the lives that he saved—the people who now have grandchildren to tell the story? But we didn't want him because of his sexual orientation."[31]

The gay rights movement's embrace of Leonard Matlovich, and the cause that he symbolized, was, in many ways, surprising. After all, the story broke in the press just weeks after the fall of Saigon, and many of the pioneers of the gay liberation movement had been connected intimately with the anti–Vietnam War movement.[32] Whereas the "homophile" movement of the early 1960s had demanded that gays be allowed to serve in the U.S. armed forces, by the late 1960s and early 1970s many gay rights activists were denouncing not just the war in Vietnam, but the American military itself. The historian Justin David Suran has even claimed that opposition to the Vietnam War and a "radical antimilitarism" were "essential" to "the creation of a High Sixties 'gay' identity."[33] New York's Gay Liberation Front (GLF), which had been founded in the immediate aftermath of the Stonewall riots, famously proclaimed its solidarity with the Vietnamese (its very name was modeled on South Vietnam's National Liberation Front), while in August 1969, the Youth Committee of the North American Conference of Homophile Organizations called on gay rights activists to "totally reject the insane war in Vietnam and refuse to encourage complicity in the war and support of the war machine." During the November 1969 Moratorium demonstrations in San Francisco, meanwhile, some 15,000 gay and lesbian protesters joined in with chants of "Ho Ho Ho Chi Minh, dare to struggle, dare to win," and some even carried placards proclaiming "Suck Cock to Beat the Draft."[34] According to one participant, the war had "helped bring thousands of gay people together in the strongest show of gay power in the history of the world. . . . Vietnam has awakened life in the midst of death."[35] Three years later, Boston's GLF called not just for "the *total* withdrawal of all United States and United States–supported air, land or naval forces from Vietnam," but for the abolition of "all aggressive armed forces."[36] Indeed, during the late 1960s, many gay liberationists came to embrace nonparticipation in the military as "a positive good," arguing that to serve in the military was to offer aid and comfort to *Amerika*'s imperialistic "war machine" and reenforce traditional heterosexual notions of masculinity.[37] During the major antiwar protests that took place in Washington, D.C., during the first weekend of May 1971, for instance, the Gay May Day Tribe declared, "War American style is a man's game, where to prove his masculinity, he must maim or kill women, children, the very old, the very young, and his own brothers. War is an extension of our own oppression because it reinforces the masculine image of males and forces them into playing roles where the end result is the death of millions of people."[38]

By the mid-1970s, the end of America's formal military involvement in Southeast Asia, together with the rapid decline of both the antiwar movement and the wider New Left, meant that the gay liberation struggle was no longer so deeply entwined with the Vietnam issue.[39] Nevertheless, many gay liberationists remained profoundly uneasy (to say the least) with the movement's very public support for a decorated Vietnam veteran and military "hero."[40] As the NGTF's Bruce Voeller recalled, "a lot of people were pissed at Lenny because he was a military hero. The very virtue that I saw in him was considered by a lot of people in the movement to be anathema."[41] Any doubts were unlikely to be assuaged by Matlovich's claims that, in Vietnam, he had merely been "an electrician . . . changing lightbulbs," or his robust opinions on the war itself.[42] Like many conservatives, he took the view that "if Vietnam was worth being there, we should have fought to win it. If it wasn't worth winning, then we should not have been there." He believed that "when you go to war and ask someone in your country to die, you have a moral obligation to end that war as fast as possible. And that means being willing to use everything in your arsenal, if need be, to protect your people." While no apologist for American atrocities like the My Lai massacre, Matlovich understood all too well that the pressures of war could have terrible consequences: "When each day you watch your buddies on both sides of you being blown away all because of some stupid orders to capture the same hill over and over again," he explained, "you become very callous toward human life."[43]

Writing privately to Matlovich in May 1975, Randy Shilts—then a young reporter in Eugene, Oregon, later a pioneering gay journalist and writer—confessed that "as a member of the peace march generation," he had a "difficult time relating to your desire to stay in the military. But I can respect and relate to the great service which you are now doing for your country."[44] Others were less forgiving. On September 27, 1975, *Gay Community News* (*GCN*), the influential Boston weekly, published a letter by Brian Kelly denouncing the Air Force sergeant: "He doesn't want freedom for Gay People, he wants 'the right' to murder and oppress women and men (Gays included) in occupied countries. Matlovich is not our brother. He doesn't stand for freedom for people, he stands for the freedom to oppress. We cannot support him if we truly believe in Liberation and Human Dignity." Claiming that support for Matlovich discredited the entire gay liberation struggle, Kelly implored activists to "demand freedom for the oppressed, not the oppressor!"[45] A few months later, John Kyper, a founder of Boston's GLF who had been arrested as a result of his "absolute opposition" to the Vietnam War, confessed his misgivings about a "gay hero who expresses, without qualification, his *love* for the Air Force." While praising Matlovich's "courage and dedication to coming out publically," Kyper urged gay rights activists to "question just where we are going before we accept Respectability as a substitute for our attempts to change this diseased society. The sellout isn't worth its price."[46]

Although others argued that the Air Force sergeant deserved support for "rocking the boat" and challenging society's taboos, or urged the gay community to put their differences to one side and maintain a united front, it was clear that Matlovich's emergence as a gay rights "hero," and the wider question of whether the movement should support homosexuals who wished to serve in the military, were deeply divisive.[47] Some activists refused point-blank to support Matlovich because of his desire to remain in the Air Force, while others jeered and heckled him at rallies.[48] Writing in early December 1975, *GCN*'s Neil Miller identified a growing "antimilitary backlash" within the gay rights movement, noting that "after a period in which private doubts were sacrificed to a perception that the military issue was a powerful consciousness-raising device among both gays and straights, gay activists are asking some hard questions about the wisdom—and morality—of gay participation in the Armed Forces."[49]

Just a few weeks earlier, for instance, the Gay Academic Union (GAU) had held its third annual conference in New York City. Even before it got underway, many of the organization's radicals had quit in protest at Matlovich having been invited to address the opening plenary. The historian John D'Emilio recalled how "for those of us who had come of age in the antiwar movement, it seemed a betrayal to honor someone who had proclaimed, 'I love the military.'"[50] In the end, the Air Force sergeant did not show up, but this did not prevent the editor of a local gay monthly from circulating a leaflet denouncing the U.S. military as "an organization of murderers" and arguing that "the struggle that some gay persons seem to be undertaking to get into or remain in the Armed Forces" was "unworthy of Gay Liberation and treasonous to our common humanity." "Our total response to the state at this level," it declared, "must be NON SERVIAM! I will not serve."[51] Other GAU members who were more sympathetic to efforts to oppose antigay discrimination wherever it was found nevertheless chided those who had accepted uncritically "the sentiments expressed in the statement [by Leonard Matlovich], 'I love the military.'" As they saw it, the U.S. military was a "repressive police force whose sole purpose is to make the world safe for American imperialism," and they warned that "privileges for the few of us must not be won at the price of endorsing a system which will continue to oppress the majority of us."[52] Meanwhile, in San

Francisco, members of Bay Area Gay Liberation (BAGL)—an organization that had been founded in early 1975 following a spate of police attacks on the city's gay population—furiously debated whether or not to cosponsor a Matlovich fundraiser. After several hours, the "pro-Matlovich" forces prevailed, but when about half of the members began to walk out, the motion was quickly rescinded (over a handful of objections) in order to avert an organizational schism.[53]

Although Matlovich noted, somewhat ruefully, that his "roughest" critics were the "left-controlled" gay media who attacked him as a "baby-bomber" and "napalmer," he does appear to have been genuinely popular among the gay rank and file, with many won over by his evident sincerity.[54] An article in the December 1975 issue of the *Advocate*, titled "Cannibalization of a Hero," noted that "every gay group in the country, it seemed, wanted Matlovich for a personal appearance. . . . Every gay group in the nation was trying to organize a benefit for Matlovich. . . . Gay people acted as if they owned him."[55] Countless gay Americans, including many in uniform, wrote to Matlovich to praise him for his bravery, courage, and "guts" for taking a stand. As one put it, "I want you to know that I consider you to be one of the most courageous men I have ever heard of, and a sterling example to all of us who are still too frightened of coming out while in the military—indeed, in any situation where the old taboos still persist."[56] Another declared that "I don't know much about the way the service awards its medals, but I'd say this action took rather more courage than stepping on a land mine."[57] Indeed, a number of gay military personnel—notably, twenty-four-year-old Navy ensign Vernon E. Berg, who had served as a missile battery officer with the Sixth Fleet in the Mediterranean, and twenty-eight-year-old Miriam Ben-Shalom, a convert to Judaism and Army staff sergeant—decided to follow Matlovich's example and challenge the military ban on homosexuals in the courts.[58]

For some historians, Matlovich's emergence as a gay rights icon signifies a narrowing of the revolutionary promise of gay liberation. As David Eisenbach has put it, "by the mid-1970s, the gay rights movement rallied around a decorated Vietnam vet who simply wanted to defend his country. The grandiose vision that the gay rights movement was part of a larger social revolution that would transform the politics of the United States was succeeded . . . by a more limited focus on securing the rights of open homosexuals to contribute to society."[59] Moreover, the movement's appropriation of military heroism—a concept that, as Simon Wendt notes in the introduction to this volume, is rooted in traditional notions of white warrior masculinity—risked legitimizing or reinforcing homonormative values.[60] In stressing his conservative beliefs and desire to settle down in a monogamous relationship, for example, Matlovich, and a good many of his supporters, valorized a particular kind of homosexual—conservative, patriotic, conventional, unthreatening. The *Advocate*, for instance, declared that "none could argue that the ideal gay version of the common man was Matlovich himself," while one supporter claimed that the Vietnam veteran had "given the gay movement a dignity that it didn't previously have." For his part, Matlovich complained that by permitting "some gay people's vices" to be "flaunted," the movement had set back the cause of "acceptance" by obscuring the fact that "we're like everyone else. . . . We're moral people. We're good people. We contribute to American society and make it a better place. . . . Like everyone else, we deserve a piece of the American pie."[61] There was precious little room here for the effeminate, the camp, or the promiscuous, to say nothing of those who understood gay liberation as a powerful revolutionary force with the potential to break down all forms of oppression and exploitation—including capitalism, militarism, and imperialism—or who argued that, far from being "carbon copies" of straight people, homosexuals had a unique and valuable insight into mainstream culture that was borne of their particular historical experience.[62]

In many ways, the movement's support for Matlovich represented a revival of the earlier "homophile" tradition of harnessing "patriotic protest."[63] In 1964, for instance, New York Mattachine, a gay rights organization that had been founded 14 years earlier in Los Angeles, had picketed an induction center in lower Manhattan to protest the military's ban on homosexuals; two years later, on Armed Forces Day, hundreds of activists had taken to the streets in several cities to highlight the military's continued discrimination against homosexual citizens.[64] This earlier generation had also argued that the automatic exclusion of homosexuals from the military and federal government damaged America's Cold War fight against the Soviet Union by excluding talented individuals from public service.[65] Appeals to patriotism and the appropriation of military heroism have also featured prominently in the recent battles over the right to repeal Don't Ask, Don't Tell. Testifying before Congress in February 2010, for instance, the National Gay and Lesbian Task Force claimed that, in the context of the War on Terror, "our nation can ill afford to squander the contributions of brave and loyal Americans who volunteer to serve in the U.S. Armed Forces."[66] The Human Rights Campaign, meanwhile, launched a "Voices of Honor" tour that featured moving testimony by both gay and straight service personnel in support of repeal (Staff Sergeant Eric Alva, the first Marine seriously wounded in the Iraq War, came out publicly in order to support the campaign).[67] Speaking at the tour's launch, Pennsylvania Democrat Patrick Murphy, a former West Point professor and Iraq War veteran, declared that "President Barack Obama has stated that if Congress can get a bill to his desk repealing Don't Ask, Don't Tell, he will sign it into law. It is now our job, and my job specifically, to quarterback this through the Congress of the United States to do just that. I cannot tell you today how long it's gonna take. All I can tell ya is that paratroopers don't quit, and paratroopers get the job done. To remove honorable, talented and committed Americans from serving in our military is contrary to the values that our military holds dear."[68]

Invoking patriotism, heroism, and military service in support of gay rights is in many ways an attractive strategy, not least because it enables activists to deploy language and symbols that resonate powerfully and widely, and can provide an effective way of building public and political support. As Steve Estes has noted, documenting the patriotism of gay service men and women "can lay a foundation for gay citizenship rights and reveal the shared ideals and experiences that bind Americans, gay and straight, together."[69] This approach, though, is not without its critics. Speaking in 2012, Martin Duberman, the playwright and veteran activist, deplored how the radicalism of gay liberation had been swept aside by an assimilationist approach that "[reduces] our critique of mainstream values to an agenda that pledges allegiance to them." "Those of us on the left," he explained, "feel much the way James Baldwin did when he asked why blacks were begging to rent a room in a house that was burning down. Wouldn't it be better, Baldwin asked, to build a new house? In the same spirit, gay radicals denounce the killing machine known as the military and have no wish to become part of it."[70] The approach taken by some gay rights organizations has even led to warnings that the movement risks becoming a cheerleader for the War on Terror. These dangers were highlighted when, in the autumn of 2001, just as Operation Enduring Freedom was getting underway in Afghanistan, the National Coalition of Anti-Violence Programs (NCAVP)—a gay rights coalition that advocates for victims of homophobia—criticized a photograph of a U.S. missile daubed with the slogan "Hijack this, fags" as a "serious instance of gay-bashing," while praising the service of "honorable" "gay, lesbian and bisexual" military personnel. When it came to the morality of the conflict itself, the NCAVP was silent.[71]

In her landmark 2007 book *Terrorist Assemblages*, Jasbir Puar showed how a sense of nationalism infused the gay rights movement in the weeks following 9/11, and explored the ways in which claims to "progressive sexuality" have been used by the U.S. state to justify its subsequent military interventions overseas (by stressing the "liberation" of Afghan women, for instance, or presenting the United States as a "safer" space for homosexuals than the Middle East). Puar wrote of the "collusion between homosexuality and American nationalism that is generated both by national rhetorics of patriotic inclusion and by gay and queer subjects themselves."[72] In laying claim to freedom, enlightenment, and other progressive values, contemporary imperialism, in Puar's reading at least, requires the rainbow flag.[73] Such a conclusion should not only give pause to anyone who holds fast to transgressive, progressive, or radical visions of gay liberation; it also frames the movement's earlier embrace of "Leonard Matlovich, military hero" in a profoundly troubling light.

NOTES

* I would like to thank Steve Estes, Mark Walmsley, and especially Amanda Kreklau for their invaluable assistance during the researching of this essay.

1. Leonard P. Matlovich to secretary of the Air Force, through Captain Dennis M. Collins, March 6, 1975, 1, in Leonard P. Matlovich Papers, series 4: Air Force Case, box 2, folder 31, San Francisco Public Library.

2. "Air Force Sergeant Feels He Is a Patriot Fighting for Freedom," *New York Times*, September 20, 1975, 15; "The Sexes: The Sergeant v. the Air Force," *Time*, September 8, 1975; Randy Shilts, *Conduct Unbecoming: Lesbians and Gays in the U.S. Military, Vietnam to the Persian Gulf* (New York: St. Martin's Press, 1993), 194–195, 198–200, 203–204.

3. On the legal challenge see Shilts, *Conduct Unbecoming*, 198–200, 202, 234–240, 240, 279, 285–87, 319–321, 362–366.

4. Naveena Kottoor, "The Gay Airman Who Took on the U.S. Military," *BBC News Magazine*, March 25, 2013; Shilts, *Conduct Unbecoming*, 210–211.

5. Lesley Oelsner, "Homosexual Is Fighting Military Ouster," *New York Times*, May 26, 1975, 33, 24; Shilts, *Conduct Unbecoming*, 75–77.

6. "Citation to Accompany the Award of the Air Force Commendation Medal to Leonard P. Matlovich," and "Recommendation for A. F. Commendation Medal," February 25, 1966, in Matlovich Papers, series 5: Subject Files, box 3, folder 6. Matlovich also helped to man machine gun posts.

7. "Citation to Accompany the Award of the Bronze Star Medal," in Matlovich Papers, series 5: Subject Files, box 2, folder 73; Shilts, *Conduct Unbecoming*, 94; "Gay Activist Leonard Matlovich, 44, Is Buried with Full Military Honors," *Chicago Tribune*, July 3, 1988; Burt A. Folkart, "Gay Activist Leonard Matlovich, 44, Dies," *Los Angeles Times*, June 24, 1988.

8. Shilts, *Conduct Unbecoming*, 185–186. For an in-depth discussion of the military's antiracism educational programs during this period, see Say Burgin, "The Most Progressive and Forward Looking Race Relations Experiment in Existence: Race 'Militancy,' Whiteness, and the DRRI in the Early 1970s," *Journal of American Studies* 49, no. 3 (2015): 557–574.

9. Sgt. Performance Report, June 18, 1974, in Matlovich Papers, series 4: Air Force Case, box 2, folder 51.

10. Leonard P. Matlovich v. Secretary of the Air Force, United States Court of Appeals for the District of Columbia, Brief of Appellant, 16, in Matlovich Papers, series 4: Air Force Case, box 2, folder 56.

11. Jay Matthews and Donnel Nunes, "Homosexual GI Fights Release from Service," *Washington Post*, May 28, 1975, A1, 6.

12. Donald P. Baker, "Family Shifts," *Washington Post*, September 17, 1975, 12.

13. See, for example, Ken Ringle, "Matlovich Adjusting to New Life Here," *Washington Post*, November 17, 1976, B1; Jeannette Smyth, "Matlovich: 'It's Not Me That's the Issue,'" *Washington Post*, October 25, 1975, A17; Shilts, *Conduct Unbecoming*, 251.

14. "Homosexual Sergeant Asks Air Force That He Not Be Discharged," *New York Times*, September 18, 1975, 12.

15. Interviewed in Mary Ann Humphrey, *My Country, My Right to Serve: Experiences of Gay Men and Women in the Military, World War II to the Present* (New York: HarperCollins, 1990), 153; Shilts, *Conduct Unbecoming*, 191; Oelsner, "Homosexual Is Fighting Military Ouster," 24; Matthews and Nunes, "Homosexual GI Fights Release from Service."

16. Jay Matthews, "Homosexual in Forces 'Test Case,'" *Guardian*, May 29, 1975, 2.

17. Michael Bedwell, *"And a Discharge for Loving One*—34 Years and Counting: Leonard Matlovich," *Gay Military Signal: The Voice of the Military Rainbow Community*, 2009, http://www.gaymilitarysignal.com/0907Bedwell.html.

18. Mike Hippler, *Matlovich: The Good Soldier* (Boston: Alyson Publications, 1989), 62

19. Kottoor, "The Gay Airman Who Took on the U.S. Military."

20. Oelsner, "Homosexual Is Fighting Military Ouster," 24; "Homosexual Sergeant Asks Air Force That He Not Be Discharged"; "Air Force Acts to Oust Homosexual Sergeant," *Chicago Tribune*, September 20, 1975, 2.

21. "Join the People of NGTF" (advertisement), *The Advocate*, October 19, 1977, 25.

22. "Air Force Sergeant Feels He Is a Patriot Fighting for Freedom."

23. Shilts, *Conduct Unbecoming*, 227; Simon Hall, *American Patriotism, American Protest: Social Movements since the Sixties* (Philadelphia: University of Pennsylvania Press, 2011).

24. "The Sexes: The Sergeant v. the Air Force."

25. "Armed Forces: No to Matlovich," *Time*, September 29, 1975; "Air Force Acts to Oust Homosexual Sergeant," W1.

26. Oelsner, "Homosexual Is Fighting Military Ouster," 33, 24; Matthews and Nunes, "Homosexual GI Fights Release From Service"; Baker, "Family Shifts"; "Air Force Acts to Oust Homosexual Sergeant"; Smyth, "Matlovich: 'It's Not Me That's The Issue' "; Martin Duberman, "Sex and the Military: The Matlovich Case (1976)," in *Left Out: The Politics of Exclusion/Essays/1964–2002* (Cambridge, MA: South End Press, 2002), 297–298, 313–314; "Armed Forces: Homosexual Sergeant," *Time*, June 9, 1975; "The Sexes: The Sergeant v. the Air Force"; "Armed Forces: No to Matlovich"; David Eisenbach, *Gay Power: An American Revolution* (New York: Da Capo Press, 2007), 262, 282.

27. Morton Kondracke, "Anita Bryant Is Mad about Gays," *New Republic* 176, no. 19 (1977): 13–14; Shilts, *Conduct Unbecoming*, 300; "SGT. Len Matlovich Takes an Active Role," *Miami Sunshine* 1, no. 1 (May 13, 1977): 1 (published by Dade County Coalition) in Matlovich Papers, box 2, folder 81, and "notes for speeches' in box 2, folder 82; Tom Matthews et al., "Battle over Gay Rights," *Newsweek*, June 6, 1977; *No More Miamis! Gay Liberation Today* (pamphlet) (New York: Pathfinder Press, 1977), https://www.marxists.org/subject/lgbtq/pamphlets/Gay%20Liberation%20Today.pdf. Matlovich also spoke in dozens of cities and raised tens of thousands of dollars to support the campaign to stop the Briggs Initiative (Proposition 6) in California, which would have prevented homosexuals from teaching in the state's public school system. See letter, Bruce Goranson, "Elect Leonard Matlovich, Supervisor, District 5," in Leonard Matlovich Papers, series 5: Subject Files, box 3, folder 13.

28. Michael Bedwell, "Taps for 'the Charles Lindbergh of the Gay Movement,'" *Gay Military Signal—The Voice of the Military Rainbow Community*, 2013, http://www.gaymilitarysignal.com/1307Bedwell.html.

29. Bedwell, "Taps for 'the Charles Lindbergh of the Gay Movement'"; Shilts, *Conduct Unbecoming*, 622–624.

30. Matlovich, interviewed in Mary Ann Humphrey, *My Country, My Right to Serve*, 154.

31. Steve Estes, *Ask and Tell: Gay and Lesbian Veterans Speak Out* (Chapel Hill: University of North Carolina Press, 2009), 209; Steve Estes, interview with Vince Patton, April 23, 2004, Veterans History Project, American Folklife Center, Library of Congress, http://lcweb2.loc.gov/diglib/vhp/story/loc.natlib.afc2001001.43230/transcript?ID=sr0001.

32. Estes, *Ask and Tell*, 35; Justin David Suran, "Coming Out against the War: Antimilitarism and the Politicization of Homosexuality in the Era of Vietnam," *American Quarterly* 53, no. 3 (2001): 452, 453, 454, 465–477. See also the numerous accounts in Tommi Avicolli

Mecca, ed., *Smash the Church, Smash the State! The Early Years of Gay Liberation* (San Francisco: City Lights Books, 2009).

33. Suran, "Coming Out against the War," 456–459, 463–464.

34. John D'Emilio, *Making Trouble: Essays on Gay History, Politics, and the University* (New York: Routledge, 1993), 242; Shilts, *Conduct Unbecoming*, 96.

35. Quoted in Suran, "Coming Out against the War," 454.

36. Charles Shively, "*Fag Rag*: The Most Loathsome Publication in the English Language," in *Insider Histories of the Vietnam Era Underground Press, Part 2*, ed. Ken Wachsberger (East Lansing: Michigan State University Press, 2012), 104.

37. Suran, "Coming Out against the War," 471–472. See also Say Burgin, "Understanding Antiwar Activism as a Gendering Activity: A Look at the U.S.'s Anti-Vietnam War Movement," *Journal of International Women's Studies* 13, no. 6 (2012): 18–31.

38. Allen Young, "Out of the Closets, Into the Streets," in *Out of the Closets: Voices of Gay Liberation*, ed. Allen Young and Carla Jay (New York: New York University Press, 1992), 20. The piece was originally published, in abridged form, in the November 1971 edition of *Ramparts*.

39. Suran, "Coming Out against the War," 477.

40. Shilts, *Conduct Unbecoming*, 252, 365–366.

41. Hippler, *Matlovich*, 62.

42. Neil Miller, "A Talk with Lenny Matlovich," *Gay Community News*, October 11, 1975.

43. Hippler, *Matlovich*, 64.

44. Randy Shilts (reporter for the *Daily Emerald*, Eugene, Oregon) to Leonard Matlovich, 1975, in Matlovich Papers, series 1: Correspondence, 1975, box 1, folder 36. See also Baird Searles to Matlovich, May 28, 1975, box 1, folder 30.

45. Brian Kelly, letter, *Gay Community News*, September 27, 1975, 4.

46. John Kyper, "Saxe-Matlovich-Morality," *Gay Community News*, January 17, 1976, 5.

47. For letters of support, see, for instance, Reine d'Amoire, *GCN*, October 11, 1975, 5; "satyr," *GCN*, November 29, 1975, 5. On opposition, see letter from Paula Cohen, *GCN*, November 1, 1975, 5; Stephanie Lee, "Lesbians in the Military: Instruments of Our Oppression," *Lesbian Tide*, November/December 1975, 14–15.

48. Suran, "Coming Out against the War," 480; David Thorstad, "Interview with John Damien," n.d. (but accompanied by letter dated November 4, 1976), *Gay Activist* (news sheet), Topical File; box 18 f.9-11 in The Gay Rights Movement, series 2: Gay Activists Alliance, reel 11; Tommi Avicolli Mecca, interview with Leonard Matlovich, *Gay News*, October 31–November 13, 1980, 14, in Leonard Matlovich Papers, series 5: Subject Files, box 3, folder 12; Hippler, *Matlovich*, 63–64, 68.

49. Neil Miller, "Anti-military Backlash Surfaces," *Gay Community News*, December 27, 1975, 3.

50. John Kyper, "Largest Conference Ever," *Gay Community News*, December 13, 1975, 1; D'Emilio, *Making Trouble*, xxxi. On the GAU, see also "Feminism and the Gay Academic Union (GAU)," in Martin Duberman, *The Martin Duberman Reader: The Essential Historical, Biographical, and Autobiographical Writings* (New York: The New Press, 2013), 265–273.

51. Miller, "Anti-military Backlash Surfaces"; John Kyper, "Largest Conference Ever."

52. Miller, "Anti-military Backlash Surfaces."

53. Ibid. On BAGL, see Dudley Clendinen and Adam Nagourney, *Out for Good: The Struggle to Build a Gay Rights Movement in America* (New York: Simon and Schuster, 1999), 335. BAGL's Jane Sica did, though, speak at a fundraiser for the Coalition to Defend Gays in the Military, held in San Francisco on February 22, 1976. See "Gays–Military Fuss," *Chicago Gay Crusader*, March 1976.

54. Suran, "Coming Out against the War," 480; Thorstad, "Interview with John Damien"; Mecca, interview with Leonard Matlovich; Hippler, *Matlovich*, 63–64, 67, 68; Shilts, *Conduct Unbecoming*, 251; David Steven Ritchkoff, "Matlovich Wows Amherst Audience," *Gay Community News*, October 11, 1975, 3.

55. Sasha Gregory-Lewis, "Cannibalization of a Hero," *The Advocate* 180 (December 1975), reprinted in *Long Road to Freedom: The Advocate History of the Gay and Lesbian Movement*, ed. Mark Thompson (New York: St. Martin's Press, 1994), 124–125.

56. Thomas J. Bass to Leonard Matlovich, September 12, 1975, in Matlovich Papers, box 1, folder 3.

57. Andrew P. Tobias (NY), May 26, 1975, in Matlovich Papers, box 1, folder 30. See also Bob Weems (Florida), May 29, 1975, box 1, folder 8; David King (Michigan), September 22, 1975, box 1, folder 21; Bob V. Meyer (Alabama), June 7, 1975, box 1, folder 1; Steven D. Turocy (Kansas), June 16, 1975, box 1, folder 15; Alan R. Stein (Colorado), September 22, 1975, box 1, folder 5.

58. Estes, *Ask and Tell*, 38–39; A Homosexual Ensign Receives Other than Honorable Discharge," *New York Times*, May 22, 1976, 21; Peter Kihss, "Homosexual Cites Pentagon View to Back Fight against Ouster," *New York Times*, March 24, 1976, 17; "The Sexes: The Bisexual and the Navy," *Time*, February 2, 1976; "Frontlines: Military Gays Fight Back," *Mother Jones* 1, no. 4 (1976): 5–6; Steve Estes, interview with Miriam Ben-Shalom, December 11, 2004, Veterans History Project, American Folklife Center, Library of Congress, http://memory.loc.gov/diglib/vhp/story/loc.natlib.afc2001001.43276/transcript?ID=sr0001. See also Humphrey, *My Country, My Right to Serve*.

59. Eisenbach, *Gay Power*, 263.

60. On these issues, see this volume's introduction.

61. http://www.leonardmatlovich.com/gallery.html (accessed May 14, 2015) (quote from July 8, 1977); "Gay Setbacks Not Disastrous, Says Activist," *Washington Star*, June 26, 1975, A10; Alan R. Stein (Colorado) to Leonard Matlovich, September 22, 1975, in Matlovich Papers, series 1: Correspondence, 1975, box 1, folder 5.

62. See, for example, Third World Gay Revolution (Chicago) and Gay Liberation Front (Chicago), "Gay Revolution and Sex Roles," in Young and Jay, *Out of the Closets: Voices of Gay Liberation*, 252–259 (originally published June 1971); Martin Duberman, "Coda: Acceptance at What Price? The Gay Movement Reconsidered" (acceptance speech for Kessler Award from Center for Lesbian and Gay Studies, December 5, 2012), in *The Martin Duberman Reader*, 365–366.

63. David K. Johnson, *The Lavender Scare: The Cold War Persecution of Gays and Lesbians in the Federal Government* (Chicago: University of Chicago Press, 2006), 201; "Craig L. Rodwell, 52, Pioneer for Gay Rights," *New York Times*, June 20, 1993, 38; Eisenbach, *Gay Power*, 40. See also Simon Hall, "The American Gay Rights Movement and Patriotic Protest," *Journal of the History of Sexuality* 19, no. 3 (2010): 536–562.

64. Suran, "Coming Out against the War," 458–459.

65. "News Release from the Mattachine Society of Washington," August 28, 1962, 1–2 in MSNY, series 3, Gay Organizations, reel 18, box 8, folder 5.

66. Testimony of the National Gay and Lesbian Task Force Action Fund for the Hearing "Don't Ask, Don't Tell" Policy, Committee on Armed Services, United States Senate, Room SD-G50, Dirksen Senate Office Building, Tuesday, February 2, 2010, http://www.thetaskforce.org/static_html/downloads/release_materials/tf_dadt_020210.pdf.

67. Matthew Rettenmund, "HRC & Servicemembers United Launch 'Voices of Honor' Tour to Repeal DADT," *Towleroad*, July 8, 2009, http://www.towleroad.com/2009/07/hrc-servicemembers-united-launch-voices-of-honor-tour-to-repeal-dadt.html; Andy Towle,

"First Marine Wounded in Iraq Comes Out of the Closet," *Towleroad*, February 28, 2007, http://www.towleroad.com/2007/02/first_marine_wo.html. See also Beth Bailey, "The Politics of Dancing: 'Don't Ask, Don't Tell,' and the Role of Moral Claims," *Journal of Policy History* 25, no. 1 (2013): 89–113, esp. 107.

68. Rettenmund, "HRC & Servicemembers United."

69. Steve Estes, "Ask and Tell: Gay Veterans, Identity, and Oral History on a Civil Rights Frontier," *Oral History Review* 32, no. 2 (2005): 27.

70. Duberman, "Coda: Acceptance at What Price?"; Adam Nagourney, "For Gays, a Party in Search of a Purpose," *New York Times*, June 25, 2000, 30; Lisa Duggan, *The Twilight of Equality? Neoliberalism, Cultural Politics, and the Attack on Democracy* (Boston: Beacon Press, 2003).

71. Duggan, *The Twilight of Equality*, 46–47; "About NCAVP: Our Mission," at http://ncavp.org/about/default.aspx (accessed November 16, 2012).

72. Jasbir K. Puar, *Terrorist Assemblages: Homonationalism in Queer Times* (Durham, NC: Duke University Press, 2007), xxiv–xv, 38–39, 41, 43.

73. See Deborah Cowen's review of *Terrorist Assemblages* in *Social & Cultural Geography* 11, no. 4 (2010): 400.

7 • DISPLAYING HEROISM

Media Images of the Weary Soldier in World War II, the Korean War, and the Vietnam War

AMY LUCKER

One of the tropes used by war photographers might be called "the thousand yard stare," or "the weary soldier." As Susan Sontag explained in *Regarding the Pain of Others*, "Certain photographs—emblems of suffering . . . —can be used like *memento mori*, as objects of contemplation to deepen one's sense of reality; as secular icons, if you will."[1] Inherent in these images is a basic instability between what the images show and how the images were and continue to be used, particularly through their publication in newsweeklies. The later lives of these images—reprinted in books and exhibited in museums—further divorce them from their original contexts and create additional tensions between images and meanings of martial heroism.

Through investigating these photographs, we might learn more about American public views and tolerances of "warrior emotion," as arbitrated by U.S. print media, and the ways in which they affected notions of the heroic. I believe we can learn much more about the experience of the soldiers and about the society and culture in which these images were received by looking through these images, beyond the first reactions of sorrow, or pity, or sadness that they bring to the viewers. At the same time, we can find evidence of the power of the media to construct and promulgate collective cultural memories about war and heroism in twentieth-century America.

Looking at specific examples of weary warrior images published, for example, on the covers of *Time* and *Life* magazines, some of the difficulties in reconciling the image itself with the use of that image become clear. My use of these particular newsweeklies is not random; they were among the most circulated and best known in their day, especially the period from World War II through the Vietnam War era. In addition, they employed some of the most well-regarded and prolific war photojournalists active in those conflicts.

There has always been an essential tension between the traditional and, in some ways, necessary image of the warrior—brave, unafraid, heroic—and the reality of the situation: that they are, above all, human. In some ways, the use of photography only exacerbates this tension; the images of the weary soldier, for example, could be surrounded by any amount of text extolling the bravery of the soldiers and affirming the necessity that they be in the Pacific, or Korea, or Vietnam in order to save the world from fascism or communism. Nonetheless, it is only the images themselves that could bring forth sympathy and show the soldier as an individual, a human, and in pain. These images, according to historian Andrew Huebner, reflect a "cultural turn from stoicism to sensitivity," displayed in images and media stories.[2]

The warrior image has passed through many stages, even within the relatively brief time period of World War II through the Vietnam conflict. And throughout this period, the mass media—including news outlets in print and on TV—have had a major impact on how the image of the soldier has been constructed. Moreover, identification with the soldier did not necessarily reflect the media's opinion of the conflict. While the media has been "blamed" for America's eventual loss in Vietnam, for example, over time it has become clear that the issue is far more nuanced and complicated. As Huebner states in his study *The Warrior Image*, "while in some ways the mainstream press, Hollywood filmmakers and other image makers may have served the purposes of administrations, in other ways—in the depiction of soldiers—they have often undermined or challenged the government's war efforts."[3] This type of depiction, insofar as it showed actual emotions, suffering, and damage, and not the overall "glory" of war, could elicit only sympathy for and perhaps empathy with the subjects of the images.

World War I depicted the soldier as we now remember him from the period's propaganda films—that is, per Huebner, "the tough, dependable, honorable GI."[4] The World War II soldier, and to some extent, the soldier in Korea, was still largely cast as a hero: "War was not about conflict between nations; it was about the hero's journey from boyhood to manhood, in which Communism was the dragon to be slain."[5] Particularly in World War II, any individual soldier was also a representation of a larger cause, a more encompassing good; his "violence had larger structure and purpose; it created personal as well as national identity."[6] But with the advances in photographic techniques, and with more photojournalists (and TV cameramen) on the battlefield during the later years of World War II, and especially during the Korean and Vietnam Wars, the weary soldier appeared more and more often, "dog-tired, battered, and suffering from the emotional strain of battle."[7] Finally, as the long Vietnam conflict came to its painful end, bringing with it extreme social divisions in the United States, the image of the soldier as victim of his government prevailed.[8]

It bears mentioning, however, that images of war never dominated the covers of *Life* or *Time*. In analyzing covers during the three conflicts discussed here, certain trends became clear. The analysis was done in a relatively unscientific manner: I looked at covers of *Life* and *Time*, primarily online, and counted how many covers featured one of the wars in question, keeping record on a spreadsheet. I counted only visual representations; if the cover text included mention of the war, but the image was not war related, then it did not count. I categorized the images in terms of image content, looking at what elements were portrayed, such as battle scenes, enemy action or personnel, enlisted men as opposed to officers, and so on. Despite ongoing myths about the quantity and quality of coverage of the Vietnam War in the popular press, in truth, war coverage (at least in terms of what was pictured on the actual covers) was highest during World War II (1941–1945), and the levels of coverage were about even during the Korean War (1950–1953) and the conflict in Vietnam (1960–1972). For *Time* magazine, the number of nonwar covers (versus war covers) was 38 percent for World War II, 66 percent during the Korean War, and 83 percent during the Vietnam War years. The numbers for *Life* magazine were similar: 58 percent, 86 percent, and 88 percent, respectively.

During the World War II years, two motifs were most prevalent on the war-related covers: images of battles and images of single, heroic soldiers. Curiously, on *Time* covers, images of enemy participants were the next most common subjects.[9] During the Korean War, the same motifs appeared most often, with battle scenes appearing more often than heroes.[10] During the Vietnam War years, battles again appeared most often, but after that, there is more diversity of subjects, including significant numbers of weary soldiers (both in groups and as individuals), as well as enemies, which were rarely pictured on covers during the Korean War.[11]

An issue in American society during the period 1940 to 1972 that is not reflected in this discussion of images of soldiers is race. In describing the approach that Luce took in representing America during this period, Wendy Kozol explains, "Beginning in the 1940s, the editors increasingly relied on images of the white, middle-class family to signify national ideals."[12] Specifically, however racialized American society and the armed forces were during this period, this is not reflected in the covers discussed here. The American armed forces were still largely segregated by race during World War II; President Truman introduced troop integration shortly before the Korean conflict. Certainly, racial factors in America—including the disproportionate numbers of nonwhite soldiers serving as infantry and therefore suffering greater rates of fatalities—were of great import and the subject of much discussion during the Vietnam War. The antiwar and Black Power movements intersected on many fronts, especially from the mid- through the late 1960s. These movements were covered by the newsweeklies, and were pictured, with images of nonwhites appearing more frequently on the covers of *Life* and especially *Time* during the Vietnam War. However, these images did not overlap with the images of soldiers and war, although the accompanying text might have discussed those interactions.[13]

A perusal of black-oriented magazines such as *Jet* and *Ebony* does not alter this conclusion, at least for the Vietnam War period of 1960 to 1972. *Jet*, which catered to a black working-class readership, had two covers that mentioned the war, and one pictured James Brown, who was going to perform in Vietnam. The covers of the black middle-class magazine *Ebony* included three that explicitly dealt with the Vietnam War; of these, the first depicted an officer, the second, black soldiers in the field, and the third, which was a collage, included one small image of soldiers.[14]

In all three wars, issues of masculinity were tightly tied to military service. As Wendy Kozol describes it, "Military exploits during the postwar years, especially the Korean War, presented *Life* with the opportunity to depict fighting men protecting the United States."[15] During the Vietnam War, too, media representations of soldiers—specifically, "the fighting man," or infantry—privileged masculinity over other categories. As Susan Jeffords states, "Vietnam representation poses the masculine bond—commitments between men that are seen to cross barriers of racial, ethnic, class, age, geographic, religious, or social differences."[16] To some extent, as the war persisted and popular opinion about it started to turn, there was a distancing of drafted soldier from military "lifer," where the divide was between infantry and the government, or soldiers and officers (the history of "fragging" during the Vietnam War supports this). Jeffords notes, "it could then be argued that (white) men were not oppressors but instead, along with women and men of color, themselves victims of a third oppressor, in this case the government."[17] As the war went on, even the enemy was identified as more sympathetic than the U.S. government, most notably by the antiwar movement. The Vietnam War was especially damaging to the image of the veteran. As Jerry Lembcke states in his well-known book on the myth of the spat-upon Vietnam War vet, "The identity crisis supposedly suffered by Vietnam veterans because they were denied the military victory of their youth might better be laid at the feet of a culture that confers manhood on warriors, but not on peacemakers."[18]

The portrayal of emotions in soldiers is thus interestingly complicated by the fact that the modern military operates under an emotional regime of stoicism and interiority, inextricably tied to conceptions of masculinity. Women did serve on the front during all three conflicts covered here. Nonetheless, the privileging of masculinity over all else dictated that women warriors be absent from the covers of mainstream newsweeklies. All three of these wars—World

War II, the Korean War, and the Vietnam War—were draft wars, and the draft involved only young men. As Erika Doss points out, this "segregation of the American population by gender [was] of unprecedented proportion and duration,"[19] and would have been particularly striking to these draftees. Women who served did so as volunteers, even if they were employed by the military. The full gender integration of American military forces that has occurred since this period is reflected in images from more recent wars, although the creep of female images echoes the slow creep of images of nonwhite soldiers. The draft is one of the factors that the three conflicts under discussion share that allows them to be grouped together, even though World War II stands out in America's collective memory. As Anna Froula writes in the preface to an edited volume on heroism and gender in war movies, "in the American psyche, WWII—the 'Good War'—remains the template with which to shape official discourse about subsequent military incursions, even when the analogy fails."[20] While both the Korean and Vietnam Wars have certainly been recast over time, neither has been able to gain the moral traction of World War II.

Of course, numbers and percentages do not change the visceral reactions that viewers experience upon seeing the effects of war on men. And front covers are only one measure of the total coverage of the wars. Despite the non-dominance of images of weary warriors in terms of numbers, and noting that they depict an incomplete story with respect to race, these images nonetheless persist in memory, and their impact diminishes little over time. What follows is a detailed visual analysis of some of these images, examining how the image of the weary warrior changed, and how it was used to powerful effect by mass media over the period of World War II through the Vietnam War.

WEARY SOLDIER IMAGES

The original model for the type of weary warrior image analyzed in this chapter comes from a painting by artist and war correspondent Tom Lea during World War II. *Life* published the painting *Marines Call It that 2,000 Yard Stare* to illustrate an article published on June 11, 1945. The painting is a 1944 portrait of a Marine at the Battle of Peleliu. The article is titled "Peleliu, Tom Lea Paints Island Invasion," and the portrait is on page 65, midway through the article, which is primarily pictorial; the article is featured in the arts section, not news. The caption underneath reads, "BATTLE FATIGUE is mirrored in the stark, staring eyes of this marine painted against the background of 'Bloody Nose Ridge.' . . . Lea's notes tell this man's story. . . . How much can a human being endure?"

By the beginning of World War II, the print media preferred photography as the technology for delivering images from the war, but paintings and drawings were sometimes still considered better for representing painful emotion. A Bill

Mauldin drawing graces the cover of *Time* on June 18, 1945. In this case, the image, captioned "Mauldin's War," depicts one of Mauldin's by then well-known characters, "Willie," who was modeled after his comrade and friend Irving Richtel, and who, along with "Joe," became synonymous with the average American GI. Mauldin, like Lea, was a soldier as well as an artist—an early version of an embedded journalist—who risked his life and suffered along with the soldiers he drew. Thus, his sympathies could not be questioned; Mauldin, too, was the average American GI.

But cover images of weary warriors were not limited to drawings or cartoons. While World War II has been historicized as the "good war," the devastating impact it had on the soldiers who fought was also documented in the most "realist" medium: photography. It may well be that the hardships were easier to acknowledge in a war that was far less divisive than the Korean War and the Vietnam War, so the editorial meaning behind such images was less loaded or problematic than in later years. For example, a cover of *Life* published on August 14, 1944, featured a resolute, if scraggly, soldier, with the caption "In Normandy." Inside the magazine, the description of the cover reads, "The tough, haggard man on the cover is one of thousands who are winning the battle for France. He is Lieut. Kelso C. Horne, of the U.S. airborne infantry. Men like Lieut. Horne saw their hardest fighting on June 6." Lieutenant Horne may be haggard, but he remains tough. His fight is valiant and, ultimately, successful.

The covers from Korea start to tell another story. Here we begin to see some of the conflicts between the editorial and political leanings of two of the most widely read newsweeklies of the day and the realities of a brutal, unforgiving war; a war that fewer Americans understood, or accepted as necessary. Indeed, whereas World War II came to be considered the "good" war (particularly in comparison to the Vietnam War), Korea became the "forgotten" war. Forgotten, despite the fact that per annum, American casualties were far higher during the Korean conflict than in either World War II or the Vietnam War.

On the January 1, 1951 cover of *Time* is another drawing, but one quite obviously meant to look as photographic as possible. Again, it depicts the average American GI as *Time* presents its "MAN OF THE YEAR / Name: American / Occupation: Fighting Man." As in World War II, photographs also graced covers during the Korean War—especially the covers of *Life*. While the editorial policies, and content, of the two newsweeklies were in accord (since both were Luce publications), *Life* was produced and marketed as the more pictorial of the two, and *Time* was the "Weekly Newsmagazine." Hence, we have a cover of *Life* from June 31, 1950, with the caption, "24th DIVISION SOLDIERS AT FRONT." The cover image, credited to Carl Mydans (who also has a photo essay, "Yanks Hit a Beach in Korea," later in the same issue), is described on page 11: "First U.S. infantry outfit to shed blood in the Korean war [sic] was the 24th 'Victory' Division, three of whose men are shown aboard a jeep in Korea. Last week the men of the 24th fought heroically to hold the key city of Taejon against superior Communist forces, then were forced to retreat under murderous fire after their commander was reported missing and the enemy had surrounded and infiltrated the town." We are told that the men "fought heroically," if unsuccessfully. Yet, their faces, especially that of the driver, reflect exhaustion, fear, perhaps resignation. Is this the face of heroism, as we have been culturally conditioned to see it? The ambiguous gender and ethnicity of the soldier sitting in the rear of the jeep adds to this image's ambiguity. He (we must believe) is one of the three men of Division 24. He is, according to the description, an American soldier. But his face is vaguely Asian, and vaguely effeminate, or delicate, lending another dimension of atypicality to the image in terms of Western conceptions of what an American soldier looks like, even if the meaning or import of the image was clear from the text.

By the mid- to late 1960s, deep into the war in Vietnam, published images became more loaded, challenging the maintenance of the status quo. It is important to note that by this time, Henry Luce had passed away, and with his absence came a more nuanced and questioning tone to the editorial content in *Time* and *Life*. Editors during this era were aware of the changing feelings of many readers toward the war, and the divisive nature of the conflict and its impact on American culture did not escape them. As reader opinions changed (evidenced, for example, in letters to the editors), so did the presentation of the war.

The cover of *Time* on June 6, 1967, is a good example. A compelling photograph by David Greenway shows a solitary American soldier, tucked into a bunker, clasping his helmet onto his head. The caption under the photo reads "Under Fire at Con Thien," and a banner laid diagonally across the top right corner reads "Rising Doubt About the War." Unlike Bill Mauldin, Tom Lea, and David Douglas Duncan in World War II, Greenway was not in the war as a soldier, but as a correspondent and photojournalist. Most of the photographers working for *Time* and *Life* during the Vietnam War were there as journalists only, not as soldiers or as draftees, but unlike most of the men they photographed, they had volunteered for their dangerous assignment. Their lives were very much threatened with every sortie; print journalists could sit in a hotel in Saigon and file their stories from safety, but photojournalists had to be in the thick of things. Consequently, they were every bit as vulnerable as the young soldiers they photographed, but were armed only with cameras. They were totally involved in the war, and the emotions they searched for and photographed must, in some way at least, have reflected their own concerns and doubts. Greenway, for example, was wounded in Vietnam and also received a commendation for saving a Marine. In fact, more than sixty journalists died covering the Vietnam War from 1955 to 1975, far more than in either World War II or the Korean War.

Life featured images from Con Thien, a U.S. Marine Corps combat base that was the site of fierce fighting from February 1967 through February 1968. "David Douglas Duncan Photographs the Marines. Inside the Cone of Fire at Con Thien" reads the text on the cover of the issue for October 27, 1967. Duncan (discussed in greater detail below) was a Marine photographer during World War II and a photographer for *Life* during both the Korean War (when some of his best-known, now iconic images were created) and the Vietnam War. The editor's note for this issue reads, in part, "In Vietnam, Duncan, as usual, went where the bitter action was—Con Thien." Again, his subject was Marines. His essay in this issue of *Life* is almost fifteen pages long and features primarily "action" shots. As is typical for Duncan's essays, the text is minimal. But the cover photograph is particularly compelling: a close-up of a Marine's young, dirt-covered face, with eyes that seem to radiate anxiety and fatigue. While there may be beauty, there is also certainly doubt. The Marine is a "man at war," but he is also unquestionably young. He is brave, he is not flinching, but we see fear. Is he a hero? Does it even matter? As the country struggled with questions about the validity of a war that in the eyes of an increasing number of Americans had been going on for far too long, and yet would go on for another five-plus years, Duncan's portrait exposed the many layers of "reality" involved in any lethal conflict.

To be sure, there is a certain commonality among all of the wars' cover images. But it is not until the Vietnam War that the images' accompanying texts, as well as the faces, display doubt about the mission. Art historian Jason Hill describes Luce's approach to using photographs, along with text and captions, to tell the specific stories he wished to tell in *Life* and other magazines, employing the presumed authority of the photograph to bolster his own biases and prejudices. He discusses how Luce used images as a "visual anchor," and how the pairing of these supposedly "transparent" and true images with "textually interpretive and value-laden captions" functioned to "effectively and persuasively advance its anti-communist, anti–New Deal, corporatist, and socially conservative perspective as a 'reality' to its many millions of readers."[21] While *Life* was promoted as a "pictorial," thus deemphasizing the text, the examples given above nonetheless make the point that even with the predominately pictorial approach, the editorial intent is clear. With the change in editorial policy after Luce's death, these images were paired with more questioning text. It is apparent that as the media reflected government policy, they also reflected changing public opinions; as described in an article investigating *Life* covers during the Vietnam War, "media coverage and other sources of social knowledge, reciprocally reinforcing each other, created a climate of increasingly critical observations of the military operation in Vietnam."[22]

Of course, Henry Luce did not invent the use of photographs as a means of political persuasion in media. Photography had a role in creating what people took to be "history" from the early days of the medium. Since photographers were able to represent the actual performance of events as they occurred, photographs became the favored means by which news media created and disseminated what viewers and readers rapidly accepted as the real history of events. Ulrich Keller, who has written extensively on the relationship between war and photography, argues, "Photo reportage established itself not just as an eminently *believable* medium but as a *persuasive, prescriptive,* and *transformative* one as well."[23] In truth, photography was deployed as a method of persuasion and was used by editors and publishers like Henry Luce to further their particular viewpoints and to convince their audience to adopt them.

At the same time, it is important to recognize that the role of the media in forming public opinion is tempered by their role in reflecting public opinion. The media, especially in the form of newsweeklies like *Life* and *Time,* were, above all, comprised of commercial enterprises. The view of the media as responsible for the U.S. defeat in Vietnam has been discussed at length and largely disproved.[24] Yet, as social divisions in the United States created more questions about the war, these questions were reflected in the media. In many ways, images from the Vietnam War question not only definitions of heroism and masculinity, but national policy as well. The doubt we see in the soldiers' eyes reflects the growing national doubt about the mission of the United States and its cause in Vietnam, which is also seen in the banner headlines on the magazine covers. These doubts, while certainly present during the Korean War, were not as boldly stated at that time, either in public or in the media. By looking more closely at some of David Douglas Duncan's images of soldiers from this period, we can delve more deeply into the issues they raised that were not perhaps as apparent at the time.

DAVID DOUGLAS DUNCAN'S KOREAN WAR IMAGES

The images created by David Douglas Duncan have become some of the best recognized photographs from the Korean War, even as (for many viewers and readers) the war itself has faded into relative obscurity. The image of Captain Ike Fenton, for instance, is an iconic "weary soldier" photograph. In Duncan's photographs of men at war, we recognize both the pain of the man and the "heroism" of the soldier, which is made clear only by the captions the photographer and editors added when using these images. The image of Fenton is one of a large series taken by Duncan as photojournalist for *Life* during the Korean War. These images were first published in *Life* in September 1950 and have been reproduced and exhibited many times since then.

That the possibility of reinterpretations (or misinterpretations) of images becomes greater when a photograph is surrounded by text or captions was clear to Duncan. In the preface to his photo memoir *This Is War!*, first published in 1951, during the war it pictured, he states: "Believing that the look in that man's eyes tells more clearly what he felt, I am presenting this book to you without a single caption. . . . To sit down now to write subtitles for these pictures, telling what *that* man *thought*, would be a mockery of the worst order. . . . The photographs reflect only what the men in this book did."[25] In a later photo memoir, Duncan again included this photo, this time with a cryptic caption—almost a poem—accompanying it: "*That Thousand Yard Stare*/Captain Ike Fenton/U.S. Marine/1950/Naktong River/Perimeter/with some problems/no radio with anybody/mostly grenades/bayonets of course/no reinforcements/that's normal because/nobody back there knows/casualties/high still climbing/suppose/gook battalion/climbing/our little hill/Yeah . . . now to worry."[26] For Duncan, the man speaks for himself, as a man, heroic in the moment because he remains standing despite the very long odds against him. Indeed, some of the subjects of other famous images from this sequence were not so lucky: they were killed during this fight to drive the North Koreans back over the Naktong River.

For example, the image of machine gunner Corporal Leonard Hayworth in tears is perhaps equally as famous as that of Captain Fenton. Hayworth was killed the morning after seeing this photo of himself in *Life*. This image went farther than comparable images in displaying emotion. Crying was not unexpected, but its depiction in *Life* could be regarded as disruptive to the image of the heroic soldier. Wendy Kozol posits, "Challenges to masculine ideals in Duncan's photographs also open up spaces in which to critique the political actions taken in the name of masculinity. . . . Alternatives to dominant male gender ideals potentially make problematic the military actions legitimized on the basis of those same ideals."[27] When Duncan showed Hayworth his published image, he took a picture of the soldier looking at himself; this image, too, was published. The seeming egocentrism of a soldier looking at a picture of himself crying was overcome only because, as Huebner describes, the "caption told viewers Hayworth had been killed the morning after seeing his picture."[28] The editorial position of *Life* under the direction of Henry Luce was clear: defense of the Korean War was a defense against the expansion of communist and anti-American ideals. Duncan's photographs viewed on their own likely posed greater questions than they did when they were published in *Life*, surrounded as they were there by text that justified the conflict and the sacrifices it required. Kozol further asserts (per Fredric Jameson) that *Life* and other mass media published challenging images because they "must address the hopes and anxieties of their audiences in order to capture their interest and sell products effectively."[29] With the editorial posturing, these "hopes and anxieties" were doubtless quelled, or at least categorized as necessary, given the situation.

Duncan's studies of soldiers are studies of modern warfare, of heroism, and of doubt. In a book review in *American Photo* of the 1990 reissue of *This Is War!*, Joe Gioia states, "His photographs are heroic narratives and sensitive studies of anguish. . . . Duncan shows the grim reality of war; his men weep as well as grin."[30] Indeed, there is more room for doubt about the war in Duncan's book than there was when these same images were published in *Life*.

When they were published in *Life*, in the issue dated September 18, 1950, the editorial decision to respect Duncan's wish to let the images speak for themselves was tempered by presenting the photographs as a "photo essay" as opposed to a news story, and also by including at least some minimal explanatory text and captions. Moreover, the editorial position is made clear by the choice of cover image, which depicts a smiling "Pinza in Hollywood," with a banner on the top right announcing that inside the issue is "Air War in Color." Not until the table of contents (on page 39), listed under "The Week's Events," do we get notice of "*This is War.* Photographed for Life by David Douglas Duncan." The photographs chosen by *Life* editors for the covers that did feature the war more often than not showed either a general or men in action. Luce's support of the war in Korea, and for the government, was well documented and would have been no surprise to the readers of the magazine at the time. Regardless of the photographer's wish that we, the viewers, consider the humanity of Ike Fenton first and foremost, the editorial choices made by Luce and others work to counter this interpretation as the only important one.

CONCLUSION

Visual depictions of soldiers at war are one of the ways by which American culture has always defined masculinity, and heroism, and these definitions have similarly helped define the body of images. As stated by cultural historian Todd Reeser, "Visual culture thus produces masculinity for culture, and conversely, cultural constructs of masculinity that exist before a visual text influence visual culture."[31] One of the changes in media depictions of soldiers has been an increasing isolation of the soldier as an individual; that is, no longer is the soldier/hero a man among men—rather, he is a man alone at war. This shift can be seen in David Douglas Duncan's images from the Korean War, and again in the many images from the Vietnam War that stressed the plight or the agony of the individual soldier.

By adding to the emotional vocabulary of the warrior image, photojournalists allowed access to a more complicated, nuanced picture of the soldier as one who, even while fighting and (perhaps) believing in the fight, nonetheless was a single human being. As Huebner says, "No longer a cultural hero just because of his contribution to a worthy collective effort, now the individual American GI was valorized in the media for his suffering as well."[32] Duncan's images from the Korean War, then, presaged what would become far more commonplace during the Vietnam War: images of soldiers whose doubt about their job was evident. But it was not until after the end of the Vietnam War that the exhaustion, fear, and tears pictured by photographers such as Duncan were considered wounds, or evidence of trauma. Rather, the viewers were told that these were heroic, masculine soldiers, who were allowed to show human feelings, but nonetheless were committed to their roles as warriors. Bloodied, perhaps, but always unbowed. Nonetheless, the wounds showed through. Despite the official lack of recognition (which would come much later, in the form of the definition of and treatment for post-traumatic stress disorder), one must see evidence of pain in these images, regardless of caption or explanation. In this way, the photograph cannot lie. Even if editorial policy was that the image was meant to tell a story of heroic triumph and meaning, the images themselves transmitted a different tale.

But it is also the case that in the period between World War II and the end of the Vietnam War, the imagery of soldiers underwent great changes. Film and media historian Kathleen McClancy informs us that by the end of the 1970s, "soldiering was depicted as both mundane and arduous, not as a story of victory."[33] Over this period, we were allowed to see soldiers as humans, as individuals, vulnerable to pain, to weariness, to the frustrations of war. These images can be, and often are, treated as examples of the art of photojournalism, allowing them to be divorced from their origins and circumstances. The humanity of the soldier is then translated into "art" so that, editorially, these images can become both a critique of war and a justification for future military conflicts. Again, and always, the intended use of the image does not necessarily accord with the feelings of the viewers upon seeing it.

Our reactions to seeing someone in pain, to seeing a weary warrior, speak to an emotional truth portrayed by the image. This truth cannot be entirely overtaken by the context of the image, by the editorial commentary that accompanies it. These images force us to doubt that the sacrifices of war are valid, and force us also to question whether heroism must require such sacrifices. In his memoirs *Photo Nomad* and *This Is War!*, David Douglas Duncan makes clear that he had similar doubts. In another close-up of another Marine, fighting in Korea in December 1950, once again we are confronted with a young man who undoubtedly would rather be anywhere else in the world. The text accompanying the image in *Photo Nomad* is another poem:

Manchurian / winds unknown to most mortals / never—forgiving / hurricane ferocity / (chill factor unknown) / -40 F. // Somewhere South / of / The Yalu River / North Korea / 9 December 1950 . . . dawn // I asked the rigid Marine // (age also unknown) / teenager or grandfather // the / Question /

idiotic or sacrilegious / under normal circumstances / quite normal there. // IF / I were God / what would you want / for Christmas? // His answer took almost forever // *"Give me Tomorrow."*[34]

NOTES

1. Susan Sontag, *Regarding the Pain of Others* (New York: Picador, 2004), 119.
2. Andrew J. Huebner, *The Warrior Image: Soldiers in American Culture from the Second World War to the Vietnam Era* (Chapel Hill: University of North Carolina Press, 2008), 279.
3. Ibid., 11.
4. Ibid., 275.
5. Kathleen McClancy, "The Iconography of Violence: Television, Vietnam, and the Soldier Hero," *Film & History* 43, no. 2 (2013): 54.
6. Ibid., 53.
7. Huebner, *The Warrior Image*, 276.
8. Ibid., 278.
9. For *Life*, the numbers are 39 percent battles and 43 percent individual "heroes." For *Time*, 21 percent battles, 57 percent "heroes," and 18 percent enemies.
10. *Life* magazine covers showed 46 percent battles, 31 percent "heroes"; *Time* covers had 65 percent battles, 32 percent individual soldiers.
11. *Life* numbers are 58 percent battles, 11 percent weary soldiers (group), and 15 percent enemies. For *Time* the numbers are 70 percent battles, 18 percent individual "heroes," 4 percent weary soldier (individual), and 5 percent enemies.
12. Wendy Kozol, Life's *America: Family and Nation in Postwar Photojournalism* (Philadelphia: Temple University Press, 1994), 56.
13. During World War II, *Time* covers featured nonwhites once, *Life* covers not at all. During the Korean War, each magazine had nonwhites on the cover twice. The numbers jumped during the Vietnam War, even allowing for the longer duration of coverage: twenty for *Life*, and twenty-seven for *Time*.
14. *Jet*, July 7, 1966; *Ebony*, March 1960, August 1968, and August 1969.
15. Kozol, Life's *America*, 169.
16. Susan Jeffords, *The Remasculinization of America: Gender and the Vietnam War* (Bloomington: Indiana University Press, 1989), xiii.
17. Ibid., xiv.
18. Jerry Lembcke, *The Spitting Image: Myth, Memory, and the Legacy of Vietnam* (New York: New York University Press, 1998), 185.
19. Erika Lee Doss, ed., *Looking at* Life *Magazine* (Washington, DC: Smithsonian Institution Press, 2001), 183.
20. Karen A. Ritzenhoff and Jakub Kazecki, eds., *Heroism and Gender in War Films* (New York: Palgrave Macmillan, 2014), xiii.
21. Jason E. Hill, "On the Efficacy of Artifice: PM, Radiophoto, and the Journalistic Discourse of Photographic Objectivity," *Etudes Photographiques* 26 (November 2010): 74.
22. Matthias Bandtel and Jens Tenscher, "Front Cover Imagery and the Social Construction of the Vietnam War: A Case Study of *Life* Magazine's Iconology and Its Impact on Visual Discourse," *Journal of War & Culture Studies* 7, no. 2 (2014): 113.
23. Ulrich Keller, "Photography, History, (Dis)belief," *Visual Resources* 26, no. 2 (2010): 100.

24. See, for example: Michael J. Arlen, *Living-Room War* (New York: Penguin Books, 1982); Peter Braestrup, *Big Story: How the American Press and Television Reported and Interpreted the Crisis of Tet 1968 in Vietnam and Washington*, abridged ed. (Novato, CA: Presidio, 1994); Daniel C. Hallin, *The "Uncensored" War: The Media and Vietnam* (Berkeley: University of California Press, 1989); William M. Hammond, *Reporting Vietnam: Media and Military at War* (Lawrence: University Press of Kansas, 1998); Susan L. Carruthers, *The Media at War* (New York: Palgrave Macmillan, 2011); Stuart Allan and Barbie Zelizer, *Reporting War: Journalism in Wartime* (New York: Routledge, 2004).

25. David Douglas Duncan, *This Is War!: A Photo-Narrative in Three Parts* (New York: Harper and Brothers, 1951).

26. David Douglas Duncan, *I Protest!* (New York: New American Library, 1968), 174–175.

27. Kozol, Life*'s America*, 171.

28. Huebner, *The Warrior Image*, 122.

29. Kozol, Life*'s America*, 172.

30. Joe Gioia, "David Douglas Duncan's Classic Returns," *American Photo* 1 (May–June 1990): 14.

31. Todd W. Reeser, *Masculinities in Theory: An Introduction* (Malden, MA: Wiley-Blackwell, 2010), 111.

32. Huebner, *The Warrior Image*, 130.

33. McClancy, "The Iconography of Violence," 51.

34. David Douglas Duncan, *Photo Nomad* (New York: Norton, 2003), 9.

8 · "FROM LOUBOUTINS TO COMBAT BOOTS"?

The Negotiation of a Twenty-First-Century Female Warrior Image in American Popular Culture and Literature

SARAH MAKESCHIN

In spite of the 1994 Pentagon rule that officially restricted women from artillery, armor, infantry, and other combat roles, the share of women among the enlisted ranks of the U.S. military increased from 2 percent to 14 percent, and the share among commissioned officers increased from 4 percent to 16 percent between 1975 and 2011.[1] In early 2013 the Obama administration overturned the Pentagon rule, arguing that in contemporary military conflicts, the reality is that women frequently find themselves in what must be considered combat situations. On January 24, 2013, Secretary of Defense Leon E. Panetta declared it a top priority of the U.S. Defense Department "to remove as many barriers as possible for talented and qualified people to be able to serve this country in uniform."[2]

Even though women already engage in and die doing the same jobs as men in the U.S. military, and the ban on women in direct combat has officially been lifted, gender equality is elusive in both the U.S. military as an institution and in contemporary discourses on female soldiers.[3] Instead, as feminist scholar Laura Sjoberg claims, women are allowed to participate in a gender-integrated military that is still dominated by "discursive structures of gender-subordination."[4] It seems that femininity is still constructed as "antithetical to soldiering."[5] This circumstance raises questions about how notions of the female warrior and female military heroism are negotiated in the early twenty-first century.

Western military culture is traditionally inclined toward celebrating an image of the true soldier characterized by a "hegemonic, heterosexual masculinity."[6] The empowerment of female soldiers[7] and the redefinition of militarized femininity and female military heroism through the daily realities of war in the twenty-first century consequently pose a massive threat to deeply entrenched patriarchal and masculinized gender structures. Francine D'Amico and Laurie Weinstein claim:

> When American women enter the United States military institution, they enter hostile territory: it is quite literally No-Woman's Land. . . . Each day, the servicewoman must (re)construct her gender identity: Should I try to be "one of the guys," that is, adopt a passing strategy hoping for male bonding to extend to include me? Or should I be "one of the girls," that is, become ultra-feminized, hoping for brotherly affection or chivalric protection? Should I try to be a "soldier," that is, aim for a seemingly gender-neutral professionalism, hoping for mutual respect? Or should I be a crusader, mounting a conscious—and personally and professionally risky—challenge to the structure of gender relations in the institutions?[8]

Over the last ten years, female soldiers have received wider media attention, while a rising number of firsthand accounts and memoirs on the war in Afghanistan and Iraq have been published by female and male members of the armed forces.[9] Many of them focus on the interrelated questions of gender, identity, "successful" soldering, valor, and heroism in the military. Given that "military women challenge notions of military masculinity and manliness," a closer examination of subjective gender experiences in U.S. military service and female soldiers' image of themselves as valiant "women warriors" can reveal much about the gendered ramifications of military heroism in twenty-first-century America.[10]

This chapter first discusses established discourses on the female soldier image and the construction of the heroic female warrior from the 1990s to the present. Second, it analyzes Jane Blair's 2011 memoir *Hesitation Kills,* focusing on her self-perception as a female soldier in the Marines, which is arguably "the most 'masculine' branch of the service."[11] Along these lines, the chapter also takes a closer look at the threats that contemporary (self-)constructions of valiant female warriors and discourses related to these hero figures seem to pose to the socioculturally entrenched masculine warrior paradigm.

As Joshua Goldstein notes, "cultures use gender in constructing social roles that enable war."[12] In Western culture, conceptions of the "good warrior," the military hero, and military valor are thoroughly interwoven with notions of masculinity. Jean Bethke Elshtain explains that there exist deeply rooted traditions that assume "an affinity between women and peace" and "between men and war."[13] In these cultural contexts, "ideals of masculinity largely overlap with those that constitute the warrior ethos (i.e., courage, honor, sacrifice for one's group, endurance and determination."[14] As a result, the warrior hero, in the words of Rachel Woodward, is "physically fit and powerful. He is mentally strong and unemotional. He is capable of both solitary, individual pursuit of his goals and self-denying contribution towards the work of the team. He is also a bit of a hero with a knack for picking up girls and is resolutely heterosexual. He is brave, adventurous, and prepared to take risks. Crucially, he possesses the abilities to conquer hostile environments, to cross unfamiliar terrain, and to lay claim to dangerous ground. . . . He is resolutely male."[15] This means that the path to becoming a war hero is clearly determined by the rules of hegemonic masculinity. The war hero and the heroic warrior thus stand in opposition to femininity and the female sex.[16]

These gendered perceptions of heroic warrior figures traditionally emphasize "violence and warfare as provinces of men and peace and nurturing as the provinces of women."[17] By this logic, the heroic female warrior not only troubles and complicates sociocultural conventions of heroism, and thus cultural self-concepts of the nation they represent, but also, even more, seems to constitute a paradox. Given the understanding that the path to military heroism is defined by maleness/masculinity, access to the status of war hero seems to be blocked for women. In the American cultural sphere, the warrior hero of the twentieth and twenty-first centuries dates back to World War II: "the stoic citizen-soldier, the masculine hero of World War II mythology."[18] Real and fictional heroic icons of military heroism such as Audie Murphy and John Wayne lastingly embodied that ideal.[19] As Debra Ramsay notes, they ultimately defined "war as a proving ground for masculinity."[20]

With these understandings of the valiant warrior remaining firmly in place, the increasing intersection of war, military heroism, and femininity or "the female" clearly constitutes a site of sociocultural conflict. Militarized masculinity, Cynthia Enloe claims, still "cannot succeed without making women also play a specifically feminine part in the militarized process."[21] Women, accordingly, are seen as fit to serve only in specifically feminine (i.e., "civic" and "supporting") roles in relation to warfare.[22]

Due to the high degree of media coverage during the 1991 Persian Gulf War, Operation Desert Shield/Desert Storm was clearly a watershed with regard to awareness of women's presence in the U.S. military. The visibility of the deployment of women in this combat mission provoked significant discussion in the United States about the extent to which female soldiers should be involved in actual military combat—the space where heroism can be proven and achieved.[23] According to Ilene Rose Feinstein, this discussion "at times approach[ed] national obsession."[24] In 1994, it resulted in an official Pentagon regulation of military assignments, the Direct Ground and Combat Definition and Assignment Rules, which legally banned women from direct combat on the ground.

9/11 and the resulting wars in Afghanistan and Iraq produced the other major peak in the debate over the role of women in the military. For one thing, in the reality of a "360-degree war," as war correspondent Ann Scott Tyson described it, a clear delineation between combat-based and support-based roles was no longer possible.[25] According to military sociologist Brenda Moore, this is because "the unpredictable nature of the attacks in this war blurs the distinction between front-line and rear areas."[26] By 2013, 280,000 female soldiers had done tours in Iraq, and 152 female soldiers had been killed while serving in Iraq and Afghanistan.[27]

At the same time, however, as many commentators noted, after 9/11, the tough, heroic, and hypermasculine man figured prominently in America's patriotic discourse as the nation searched for consolation and security after having been attacked on home soil. In the context of these post-9/11 discourses, women were confronted with a cultural backlash assigning them the role of the helpless victim or emotional caretaker. This case was put forward by a number of renowned scholars, including military historian Martin van Creveld, who claimed not only that feminist scholars had inflated the history of female warriors, but also that gender integration in the U.S. military had led to its decline.[28] Van Creveld argued that as more women entered the armed forces, its members would "become both less willing to fight and less capable of doing so."[29] This had an impact on public discourses pertaining to whether female soldiers should play an active role in military conflicts. Among the most discussed stories were those of Jessica Lynch and Lynndie England, two female soldiers who served in Afghanistan and Iraq. Frequently depicted as the "stereotypical fragile, domestic, feminine woman" versus the "gender-bending hillbilly pervert," Lynch and England were the protagonists of the most media-driven and analyzed stories of female soldiers in the post-9/11 era.[30]

One narrative that emerged in this post-9/11 context, but which had been in existence for at least a quarter of a century, revolves around the belief that women cannot meet the requirements for being a "real" soldier in combat due to their biological limitations: women are seen as weaker than men, both physically and emotionally.[31] According to critics such as Jason Hartley, a member of the infantry during the invasion of Iraq in 2003 who wrote a memoir about his war experience, other female physiological disadvantages that render it impossible for women to be real warriors include menstruation, pregnancy, the female urinary system, aging, and the incompatibility of the female physiognomy (e.g., breasts) with the use of weapons or armor. Many female soldiers' personal accounts of their experiences in the U.S. military address the physiological differences that Hartley perceived as disadvantages, but refute his argument, offering stories that reveal women's ability to find creative solutions to overcome the challenges that arise as a result of these differences (e.g., going to the bathroom in a vehicle on mission).[32]

Other widely held perceptions of women's unsuitability for the job of the valiant warrior have been subsumed under the tropes of the "woman in peril," the "damsel in distress," and the "beautiful soul."[33] For example, Van Creveld, one of the most vociferous critics of a gender-integrated military, claims that "women's attempt to improve their social positions by joining the military has not only failed but backfired. Instead of showing they are equal to men, it has proved they cannot do without special protection."[34] Interestingly, the female servicewoman Kayla Williams uses the term "damsel in distress" disparagingly in her 2006 autobiography *Love My Rifle More than You* when explaining her unwillingness to call for help in a situation where she is threatened by a male fellow soldier: "The shame of being in a position where you might have to do that. Yell for help. Like some damn damsel in distress."[35]

The melodramatically staged rescue of Jessica Lynch, pictured in a widely disseminated, iconic photograph lying on a stretcher surrounded by a bunch of male Marines who had saved her, most prominently evokes these tropes in the post-9/11 era.[36] Jessica Lynch—the helpless "little thing"—was depicted as a sweet and innocent "girl from next door," the "petite blonde who joined the Army to get an education and become a kindergarten teacher," who had to be "saved from danger" by a unit of "heroic males." The discursive construction of Jessica Lynch as the victimized female soldier who is "everyone's daughter, everyone's sister," can be seen as a textbook example of the woman in peril narrative.[37]

Another narrative dominating mainstream public discourse on the female warrior during the 1990s and early twenty-first century is the traditional Western understanding that women are "incapable of violent response."[38] According to Laura Sjoberg, there exists a culturally constructed perception of a naturally given "tension between ideal femininity and women's violence."[39] This idea is addressed in female soldiers' accounts of their experiences in battle, as for example in Kirsten Holmstedt's *Band of Sisters*, where Marine Corps captain Amy McGrath discusses at length her view that killing enemies is part of her job as a fighter pilot.[40] Because women engaging in violence corrupts "our image of women as both generally and specifically innocent," incidents of female soldiers acting violently are interpreted as ambiguous or even transgressive oddities.[41] According to Eileen Berrington and Päivi Honkatukia, "pathological deviance from prescribed feminine norms" is frequently "identified as the prime cause" of what is perceived as transgressive violent behavior.[42] In her autobiography, servicewoman Kayla Williams relates that she was not a "typical" girl, preferring to hang out with boys and feeling comfortable in the male-dominated punk rock scene in her hometown. She explains that her motivation to join the military was to prove wrong her violent husband, who did not believe she could "make it in the military."[43] What makes Williams's tomboyish self-description stand out is the fact that her account inadvertently reaffirms the narrative the "abnormal woman."

While the "tough," "bold," and "violent" warrior-like female soldier who physically trumps and humiliates her male fellow soldier is usually considered a "ballbuster," women who fail to perform as well as their male counterparts are also not accepted as members of the "heroic warrior community."[44] Commenting on this truism, Williams notes in her autobiography: "When women are good at what they do, they are not characterized as assertive. They are accused of being ballbusters or bitches."[45] Or, as Marine Mikiela Montoya explains in Helen Benedict's *The Lonely Soldier: The Private War of Women Serving in Iraq*: "You know how I told you there are only three kinds of female you're allowed to be in the military—a bitch, a ho, or a dyke?"[46]

The discursive construction of Lynndie England and her prominent involvement in the torturing and sexual degradation of prisoners at Abu Ghraib prison can be seen as exemplary of the dyke narrative, and has been subsumed under the trope of the fallen woman.[47] England frequently appeared in American discourse as Jessica Lynch "gone bad": "For all the tangled nudes, the hideous hoods, the dangling wires and the dog leash, perhaps the single most shocking thing about the images from Abu Ghraib prison is the woman in so many of the pictures: smiling broadly or giving a thumbs up or just standing casually in the demented scene as if posing in a college dorm. It's the all-American face of Private First Class Lynndie England. The girl next door, a Jessica Lynch gone wrong."[48] As this quote makes clear, because she is a woman, England's acts of torture and violence have a specifically disturbing character that needs to be explained, while the gender of the male perpetrators received little attention.[49] *Salon* wondered in May 2004, "How could women do that?," supposedly because female soldiers should "be a civilizing influence on the military."[50] Instead, as the title of one tabloid news story suggested, England was a "Small-Town Girl Who Became an All-American Monster."[51] *Newsweek*, like other publications, sought to "explain" England and her actions, interpreting England as a "pixie-ish tomboy" who became a "poster girl for sexual humiliation and degradation at Abu Ghraib."[52] Others commented on England's otherness by bringing up her childhood growing up in a trailer home, her speech impediment and learning disabilities, her failed marriage, and the fact that she does not conform to dominant American beauty standards.[53] Belinda Morrissey calls this process of constructing violent women as inhuman, abnormal, and "gone wrong" a form of "monsterization."[54] In a piece in the *Washington Post* about female soldiers involved in the Abu Ghraib torturing, sociologist Melissa Sheridan Embser-Herbert asked why England had participated in such a "degrading act."[55] Embser-Herbert defined this form of aggression as male, and mused, did the female soldiers want "to be accepted as 'one of the boys'? Was this a way of fitting in?"[56] Others raised similar questions, noting, for instance, "To prove their worth, many female soldiers, police officers or prison warders too easily shed the distinctions of their sex in a drive to be tougher, more aggressive, less forgiving than any of their male colleagues. To do otherwise, they imagine, is to appear weak and inferior."[57]

Another narrative that has been strikingly prominent over the last twenty-five years focuses on the "problematic" of women in war as sexual objects. First, the susceptibility of women to sexual violence is seen as a crucial factor that determines their unsuitability for real soldiering. According to Laura Browder, the old stereotype that women cannot "competently serve" because sexual weakness makes them "especially vulnerable" remains firmly in place in the twenty-first century, notwithstanding the fact that female soldiers disproved this narrative during the first Gulf War. According to this argument, captured female combatants who are subjected to torture and sexual abuse by the enemy are much more vulnerable than captured men. This "vulnerability" disqualifies female soldiers from walking the path of a true heroic warrior. Most female soldiers' accounts, particularly in the context of the wars in Afghanistan and Iraq, hardly ever touch upon this issue as a problem. Instead, they regard sexual vulnerability as a problem within the military itself, where sexual harassment is a daily occurrence and rape takes place frequently.[58]

Although studies have shown that the presence of women does not interrupt the cohesion of gender-integrated units, another claim that is frequently made is that female soldiers have a negative impact on the male collective.[59] This idea is firmly established in both academic and public discourse. According to MacKenzie, "The cohesion hypothesis conflates social and task cohesion in that it presumes that women disrupt the trust and camaraderie of men (social cohesion), and therefore disrupt troop effectiveness (task-cohesion)."[60] A commentary in the *Chicago Tribune* with regard to the gender integration of the U.S. military argued, "Men's lives will also be put at greater risk if women are in combat. The reasoning should be obvious. Plainly put, men tend to like women quite a lot and either will be tempted to express their attraction, and/or will want to protect their female companions. Scoff if you must, but blame Nature."[61] Among male members of the U.S. armed forces, similar perceptions are prevalent. Infantry man Joshua Christopher Hartley argues: "The average grunt is fairly in touch with his primal self and therefore wants generally only two things: to fuck and to fight, in that order. And the main reason they fight is to be tough and therefore attract more women with whom they can fulfill their desire to fuck. As soon as there are any women within spittin' distance, prime directive number one kicks in, and all things, especially job discipline, go straight to hell."[62] In the eyes of critics like Hartley, these biologically determined sexual needs, as well as the natural urge to act as protector, are inevitably triggered by the presence of women. The female soldier therefore automatically disrupts the "band of brothers" and compromises male battle discipline and effectiveness.[63] Yet, many lesser known accounts written by female soldiers contradict that argument. Many report that they felt well accepted as "one of the guys" due to their performance as soldiers, without explicit reference to established gender expectations.[64]

Interestingly, there also are female soldiers who are largely ignored by the public for their displays of military heroism. Lori Piestewa and Shoshana Johnson, who were taken captive along with Jessica Lynch, received very little public and media attention presumably because their stories did not sufficiently fit the "innocent victim" narrative in which a captured female soldier is rescued by a heroic unit of male soldiers. Unlike Lynch, Piestewa and Johnson actually engaged in combat, killing and injuring enemies, respectively.[65] A congressman from Piestewa's home state, Arizona, who had spoken to military officials, noted: "She fought. She drew her weapon and fought. . . . It was her last stand. She fought and died valiantly with courage and honor."[66] This narrative of the heroic Hispanic "Lady Warrior," as her family called Piestewa, never found its way into public discourse. Johnson, an African American servicewoman, discussing the limited attention she received in the media, told *CBS News* in a telephone interview, "It was kind of hurtful. . . . If I'd been a petite, cutesy thing, it would've been different."[67] Both Piestewa and Johnson were rendered invisible in the rescue narrative because their racial Otherness and their embodiment of real (female) warrior heroism posed too great a threat to the masculinity of the military's heroic male collective.[68] Cynthia Enloe described this phenomenon as follows: "Women *as women* must be denied access to 'the front,' to 'combat,' so that men can claim a uniqueness and superiority that will justify their dominant position in the social order. Women may serve the military, but they can never be permitted to *be* the military. They must remain 'camp followers.'"[69] In this context, it is not surprising that the U.S. media referred to Shoshana Johnson as a POW who had "planned on cooking, not fighting," and who wanted to "wield a whisk, not a rifle" when she entered the army.[70]

In popular culture, American discourses on the role of the heroic female warrior were negotiated in an only slightly more nuanced manner in the 1990s. Especially after women were officially banned from combat in 1994, Hollywood joined the debate, processing the American public's ambivalence to the issue of women in the military. Among the films released in the late 1990s are *Courage under Fire* (1996), *GI Jane* (1997), *Starship Troopers* (1997), *Soldier's Sweetheart* (1998), and *The General's Daughter* (1999). These films negotiate the aforementioned stereotypes of the female soldier that had been established in mainstream public discourse, taking different views of the female warrior as a sociocultural "problem." Although they offer different perspectives on the issue, they all promulgate a view of the unacceptability of the heroic female warrior.

Courage under Fire (1996), with its story centering on whether a female helicopter pilot should posthumously receive a Medal of Honor, tackles the questions of whether women can ever be fully accepted as heroic soldiers and whether they can function as military leaders without harming the heroic male collective. *G.I. Jane* (1997), the fictional story of the first woman training to become a member of a U.S. Navy reconnaissance team (similar to the Navy Seals), considers whether the female body is physically and mentally up to the demands of combat and warfare. The sci-fi war film *Starship Troopers* (1997) and the Vietnam War film *A Soldier's Sweetheart* (1998) engage the question of whether the presence of female warriors inevitably leads to the weakening of the male collective. The last pre-9/11 film about the female warrior, *The General's Daughter* (1999), tells the story of an on-base rape and murder of a high-ranking general's daughter who was trying to follow in her father's footsteps. It explores the issue of female sexuality, asking whether, considering the biological laws of nature, an integrated military will ever be possible. Interestingly, all of these films leave the audience with the impression that the renegotiation of gender structures in the military is a highly difficult task. Also, on a subtextual level, they all float the idea that, considering the potentially lethal environment, combat and war might not be the right time and place to enforce the undeniably necessary changes with regard to existent sociopolitical gender norms.[71] What is of further interest is that this heyday of films dealing with the female warrior and female military heroism occurred duing a rather quiet time for the United States, from a military perspective.

Although war and war-related films and television series remained in vogue after 9/11, it is striking that there is no noteworthy post-9/11 mainstream film that featured a female soldier in a central role. Popular movies and TV miniseries such as *Home of the Brave* (2006), *Generation Kill* (2008), *The Hurt Locker* (2008), *The Messenger* (2009), *Green Zone* (2010), *Lone Survivor* (2013), and *American Sniper* (2014) all offer traditional representations of the American soldier as hypermasculinized warrior hero.[72] *American Sniper*, for example, was characterized as a revisionist celebration of "frontier masculinity" that could be truly lived out only on the battlefield of Iraq, away from the threat of "domestic femininity."[73] At the same time that popular culture was promoting these revisionist gender narratives with regard to the military, there were already more than 300,000 women on tour in Iraq—a war distinguished by ending the clear distinction between combat and noncombat zones. Iconic gender binaries of women as being in need of protection (victims) or naturally confined to the role of caretakers, and men as protectors and potent agents (warriors) were clearly reestablished; in other words, female military heroism was rendered invisible on the screen. Representations of female warriors in American popular culture after 9/11 echo the mainstream public discourse on female soldiers in the United States.

In the last few years, however, the realities of the War on Terror have brought about a conspicuous shift in the representation of the twenty-first century's female warrior in American popular culture. Recent debates about the increasing technologization of warfare, including the use of drones and its impact on established understandings of military masculinity and heroism, have triggered a renewed engagement with the heroic female warrior.[74] The movie rights to two memoirs by female soldiers were acquired by Hollywood producers in 2015: Major Mary Jennings Hegar's memoir *Shoot Like a Girl: How One Woman's War against the Taliban Led to Her Victory over the Department of Defense* and Gayle Tzemach Lemmon's *Ashley's War: The Untold Story of a Team of Women on the Special Ops Battlefield*.[75] Fiction about the female warrior and female military heroism has been on the rise, too; notable titles include Helen Benedict's *Sand Queen* (2011), Peggy Tibbetts's *PFC Liberty Stryker* (2012), George Brant's *Grounded* (2013), and Cara Hoffman's *Be Safe I Love You* (2014). These two developments—the rising visibility of the heroic female warrior in popular culture, and the emerging discourse on remote warfare and its impact on soldiering—are intertwined. As conventional warfare is increasingly replaced by high-tech warfare, the mastery of technology has become a new essential skill of the twenty-first-century warrior, rendering physical strength, endurance, and bravery secondary. Under these circumstances, it may be that a door has opened for the female warrior to access both the heroic (male) collective of the military and the public and popular cultural discourses on this issue.[76]

Jane Blair's memoir *Hesitation Kills* offers significant insights into the rekindled interest in the valiant female warrior and her potential acceptability in American society and in the masculinity-driven sphere of the U.S. military. *Hesitation Kills* stands out among recent publications penned by female soldiers because of its positive reception by the American mainstream media.[77] Although Blair has been described as having gone from "Louboutins to combat boots,"[78] the image of herself that Blair presents in the book revolves primarily around her femaleness and femininity. At the same time, though, Blair claims that she never thought about her femaleness "until some backwater, hillbilly Marine decided not to salute me because he 'didn't salute female officers.'"[79]

In the book's promotional blurb, Jane Blair introduces her memoir as "one of the only books written by a woman who has experienced combat first hand,"[80] stating that her "aerial reconnaissance unit was assigned to travel ahead of and alongside combat units throughout the initial phase of Operation Iraqi Freedom,"[81] and noting that her book is meant to "convey the immediacy of life in the military, not just for a woman but for all Marines."[82] In addition, Blair aims to address "the struggles specific to women, including being respected as a Marine rather than dismissed as the weaker sex."[83]

Although Blair claims that she does not regard her sex or gender as an obstacle to her self-understanding as a soldier, she does not deny the challenges that long-standing gender hierarchies pose in the U.S. military. We learn that Blair successfully dealt with these challenges, as she holds a leading officer rank in her reconnaissance unit, where she "successfully learns . . . what it truly means to be a leader."[84] She notes that her sex/gender did not preclude her from achieving her position, and further elaborates that she did not join the Marines for money or because it was a viable career option: "I wanted that abstract, intangible quality that Marines seem to magically possess . . . a mixture of a warrior mentality, courage, and leadership."[85] As Blair goes on to explain, due to her top performance in the selection process, she sees herself as having fully qualified for a membership in "the Corps": "Boot camp and OCS were welcome challenges for me . . . and I excelled. After seeing more than 50% of the females drop from my officer class, we knew that those who remained belonged there. When I earned my commission, I was not skirting by; I did my best to excel."[86] Her natural feeling of rightfully occupying her (leadership) position in the Marine Corps is based on her perception of having—as a woman—successfully met the Marine Corps's male-dominated requirements. Citing the Amazons, Joan of Arc, and Israeli and Soviet female soldiers as positive examples of women in combat, Blair explains that while the female warrior "is not a new concept," it was driven out of American society, where the ideal woman is constructed as weak and soft: "Just look in any *Vogue* at the emaciated but often physically unfit women who are deemed beautiful. Meanwhile, in *GQ*, equally beautiful men are expected to maintain their physique through weight lifting and exercise. If women were held to that standard of physical fitness, we'd have much different expectations of them. Women would no longer be victims, portrayed as fragile creatures in need of men's care and protection."[87]

Fighting against this representation of women, Blair's narrative of her time in Iraq focuses on her own psychological and physical resilience and strength. Several accounts of her deployment zero in on situations when she proves her physical strength and endurance on combat missions: "Sand in teeth, in food, in eyes, in everything, made living in this place dismal. The shift in temperature was also extreme. . . . I cursed the weather every day and did push-ups and sit-ups in the sand. My thinking was that as everything else sucked, I might as well get some exercise while getting my face pelted."[88]

Discussing her ability to endure such circumstances, Blair contrasts her experience with the representations of femininity presented in *Vogue*, stylizing herself into a counterimage: "It had been eleven days since my last shower. I couldn't smell myself past the layers of caked sand on my clothes. . . . I lived like an animal. I hadn't shaved my legs or groomed myself in months. My hair was an itchy, matted mess. I didn't care at this point if I had to cut it all off."[89] "Survival and mission," as Blair puts it, "are the two essentials" in combat.[90] Her willingness and ability to endure all combat-related physical hardships is a recurring theme in the memoir. Blair also makes clear that her female biology did not interfere with what was required of her as a soldier in combat. "Thankfully," she notes, "my period had miraculously stopped. I wasn't sure if it was due to stress or malnourishment, but many of the females were in the same situation."[91]

Another aspect Blair returns to time and again is her psychological strength and impassivity. She characterizes herself as "untypical" in that "deployment meant leaving a wife or girlfriend behind. But as a female Marine, it meant leaving my husband—but not behind. Peter had been called the week before."[92] Countering traditional gender roles, Blair does not stay behind in the safe environment of the home. She follows her husband into battle, leaving behind any emotional attachment: "The once incessant thoughts of my husband had been replaced by a strange state of indifference. I remained focused, like some feral animal in search of food. Instinct, adrenaline, and existential nothingness. My feelings just switched off, and I felt nothing."[93] Blair's description of herself as a feral animal, fully able to shut off emotions that might distract or limit her, substantially negates the idea of the woman as an emotionally soft "beautiful soul" and replaces it with an image reminiscent of the prototypical male heroic warrior type.[94] Her "in-case-I-die" letter addressed to her husband further amplifies her hard-boiled image: "I know you are going to open the letter whether I die or not, so I love you. In the event that I am dead, shit, I guess I fucked up somehow. Sorry."[95]

The warrior image presented by Blair also challenges the assumption that women are inherently incapable of being truly heroic warriors because of their inability to engage in aggressive or violent behavior. Blair depicts herself as different, and addresses this in the memoir's title—*Hesitation Kills: A Female Officer's Combat Experience in Iraq*—which was inspired by one of her captains who warned that hesitating to use a weapon in combat will certainly mean death. A quote that introduces one of the early chapters further suggests that Blair is not only willing to kill to defend herself, but also willing to risk her life in order to protect others: "We sleep safe in our beds because rough men stand steady in the night to visit violence on those who would do us harm."[96] With this quote, Blair styles herself in the tradition of the male protector.[97] At another point in the memoir, Blair makes clear that she has no qualms about killing if necessary, claiming for herself an instinct associated with the male warrior paradigm. She recounts, with her "M16 downrange . . . [I was] ready to kill anything [to] keep my Marines safe as best as I can."[98] The weapon, with which she claims to be connected in a very intimate symbiosis, is a source of her empowerment, and Blair's description of her relationship with her weapon questions traditional perceptions of female violent agency: "My M16 was my lifeblood, my security blanket . . . [it was] almost a sexual thing."[99] Her accounts deny the male warrior's monopoly on the proactive use of violence.

Blair projects an image of "militarized femininity" that holds that as long as a female soldier can meet the requirements for being a heroic warrior, she should be fully accepted in that role. Blair's self-concept as a female warrior adheres to the deeply rooted traditional gender perception within the military that becoming a true heroic warrior depends on denying, or at least controlling, your femininity.[100] For Blair, the female heroic warrior is acceptable as long as she is able to make it "as a man": "While I perceived myself as six-foot, four-inch hard-ass, I was in actuality a petite five-foot, four-inch female. But as a Marine, I've got no qualms about living up to the standard that all Marines must. . . . The females were treated the same as men for the most part, as long as they were Marines before they were anything else."[101]

Blair repeatedly promotes qualities she sees as positive in a female warrior by defining herself in opposition to her fellow female soldiers. She recounts the story of a female Marine who, instead of securing an attacked battle position as ordered, is found by Blair and her executive officer hiding in her vehicle, and makes clear how much she detests such behavior: "I felt especially embarrassed that it was a female Marine. A cowardly female Marine was just what we needed in front of the grunts. Freaking awesome."[102] Blair accuses female soldiers who display moral or physical weakness of destroying what female soldiers like her have achieved. Her criticisms of "weak" women is countered by her descriptions of female comrades she respects, such as Sergeant Major Bowen: "She was a statuesque woman, resembling a female bodybuilder, the type who didn't take crap from anyone. She emanated some kind of superwoman rays. I was pretty sure she could take down someone with one punch."[103]

While Bowen is praised for her "superwomanly" qualities, her fellow soldier, Corporal Parker, is singled out for her fearlessness and toughness: "Her presence alone was both sincere and stern. She wouldn't take anyone's bullshit, and they all knew it. . . . She was the only Marine who did not flinch when she mentioned her time going through . . . SERE, a reenactment of prison camp."[104] As Blair says, "She made steel look soft."[105] Those women positively described by Blair share qualities traditionally associated with the male ideal of the heroic warrior: physical and mental strength, endurance, and toughness. As these examples from Blair's memoir suggest, female members of the armed forces frequently engage in a gender performance emphasizing masculine values and qualities in order to prove their willingness and ability to participate in the masculinized space of the military. Indeed, militarized femininity often expresses itself in extreme masculine conduct. This entails "defining [yourself] against the negative qualities associated with women, such as, for example, crying, being compliant or emotional, or simply having PMS."[106] Moreover, this performance often requires distancing oneself from other women or "sisters-in-arms," using vulgar language, and bonding with male fellow soldiers to become a member of the "brotherhood."[107]

Although Blair frequently emphasizes her personal success at overcoming established preconceptions about female soldiers, she does not deny the existence of gender-discriminatory attitudes in the military. On duty with the unit's medic—with whom she has a positive relationship—he openly tells her, "I don't think females should be in combat. . . . Most females I've seen out here are emotional basket cases. You should hear some of the things they do. Women are too emotional. They're not conditioned for this type of environment."[108] Blair responds confidently: "You think the men are conditioned for this? Wait until the bullets start flying and see how many of your fearless boys wet themselves."[109] In general, though, she rarely expresses a feeling of "in-betweenness" or exclusion on account of her sex/gender. Instead, a number of accounts underline her positive feeling of belonging in the military community, where being an accepted brother-in-arms is a reality: "Prewar camps provided a tremendous sense of camaraderie. I met old friends from my earlier enlisted years in the Corps again. . . . It was amazing how the old-boys network connected everyone."[110] From her perspective, being one of the few female soldiers in the unit does not pose an obstacle to becoming a well-connected member of the "old-boys network." Instead of feeling excluded, Blair believes that she occupies an acknowledged and much-appreciated position among her fellow soldiers.

Interestingly, Blair also appropriates the Marines' "heroic" rescue of Jessica Lynch, the Iraq war's most iconic woman in peril,[111] in her memoir. The inclusion of Lynch's story, which, according to Lana Obradovic, "served to perpetuate gendered myths about women in the military,"[112] is noteworthy. As discussed above, Blair herself is able to meet masculinized warrior standards, and has become an integrated member of the "heroic community" of the Marines.[113] In her account of the rescue, Blair describes how her reconnaissance unit was engaged in frontline combat at An Nasiriyah, where they were confronted with "militia-style" fighting and "asymmetric warfare."[114] Because Blair's unit had proven itself to be dependable, the infantry brigade in charge told them they would be participating in the rescue of POWs in An Nasiriyah.[115]

Blair indirectly claims to have been a member of the "heroic" team that rescued Jessica Lynch by stating that she provided crucial "aerial reconnaissance" for the rescue mission.[116] At the same time, she makes no mention of Lynch's fellow POWs such as Shoshana Johnson, who engaged the enemy in battle and was severely wounded during the capture, thus displaying behavior characteristic of a warrior hero. Instead, Blair focuses on Jessica Lynch, and her description of what supposedly led to Lynch's capture underlines the image of Lynch as a helpless damsel in distress: "The story he [a fellow soldier] had heard, which he vouched was the only authentic story, told of Lynch running from her vehicle after it crashed into another vehicle while the convoy was taking fire. He said she then ran into a nearby neighborhood where some Iraqis tried to help her. Not understanding the language, she thought they were trying to hurt her and fired at them. They retaliated by firing shots at her, and brought her injured body to the hospital."[117] In this story, Lynch clearly fails to meet the requirements of the heroic warrior: she freaks out and loses control in a combat situation. Blair denounces stories that Lynch gunned down "a platoon of Iraqis before being captured" as "sheer nonsense."[118] In opposition to the "failed" female warrior Lynch, Blair assumes the role of the accepted and indispensable member of the "heroic warrior collective" that successfully rescued Lynch: "As we reported the information to Task Force Tarawa, they told us to remain in place. 'We're going to do the extract now and we want you all there.'"[119]

It is clear that Blair's take on the heroic female warrior does not entail a reconsideration of established gender hierarchies or gender stereotypes. Instead, she demands that the masculinity-driven heroic collective accept females who are able to fulfill established rules of admission. Thus, the female warrior image offered in *Hesitation Kills* remains rooted in the masculine-warrior paradigm.[120] Despite the elimination of legal gender barriers in America's military of the twenty-first century, the sociopolitical and cultural understanding of soldiering and the heroic warrior remain deeply entrenched in traditional expectations defined by hegemonic masculinity. The female warrior, it seems, is thus still required "to emulate . . . masculine gender characteristics, and . . . not to show any of the perceived weaknesses associated with femininity, all while walking a gender-role tightrope where they do not deconstruct the gender dichotomies on which sociopolitical relationships are founded."[121]

NOTES

1. U.S. Department of Defense, "Direct Ground Combat Definition and Assignment Rule," January 13, 1994, http://big.assets.huffingtonpost.com/irectGroundCombatDefinitionAndAssignmentRule.pdf; Eileen Patten and Kim Parker, "Women in the U.S. Military: Growing Share, Distinctive Profile," *Pew Social Trends*, December 22, 2011, http://www.pewsocialtrends.org/files/2011/12/women-in-the-military.pdf.

2. Leon Panetta, "Statement on Women in Service," U.S. Department of Defense, January 24, 2013, http://archive.defense.gov/speeches/speech.aspx?speechid=1746.

3. For more on gender-equality in the military, see Helena Carreiras, *Gender and the Military: Women in the Armed Forces of Western Democracies* (London: Routledge, 2006); Paige Whaley Eager, *Waging Gendered Wars: U.S. Military Women in Afghanistan and Iraq* (Farnham, UK: Ashgate, 2014).

4. Laura Sjoberg, "Agency, Militarized Femininity and Enemy Others: Observations from the War in Iraq," *International Feminist Journal of Politics* 9, no. 1 (2007): 84.
5. Lana Obradovic, *Gender Integration in NATO Military Forces: Cross-National Analysis* (Farnham, UK: Ashgate, 2014), 34.
6. Christine Eifler and Ruth Seifert, *Gender Dynamics and Post-Conflict Reconstruction* (New York: Peter Lang, 2009), 40.
7. The term *female soldier* is used interchangeably with the term *female combatant.*
8. Francine D'Amico and Laurie Weinstein, *Gender Camouflage: Women and the U.S. Military* (New York: New York University Press, 1999), 5.
9. See, for example, Kayla Williams, *Love My Rifle More than You: Young and Female in the U.S. Army* (New York: W.W. Norton and Company, 2005); Shoshanna Johnson, *I'm Still Standing: From Captive U.S. Soldier to Free Citizen—My Journey Home* (New York: Simon and Schuster, 2010); Heidi Spiers Kraft, *Rule Number Two: Lessons I Learned in a Combat Hospital* (New York: Little, Brown and Company, 2012); Tracy Crow, *Eyes Right: Confessions from a Woman Marine* (Lincoln: University of Nebraska Press, 2012); Myoka Hikiji, *All I Could Be: The Story of a Woman Warrior in Iraq* (Palisades, NY: Chronology Books, 2013).
10. Karen Ritzenhoff, *Heroism and Gender in War Films* (Berlin: Springer, 2014), xxiii.
11. Dana Britton and Christina Williams, "'Don't Ask, Don't Tell, Don't Pursue': Military Policy and the Construction of Heterosexual Masculinity," *Journal of Homosexuality* 30, no. 1 (1995): 16.
12. Joshua S. Goldstein, *War and Gender: How Gender Shapes the War System and Vice Versa* (Cambridge, UK: Cambridge University Press, 2003), 249.
13. Jean Bethke Elshtain, *Women and War* (Chicago: Chicago University Press, 1984), 4.
14. Siniša Malesevic, *The Sociology of War and Violence* (Cambridge, UK: Cambridge University Press, 2010), 286.
15. Rachel Woodward, "Warrior Heroes and Little Green Men: Soldiers, Military Training, and the Construction of Rural Masculinities," *Rural Sociology* 65 no. 4 (2000): 643–644.
16. See R. W. Connell and James W. Messerschmidt, "Hegemonic Masculinity: Rethinking the Concept," *Gender & Society* 19, no. 6 (2005): 829–859. A soldier's failure to meet the requirements of the warrior hero is frequently negatively equated with being female. See R. Claire Snyder, "The Citizen-Soldier Tradition and Gender Integration of the U.S. Military," *Armed Forces & Society* 29, no. 2 (2003): 192. On the concept of "military masculinity," see, for example, Graham Dawson, *Soldier Heroes: British Adventure, Empire and the Imagining of Masculinities* (London: Routledge, 1994); Barry McCarthy, "Warrior Values: A Socio-Historical Survey," in *Male Violence,* ed. John Archer (London: Routledge, 1994), 666–687; Marcia Kovitz, "The Roots of Military Masculinity," in *Military Masculinities: Identity and the State,* ed. Paul R. Higate (Westport: Praeger, 2003), 111–124.
17. Jennifer Lobasz, "The Woman in Peril and the Ruined Woman: Representations of Female Soldiers in the Iraq War," *Journal of Women, Politics & Policy* 29, no. 3 (2008): 308.
18. Andrew Huebner, *The Warrior Image: Soldiers in American Culture from the Second World War to the Vietnam Era* (Chapel Hill: University of North Carolina Press, 2007), 130.
19. See, for example, *Fighting Seabees* (1944), *Sands of Iwo Jima* (1949), *Operation Pacific* (1951), *From Here to Eternity* (1953), *To Hell and Back* (1955).
20. Debrah Ramsay, *American Media and the Memory of World War II* (London: Routledge, 2015), 49.
21. Cynthia Enloe, *Does Khaki Become You: The Militarization of Women's Lives* (Boston: South End Press, 1983), 73. Male-female gender structures in this context have been

traditionally determined by binaries such as "strong/weak, active/passive, reason/emotion, technology/nature." See Lobasz, "The Woman in Peril," 308.

22. Goldstein, *War and Gender*, 9, 87; D'Amico and Weinstein, *Gender Camouflage*, 4–6.

23. According to Gregory Morgan, "the media coverage of the Persian Gulf War marked the beginning of a new era in war reporting." See Gregory W. Morgan, "Media," in *Persian Gulf War Encyclopedia: A Political, Social, and Military History*, ed. Spencer C. Tucker (Santa Barbara, CA: ABC-CLIO, 2014), 294–295. By February 1991, 37,000 women were deployed in the Gulf. See Paul Harris, "Women in Combat: U.S. Military Officially Lifts Ban on Female Soldiers," *Guardian*, January 25, 2013, http://www.theguardian.com/world/2013/jan/24/us-military-lifts-ban-women-combat; Jon Nordheimer, "Women's Role in Combat: The War Resumes," *New York Times*, May 26, 1991, https://www.nytimes.com/books/97/06/15/reviews/military-gulf.html. On the public debate on women in combat, see, for example, "War and the Second Sex," *Newsweek*, August 4, 1991, http://www.newsweek.com/war-and-second-sex-202970; Nordheimer, "Women's Role in Combat"; Amy Eskind, "Women Soldiers: Prisoners of Army Discrimination," *Los Angeles Times*, April 28, 1991, http://articles.latimes.com/1991-04-28/opinion/op-1299_1_women-soldiers; Jayne Hendel, "Female ROTC Cadets: Women Warriors," *Rolling Stone*, October 3, 1991, http://www.rollingstone.com/culture/features/women-warriors-19911003?page=3; Elaine Sciolino, "Female P.O.W. Is Abused, Kindling Debate," *New York Times*, June 29, 1992, http://www.nytimes.com/1992/06/29/us/female-pow-is-abused-kindling-debate.html.

24. Ilene Feinman, *Citizenship Rites: Feminist Soldiers and Feminist Antimilitarists* (New York: New York University Press, 2000), 160; Laurie Lee Weinstein and Christie C. White, *Wives and Warriors: Women and the Military in the United States and Canada* (Westport, CT: Greenwood, 1997), xv.

25. Ann Scott Tyson, "For Female GIs, Combat Is a Fact," *Washington Post*, May 13, 2005, http://www.washingtonpost.com/wp-dyn/content/article/2005/05/12/AR2005051202002.html.

26. Michele Norris, "Roles for Women in U.S. Army Expand," *NPR*, October 1, 2007, http://www.npr.org/templates/story/story.php?storyId=14869648.

27. For additional statistics, see Patten and Parker, "Women in the U.S. Military"; Rod Nordland, "For Soldiers, Death Sees No Gender Lines," *New York Times*, June 21, 2011, http://www.nytimes.com/2011/06/22/world/asia/22afghanistan.html.

28. Patricia Leigh Brown, "Heavy Lifting Required: The Return of Manly Men," *New York Times*, October 28, 2001, http://www.nytimes.com/2001/10/28/weekinreview/ideas-trends-heavy-lifting-required-the-return-of-manly-men.html; Andrea Sachs, "Susan Faludi on 9/11 Myths and Truths," *Time*, October 15, 2007, http://content.time.com/time/arts/article/0,8599,1671642,00.html; Ann Tickner, "Feminist Perspectives on 9/11," *International Studies Perspectives* 3 (2008): 235; Susan Faludi, *The Terror Dream: Myth and Misogyny in an Insecure America* (New York: Palgrave Macmillan, 2007), 112–113; Martin Van Creveld, *Men, Women, and War: Do Women Belong in the Front Line?* (London: Weidenfeld Military, 2001), 228.

29. Van Creveld, *Men, Women, and War*, 236–237. See also Kingsley Browne, *Co-ed Combat: The New Evidence that Women Shouldn't Fight the Nation's Wars* (London: Penguin Books, 2007).

30. Colleen Krepstekies, "News Media Representations of Women in the U.S. Military Post September 11, 2001" (master's thesis, University of South Florida, 2010), 8, http://scholarcommons.usf.edu/etd/3645; Carol Mason, "The Hillbilly Defense: Culturally Mediating U.S. Terror at Home and Abroad," *National Women's Studies Association Journal*

17, no. 3 (2005): 39–63. On the ways in which Lynch and England were covered by the U.S. media, see John Howard and Laura Prividera, "Rescuing Patriarchy or Saving Jessica Lynch: The Rhetorical Construction of the American Woman Soldier," *Women and Language* 27, no. 2 (2004): 89–97; Sara Struckmann, "The Articulation of Lynndie England to Abu Ghraib: Gender Ideologies, War, and the Construction of Reality," *Journal of Magazine & New Media Research* 11, no. 2 (2010): 1–23; Sine Nørholm Just, "Embattled Agencies: How Mass Mediated Comparisons of Lynndie England and Jessica Lynch Affect the Identity Positions Available to Female Soldiers in the US Army," *Scandinavian Journal of Management* 22, no. 2 (2006): 99–119.

31. Gerard DeGroot, "A Few Good Women: Gender Stereotypes, the Military, and Peacekeeping," *International Peacekeeping* 8, no. 2 (2001): 23.

32. Jason Christopher Hartley, *Just Another Soldier: A Year on the Ground in Iraq* (New York: HarperCollins, 2005), 95; Anthony King, *The Combat Soldier: Infantry Tactics and Cohesion in the Twentieth and Twenty-First Centuries* (New York: Oxford University Press, 2013), 23; Stephan Manninger, "Women in Combat: Reconsidering the Case against the Deployment of Women in Combat-Support and Combat Units," in *Women in the Military and in Armed Conflict*, ed. Helena Carreiras and Gerhard Kümmel (Berlin: Springer, 2008), 9–16. For examples of women's arguments against such arguments, see Kirsten Holmstedt, *Band of Sisters: American Women at War in Iraq* (Mechanicsburg, PA: Stackpole Books, 2008), 224; Helen Benedict, *The Lonely Soldier* (Boston: Beacon Press, 2010), 100–102.

33. Lobasz, "The Woman in Peril," 326; Stacey Lyn Peebles, *Welcome to the Suck: Narrating the American Soldier's Experience in Iraq* (Ithaca, NY: Cornell University Press, 2011), 79; Elshtain, *Women and War*, 4.

34. Van Creveld, *Men, Women, and War*, 234.

35. Williams, *Love My Rifle*, 208.

36. See the photo and video promoted by U.S. Army Central Command: "Rescue of POW U.S. Private First Class Jessica Lynch," *Getty Images*, April 2, 2003, http://www.gettyimages.de/detail/nachrichtenfoto/this-handout-photo-from-central-command-shows-the-nachrichtenfoto/1891245 (accessed September 15, 2014).

37. Jerry Adler, "Jessica's Liberation," *Newsweek*, April 13, 2003, http://www.newsweek.com/jessicas-liberation-134567 (accessed December 27, 2014); Patrick Rogers, "Saved from Danger," *People Magazine*, April 21, 2003, http://www.people.com/people/archive/article/0,,20139817,00.html (accessed December 27, 2014); Lauren Johnston, "Hero's Welcome for Jessica Lynch," *CBS News*, June 22, 2003, http://www.cbsnews.com/news/heros-welcome-for-jessica-lynch/ (accessed December 14, 2014); Rogers, "Saved from Danger"; "CNN LIVE TODAY: Family of Jessica Lynch Celebrating Her Rescue," *CNN*, April 2, 2003, http://edition.cnn.com/TRANSCRIPTS/0304/02/lt.05.html (Accessed December 5, 2014); Lobasz, "The Woman in Peril"; Lindsey Feitz and Joane Nagel, "The Militarization of Gender and Sexuality in the Iraq War," in *Women in the Military and in Armed Conflict*, 201–225; Deepa Kumar, "War Propaganda and the (Ab)uses of Women Media Constructions of the Jessica Lynch Story," *Feminist Media Studies* 4, no. 3 (2004): 297–313.

38. Lorraine Dowler, "Women on the Frontlines: Rethinking War Narratives Post 9/11," *Geo Journal* 58 (2002): 160.

39. Sjoberg, "Agency, Militarized Femininity and Enemy Others," 85.

40. Holmstedt, *Band of Sisters*, 111.

41. Laura Sjoberg and Caron E. *Gentry, Mothers, Monsters, Whores: Women's Violence in Global Politics* (London: Zed Books, 2007), 15; Laura Browder, *When Janey Comes March-*

ing Home: Portraits of Women Combat Veterans (Chapel Hill: University of North Carolina Press, 2010), 5.

42. Eileen Berrington and Päivi Honkatukia, "An Evil Monster and a Poor Thing: Female Violence in the Media," *Journal of Scandinavian Studies in Criminology and Crime Prevention* 3, no. 1 (2002): 65.

43. Williams, *Love My Rifle,* 21, 41.

44. Peebles, *Welcome to the Suck,* 93; Rikke Schubert, *Super Bitches and Action Babes: The Female Hero in Popular Cinema, 1970–2006* (Jefferson, NC: McFarland, 2007), 180; Matthew Evangelista, *Peace Studies: Critical Concepts in Political Science,* vol. 3 (London: Taylor and Francis, 2005), 233; Bruce Fleming, *Bridging the Military-Civilian Divide: What Each Side Must Know about the Other—And about Itself* (Lincoln, NE: Potomac Books, 2010), 265.

45. Williams, *Love My Rifle,* 278.

46. Benedict, *The Lonely Soldier,* 167.

47. See Howard and Prividera, "The Fallen Woman Archetype: Media Representations of Lynndie England, Gender, and the (Ab)uses of U.S. Female Soldiers," *Women's Studies in Communication* 31, no. 3 (2008): 287–311; Browder, *When Janey Comes Marching Home,* 7; Lobasz, "The Woman in Peril," 328.

48. Claudia Wallis, "Iraq: Inside Abu Ghraib: Why Did They Do It?" *Time,* May 17, 2004, http://content.time.com/time/magazine/article/0,9171,994178,00.html. The "fallen woman" trope was also applied to England in popular culture. The Rolling Stones, for instance, wrote the song "Dangerous Beauty" about Lynndie England. See Tara McKelvey, "A Soldier's Tale: Lynndie England," *Marie Claire,* May 19, 2009, http://www.marieclaire.com/politics/news/a170/lynndie-england-1/.

49. Ramzi Kassem, "Gendered Erasure in the Global War on Terror: An Unmasked Interrogation," in *Gender, National Security, and Counter-Terrorism: Human Rights Perspectives,* ed. Margaret L. Satterthwaite and Jayne C. Huckerby (London: Routledge, 2013), 27. See also Lila Rajiva, "The Military Made Me Do It," in *One of the Guys: Women as Aggressors and Torturers,* ed. Tara McKelvey (Emeryville, CA: Seal Press), 217–228.

50. Cathy Hong, "How Could Women Do That?," *Salon,* May 7, 2004, http://www.salon.com/2004/05/07/abuse_gender/.

51. See McKelvey, "A Soldier's Tale."

52. Evan Thomas, "Explaining Lynndie England," *Newsweek,* May 14, 2004, http://www.newsweek.com/explaining-lynndie-england-128501. See also James Dao, "The Struggle for Iraq: The Soldier: From Picture of Pride to Symbol of Abuse," *New York Times,* May 7, 2004, http://www.nytimes.com/2004/05/07/us/the-struggle-for-iraq-the-soldier-from-picture-of-pride-to-symbol-of-abuse.html; Maki Becker "The Face behind the Nation's Shame: The Woman at the Center of Iraqi Abuse Scandal," *New York Daily News,* May 7, 2004, http://www.nydailynews.com/archives/news/face-behind-nation-shame-woman-center-iraqi-abuse-scandal-article-1.651516.

53. Richard Cohen, "Victimizer and Victim," *Washington Post,* May 6, 2005, http://www.washingtonpost.com/wp-dyn/content/article/2005/05/05/AR2005050501682.html; Neva Chonin, "The Lynndie Hop," *San Francisco Chronicle,* August 29, 2004, http://www.sfgate.com/entertainment/article/THE-LYNNDIE-HOP-2697965.php. See also Marita Gronnvoll, "Gender (In)Visibility at Abu Ghraib," *Rhetoric & Public Affairs* 10, no. 3 (2007): 371–398.

54. Belinda Morrissey, *When Women Kill: Questions of Agency and Subjectivity* (London: Routledge, 2003), 174. See also the interview with Lynndie England in David Jones, "Why the Hell Should I Feel Sorry, Says Girl Soldier Who Abused Iraqi Prisoners at Abu Ghraib

Prison," *Daily Mail,* June 13, 2009, http://www.dailymail.co.uk/news/article-1192701/Why-hell-I-feel-sorry-says-girl-soldier-abused-Iraqi-prisoners-Abu-Ghraib-prison.html.

55. Melissa Sheridan Embser-Herbert, "When Women Abuse Power, Too," *Washington Post,* May 16, 2004, http://www.washingtonpost.com/wp-dyn/articles/A28340-2004May14.html.

56. Ibid.

57. Lawrence James, "What Turns a Woman into a Savage?," *Daily Mail,* May 7, 2004, https://www.highbeam.com/doc/1G1-116360146.html.

58. Browder, *When Janey Comes Marching Home,* 7; Nicholas Kristof, "A Woman's Place," *New York Times,* April 25, 2003, http://www.nytimes.com/2003/04/25/opinion/a-woman-s-place.html; "Abused Gulf War POW Describes Her Ordeal: Flight Surgeon Says It's All a Part of War," *Baltimore Sun,* June 29, 1992, http://articles.baltimoresun.com/1992-06-29/news/1992181107_1_cornum-gulf-war-prisoner-of-war; Holly Allen, "Gender, Sexuality and the Military Model of U.S. National Community," in *Gender Ironies of Nationalism: Sexing the Nation,* ed. Tamar Mayer (London: Routledge, 2012), 318; Helen Thorpe, *Soldier Girls: The Battles of Women at Home and at War* (New York: Scribner, 2015), 223; Browder, *When Janey Comes Marching Home,* 132–148.

59. Goldstein, *War and Gender,* 201; Van Creveld, *Men, Women, and War,* 185–186; Manninger, "Women in Combat," 1.

60. Megan MacKenzie, *Beyond the Band of Brothers: The US Military and the Myth that Women Can't Fight* (Cambridge, UK: Cambridge University Press, 2015), 145.

61. Kathleen Parker, "Women in Combat Put Men at Risk," *Chicago Tribune,* December 15, 2015, http://www.chicagotribune.com/news/opinion/commentary/ct-combat-women-military-men-parker-perspec-1214-jm-20151214-story.html.

62. Hartley, *Just Another Soldier,* 93.

63. See Annica Kronsell, *Gender, Sex, and the Post-National Defense: Militarism and Peacekeeping* (Oxford: Oxford University Press, 2012), 60.

64. Thorpe, *Soldier Girls,* 36–37; Holmstedt, *Band of Sisters,* 101–102; Holmstedt, *The Girls Come Marching Home: Stories of Women Warriors Returning from the War in Iraq* (Mechanicsburg, PA: Stackpole Books, 2009), 110.

65. Gary Younge, "What about Lori?," *Guardian,* April 10, 2003, http://www.theguardian.com/world/2003/apr/10/iraq.garyyounge; William Douglas, "Two POWs, One an American Icon, the Other Ignored: Jessica Lynch's Story, Some of It Hyped, Made Her a Star. Shoshana Johnson Faded Away," November 8, 2003, http://articles.philly.com/2003-11-08/news/25462945_1_jessica-lynch-shoshana-johnson-disability-benefits. For a discussion on whiteness and racism in this context, see, for example, Daniela Baroffio-Bota, *The Female Soldier: Mediating Promises and Problematics of Femininity, War, and the Nation* (Los Angeles: University of Southern California Press, 2006); Obradovic, *Gender Integration,* 25; Monica J. Casper and Lisa Jean Moore, *Missing Bodies: The Politics of Visibility* (New York: New York University Press, 2009).

66. Jeordan Legon, "Mom, Soldier and Hopi Indian: 'She Fought and Died Valiantly,'" *CNN,* 2005, http://edition.cnn.com/SPECIALS/2003/iraq/heroes/piestewa.html.

67. "First Female Black POW Speaks Out in Book," *CBS,* February 3, 2010, https://www.cbsnews.com/news/first-female-black-pow-speaks-out-in-book/.

68. Kim Rygiel, *(En)Gendering the War on Terror: War Stories and Camouflaged Politics* (London: Routledge, 2007), 83; France Winddance Twine, *Girls with Guns: Firearms, Feminism, and Militarism* (London: Routledge, 2013), 46; Simona Sharoni, Julia Welland, et al., *Handbook on Gender and War* (Cheltenham, UK: Edward Elgar Publishing, 2016), 275.

69. Enloe, *Does Khaki Become You*, 15 (emphasis in the original).
70. "POW Planned on Cooking, Not Fighting," *CNN*, March 26, 2003, http://edition.cnn.com/2003/US/03/25/sprj.irq.pow.johnson/index.html.
71. See, for example, A. Susan Owen, Sarah R. Stein, and Leah R. Vande Berg, "It's a Dick Thing: Ambivalent Coding of American Female Soldiers in Gulf War Narratives," in *Bad Girls: Cultural Politics and Media Representations of Transgressive Women* (New York: Peter Lang, 1997), 197–231; Rikke Schubart, "Disturbing Creature: The Female Soldier in War Film," in *Super Bitches and Action Babes*, 249–270.
72. See Steven Cohan and Ina Rae Hark, *Screening the Male: Exploring Masculinities in Hollywood Cinema* (New York: Routledge 1993); Jeff Birkenstein and Anna Froula, *Reframing 9/11: Film, Popular Culture and the "War on Terror"* (New York: Bloomsbury Publishing, 2010); Faludi, *The Terror Dream*.
73. Alex Trimble-Young, "American Sniper Revisionist Western," *Salon*, February 19, 2015, http://www.salon.com/2015/02/19/american_sniper_is_not_a_war_movie_its_a_classic_revisionist_western_and_one_of_eastwoods_finest/.
74. See, for example, Robert Myer's play *Unmanned* (2012). It deals with how drone warfare and its "remote-controlled warfare from the office chair in the desert" challenge the concept of masculinity and the heroic warrior. See also the recent film *Good Kill* (2014).
75. "Reese Witherspoon to play U.S. soldier killed in Afghanistan," *Guardian*, March 12, 2015, http://www.theguardian.com/film/2015/mar/12/reese-witherspoon-film-ashley-white-us-woman-soldier-killed-afghanistan-frontline; WITW Staff, "Air Force Memoir 'Shoot Like A Girl' Movie Adaptation Given Green Light," *New York Times*, June 25, 2015, http://nytlive.nytimes.com/womenintheworld/2015/06/25/air-force-memoir-shoot-like-a-girl-movie-adaptation-given-green-light/.
76. See, for example, the panel discussion by the United States Studies Center at the University of Sidney (Australia): "Drones, Gender, and Identity in the New American Way of War" on the occasion of the screening of George Brant's play *Grounded*, May 12, 2015, http://ussc.edu.au/events/Drones-gender-and-identity-in-the-new-American-way-of-war.
77. See, for example, Memorial Day interviews by CNN and Fox. Appearing on television, Blair, most of the time, sported a feminine look, verging on the stereotypical feminine; "Marine Jane Blair, Author of 'Hesitation Kills' on *Fox and Friends*," YouTube, May 30, 2011, https://www.youtube.com/watch?v=_sa5IRIF500.
78. Heather Haddon, "Louboutins to Combat Boots," *New York Post*, June 19, 2011, http://nypost.com/2011/06/19/louboutins-to-combat-boots/.
79. Jane Blair, *Hesitation Kills: A Female Marine Officer's Combat Experience in Iraq* (Lanham, MD: Rowman and Littlefield, 2011), 16.
80. Blair, *Hesitation Kills*.
81. Ibid.
82. Ibid.
83. Ibid.
84. Ibid.
85. Ibid., 17.
86. Ibid.
87. Ibid., 20.
88. Ibid., 58.
89. Ibid., 133.
90. Ibid.
91. Ibid., 172.

92. Ibid., 8.
93. Ibid., 97.
94. Ibid., 214.
95. Ibid.
96. Ibid., 39.
97. Seema Shekhawat, *Gender, Conflict and Peace in Kashmir: Invisible Stakeholders* (Cambridge, UK: Cambridge University Press, 2014), 7.
98. Blair, *Hesitation Kills*, 107.
99. Ibid., 34–35.
100. Melissa S. Herbert, *Camouflage Isn't Only for Combat: Gender, Sexuality, and Women in the Military* (New York: New York University Press, 1998), 45.
101. Blair, *Hesitation Kills*, 16–17.
102. Ibid., 147.
103. Ibid., 42–43.
104. Ibid., 14.
105. Ibid.
106. Peebles, *Welcome to the Suck*, 87.
107. Browder, *When Janey Comes Marching Home*, 8.
108. Blair, *Hesitation Kills*, 80.
109. Ibid.
110. Ibid., 40.
111. Lobasz, "The Woman in Peril," 305.
112. Obradovic, *Gender Integration*, 22.
113. Blair rarely expresses a feeling of being excluded from the corps on account of her sex or gender. See Blair, *Hesitation Kills*, 40.
114. Blair, *Hesitation Kills*, 109.
115. Ibid., 139.
116. Ibid.
117. Ibid., 139.
118. Ibid. 187.
119. Ibid., 139–140.
120. Karen O. Dunevin, "Military Culture: Change and Continuity," *Armed Forces & Society* 20, no. 4 (1994): 533.
121. Laura Sjoberg and Sandra Via, *Gender, War, and Militarism: Feminist Perspectives* (Santa Barbara, CA: ABC-CLIO, 2010), 44.

9 • FROM WARRIOR TO SOLDIER?

Lakota Veterans on Military Valor

SONJA JOHN

Native American men and women are strongly represented in the U.S. armed forces. Indeed, they have more members per capita in the military than any other ethnic group. Explanations for this situation compose the grand narrative of the "warrior-to-soldier" theme that constructively links a specific ethnic background to an alleged natural predisposition for military life. Lakota[1] men in particular have been confronted with expectations that arose through the mythical heroization of warriors and war chiefs such as Crazy Horse and Sitting Bull that were disseminated through American mass media. As a result, in films, novels, and internet games, contemporary Lakota soldiers are still being depicted as naturally belonging on the battlefield. Scholarly texts also utilize racial categories as the major paradigm through which to conceptualize Indigenous masculinity and military life. In general, Native Americans continue to be represented as "traditional" in an unmoving, static, premodern or antimodern sense. Stuart Hall sees representation—the connection of meaning and language to culture—as having interactive relationships to create a "circuit of culture" in which representation and misrepresentation build identities and reflect ideologies.[2] While misrepresentations are usually viewed negatively for constituting epistemological violence, I want to employ them here constructively by analyzing the causes and effects of the warrior-to-soldier grand narrative in order to challenge the often repeated assumption about the "natural" nature of Native American service members. Conceptualizing a deeper, anticolonial critique of related military heroism discourses requires being more vigilant about the way we unravel the normative frameworks that help construct, perpetuate, and challenge racial and gender hierarchies. It requires adjusting the critical aperture through which we render competing truth claims about heroism, and the ambiguous functions that "Indian warrior" stories have served in U.S. history. Military heroism narratives about "natural warriors," I argue, help to construct and perpetuate racial hierarchies in the United States, upholding the ultimate national hero as a white, male, masculine, heterosexual soldier.

Native "traditions" that predate the settler state produce sensations, desires, anxieties, and optimisms. I try to understand what these aspirations are and how they function as social technology for consolidating the imperial and genocidal history of the U.S. military. The military was and is a central instrument in the project of settler colonialism, which has as its goal the removal, dispossession, and too often, the elimination of Native peoples in the Americas. In one of the most cited works on the subject, comparative historian Patrick Wolfe pinpointed the ongoing eliminationist nature of settler colonialism.[3] In the Lakota context, the unlawful—according to the U.S. Supreme Court decision of 1980—annexation of the Black Hills in 1877 and the Wounded Knee massacre in 1890 attest to that brutal history.[4] Over the past years, contributions by Natives to the military have been celebrated with code talker memorials, photo books, and blogs related to the U.S. military (so-called miliblogs).[5] Celebrating Native involvement in the armed forces clearly raises questions of representation, recognition, and reconciliation. Such terms as *reconciliation*, for instance, are highly problematic from a normative perspective, because the historical violence of settler colonialism is not over; it is ongoing.[6] Patrick Wolfe has indicated that settler colonialism and imperial colonialism are not to be discussed in terms of historical events but as a sturdy, enduring structure, and in this sense, not as an event but as ongoing practice. Following Elizabeth Povinelli, who suggests that before one can develop a "critical theory of recognition," one needs to better understand the cunning of recognition,[7] I attempt to analyze critically the aspiration of liberation that is entailed in wedding Native "warrior traditions" like powwows and sweat ceremonies with U.S. military culture. According to Povinelli, the "cunning of recognition lies exactly in this play of parentheticals: Be (not) Real; Be (not) Alterior."[8] In this chapter, I ask how characteristics of heroic Native soldiers were portrayed in scholarship, and how these representations correspond with accounts given by Lakota veterans themselves. I also explore how such representations affect the life experiences of contemporary Native soldiers and veterans.

To investigate the changes of Lakota (self-)perceptions in and through the military, as well as the strands of continuity and change Lakota veterans face, between 2012 and 2015 I conducted interviews with thirty-seven veterans from Lakota reservations in South Dakota who served in World War II, the Vietnam War, and the wars in Afghanistan and Iraq. To accommodate the limited space available here, I mainly draw on the accounts of two individuals from the Pine Ridge Reservation, and complement their reports with the accounts of three additional interviewees. Their answers reveal commonalities that could be found in all the interviews. They are Ivan Star Comes Out, who joined the Army in 1967 and was deployed to Vietnam, and his son, Ivan Starr, who served as a Marine from 2006 to 2014 and was deployed to Iraq and a number of Latin American countries. I conducted formal interviews in 2012 and follow-up interviews in 2015 with both of them. Moreover, I have had conversations with Lakota people about military experiences since 1997, when I first stayed at Pine Ridge. Since then I have continuously engaged with the community, studying, visiting, living, and working on the reservation. This connection informs my approach; my primary interpretative mode is interdisciplinary and decolonial. I trace the legacies of the colonial "warrior-to-soldier" narrative and interpret their impact through the lens of Indigeneity with its central concepts of relationship, reciprocity, and respect, while relying on oral history methodology and the practice of listening. Providing access to the individual voices of these men, the interviews are a vital and central source to comprehend the expectations U.S. society has of Lakota soldiers and to understand the tensions between Western and Indigenous notions of the heroic.

The chapter's first section provides a definition of Lakota heroism, which is meant to show the similarities and differences between the definitions discussed in this volume's introduction and Native interpretations of the term and the values it entails. I then sketch out the basic characteristics of the "warrior-to-soldier" narrative by analyzing the formulations of Native worth, with an emphasis on "warrior traditions" and ceremonial practices. In order to interpret the connections between expectations and actual military experiences, this chapter examines the specific interweaving of social and cultural constructions of Lakota war heroes.

A HERO: THE GOOD RELATIVE

Generally, heroines and heroes are constructed in conversations about heroic acts. In general, heroism studies have found that heroes are people who do something that is moral, and that they are highly competent.[9] A hero upholds the social values and the social order of the community and, as a result, personifies its value system. Heroes in the United States include family members, athletes, statesmen, soldiers, as well as fictional characters, all of whom are regarded highly because they stand for cherished values such as generosity, self-sacrifice, struggle, persistence, and faith. Common character traits include intelligence, strength, resilience, selflessness, charisma, reliability, and the ability to care and inspire.[10] While many dominant American values resemble Lakota cardinal values of generosity (*wacantognaka*), wisdom (*woksape*), fortitude/respect (*wowacintanka*), and courage (*woohitika*), there are two significant differences between the value systems. For one, Lakota who act according to common values are not put on a pedestal, but are seen as fulfilling their basic duties to the community. Value is given to the *ikce wicasa*, the common man, who proves to be a good relative and lives according to kinship laws. Dakota ethnologist and novelist Ella Deloria expresses this idea in her historical novel *Waterlily* through a character who praises a tribal member's husband by saying, "He was liked by all because he was a good relative to all."[11] Hence, debates on heroism among the Lakota tended to revolve around "everyday heroes," ordinary people who are lauded for their selfless service and sacrifice for the community. Accordingly, in Native nations in the Americas, Indigenous war heroes' reputations are determined not only by their deeds on the battlefield, but also by their willingness to honor their duties to their people. As Anishinaabe writer Niigaanwewidam James Sinclair points out, every part of Indigenous cultures is about being a good relation.[12] According to Taiaiake Alfred (Mohawk), professor of Indigenous governance, the way to confront the dominant media-informed stereotypes of Indigenous masculinity, such as the "bloodthirsty warrior" or the "noble savage," is "to put the image of the Native male back into its proper context, that of family."[13] The English word *warrior* is a very narrow interpretation of the Lakota word *akicita*. *Akicita* can mean warrior, soldier, or policeman. It has also been used as a verb meaning "to hunt for another." Ivan Star Comes Out quoted Sitting Bull's (Hunkpapa Lakota) definition of a warrior in a newspaper article criticizing the manner in which stereotypical narratives of the warrior tradition are being upheld: "A warrior is not someone who fights, for no one has the right to take another life. The warrior for us is the one who sacrifices himself for the good of others. His task is to take care of the elders, the defenseless, those who cannot provide for themselves, and above all, the children, the future of humanity."[14] Lakota *akicita* live with the expectation that they will protect and provide for their immediate relatives and the wider community—an idea of masculinity that contrasts sharply with the individualistic heroism depicted in colonial representations of Native leaders.

The second difference is the notion of deadly sacrifice. The English word *hero* is derived from the Greek word for hero or warrior. It literally means protector or defender. The original Hero in Greek mythology was a priestess of Aphrodite, the goddess of love. When her lover Leander was lost at sea in a storm, Hero, in her grief, drowned herself. This myth may have given rise to the notion of a hero sacrificing his or her life for a greater ideal or good. Oral history among the Lakota holds that a war hero is someone who is strong, athletic, skilled, and strategically intelligent; someone who gets involved in dangerous situations but survives. The highest deed in battle is to count coup: to touch the enemy while escaping unharmed, and to spare the life of an enemy in battle, rather than kill them when presented with the opportunity. This act of generosity and courage remains with the warrior forever as a testament of his manhood. Celebrating a Lakota war hero is celebrating life, not death.[15]

In the Native American context, heroism is clearly in the eye of the beholder. Lakota leaders like Red Cloud, Sitting Bull, and Crazy Horse were heroes for some and villains for others. The Lakota take pride in the fact that they have never been defeated in war by the settler military; they always defeated the U.S. army in battle, most prominently at the Battle of the Greasy Grass (Little Bighorn), which is commemorated in a national holiday celebrated annually on Lakota reservations in late June. Joseph Campbell, a founder of heroism scholarship, acknowledged that "you could be a local god, but for the people whom that local god conquered, you could be the enemy. Whether you call someone a hero or a monster is all relative."[16] The military-government establishment depended on racialist distinctions when dehumanizing enemies and subjects, but it also needed to cover up racial degradation and differences when demanding support from young men and women of diverse backgrounds. In this article, I am concerned with the multiple meanings of these essentialist constructions and their impact on Native American soldiers and veterans.

While Lakota war leaders may be perceived differently in internal debates—as complex characters with flaws—their story line of fierce warriors was soon appropriated and exploited by the U.S. military, the sports industry, and advertisers of various sorts as a bearer of certain messages, values, and gender norms, including the idea of achieving success through hard work, team spirit, and strong masculinity. As several chapters in this volume show, most ethnic minorities in the United States assigned tremendous social, cultural, and political importance to the acknowledgement of their military heroism, and reached for increased visibility on the battlefield. By contrast, Native Americans, to this day, reject the Native American warrior stereotype and the ways it is appropriated in U.S. military culture. Military equipment carries names like "Apache" or "Tomahawk." Enemy territory is referred to as "Indian Country." Osama Bin Laden was assassinated in "Operation Geronimo." While some of these cultural appropriations may indicate that the U.S. military is slowly coming to terms with its ideological origins in American imperialism, the fact that the Black Hills have not been returned to the Lakota and that treaty territory is being compromised in favor of the Dakota Access Pipeline on the Standing Rock Reservation suggest otherwise.[17]

In general, rhetorical appreciation of non-Native service in American wars is based less on racial distinctions than on qualities of character—that is, qualities of a heroic character that lives up to the high ideals of duty, sacrifice, and courage. This "Americanism," as defined by President Theodore Roosevelt in the early twentieth century, is guided by the ideal of inclusivity that favors commitment over descent. The appreciation of Native American service members, however, is based on race, since Native Americans are presented—by descent—as the naturally occurring impersonation of these qualities. Kevin R. Kemper reminds us in his work on historical and contemporary representations of Apache leader Geronimo that his heroization in America's mainstream narrative followed an agenda: "American soldiers inflated their own manhood by making sure the American public thought of [a Native war chief] as a fierce warrior and of the soldiers as the conquerors of a fierce warrior."[18] This also explains the masculine-heroic representations of the Lakota leaders Sitting Bull, Red Cloud, and Crazy Horse. It is an example of fallaciously increasing one's own manhood at the expense of others, and/or is one mechanism to perpetuate racial hierarchies in the United States. This representation of the aggressive and martial potential of Lakota masculinity, echoed even in scholarly writing, contributed substantially to the long-term perceptions of Lakota men. An example of an academic text representing the warrior-to-soldier narrative is the book chapter "War, Masculinity, and Native Americans" by Kathleen Glenister Roberts, who repeats certain aspects of or myths about the narrative.[19] Against the backdrop of this history, I challenge three often repeated assumptions regarding (1) Native motivations to join the military in order to protect the homeland, (2) the notion of naturally belonging on the battlefield, and (3) the role of ceremonies and powwows to transition Indigenous soldiers back into civilian life. I argue that white America's embrace of Native traditions is a form of reconciliation without redistribution.

MOTIVATIONS TO JOIN THE MILITARY

Dakota environmental scholar and activist Winona LaDuke has asked, " How did we move from being the target of the U.S. military to being the U.S. military itself?"[20] It is a question often posed about Native American veterans and service members, especially where Lakota people are concerned. The mass grave for the victims of the 1890 massacre at Wounded Knee lies at the center of the Pine Ridge Reservation, where the 7th Cavalry shot defenseless Lakota men, women, and children. The massacre was canonized by the U.S. military as a heroic *battle,* for which more than twenty soldiers received the Medal of Honor. It took the occupation of Wounded Knee by the American Indian Movement in 1973, requests by two Wounded Knee survivors associations in preparation for a centennial memorial in 1990, and much soul-searching on the part of the U.S. government in the twenty-first century to consider rescinding the medals.[21] Another request by the survivors associations was not met; instead of a formal apology, Congress issued a mere statement of "regret" for the wrongdoings of the past. An official apology, by contrast, would have provided grounds for reparations claims, which the U.S. government sought to avoid. By the time Ivan Starr enlisted in 2006, it was well established among the Lakota that the 1890 massacre may be partly responsible for their distress, grief, and intergenerational trauma, with all its psychological and social implications. Unlike his father, Starr did not want to join the U.S. Army, but rather the Marine Corps, because one, he "did not want to end up in the 7th Cavalry," and two, several cousins had already joined the naval infantry.[22] Primarily, though, his desire to enlist was spurred by the prospect of educational benefits. This is not specific to Native Americans; after all, information about educational benefits is at the very top of the FAQ list on the Marines website.[23] Winona LaDuke, examining why so many Native Americans join the armed forces, concludes that economic deprivation, domination, and racism explain the high levels of Native enlistment. Paying attention to attitudes among Native Americans and African Americans—groups who have the least reason to fight for "their" country—adds insights into the inner workings of U.S. nationalism and how it gained hegemony over individual men. Since the earliest encounters with settlers, Indigenous men served as scouts or allies for European and American armies, and the number of Native service members has continually increasead since World War I. After the official closing of the frontier in 1890, a substantial number of "show Indians" were hired for Wild West shows touring in North America and Europe.[24] These shows may have been the first instances of Natives performing "traditions" for non-Native audiences, which created expectations that subsequent generations of Indigenous people would perform "authenticity." Among the veterans interviewed for this study, only Gerald Ice of Wounded Knee reported "playing Indian" in the 1980s, after leaving the service and not being able to find work on the reservation.[25] The commercial success of the novel *Bury My Heart at Wounded Knee* added to the wider public knowledge of the occupation of Wounded Knee by Indigenous "warriors." Lakota "warriorhood" had reentered public consciousness, which is one of the reasons why Gerald Ice was invited to act in films and to speak at events about the "Indian fight."

In an attempt to find a way out of alcoholism on the reservation, Gerald Ice enrolled in a relocation program and attended San Diego City College. Although he reportedly did not pass the required entrance test, he still made his way from continuing education centers in San Diego and through community colleges into university—not as a student, but as a public speaker. After speaking at the San Diego Indian Center, he was referred to higher education institutions to talk about Custer's last stand. Years later, his status as a Vietnam War veteran, combined with his genealogical lineage to Black Elk and Crazy Horse, served to legitimate him as "spiritual leader," a role he performs for Native and non-Native audiences.

Although research has shown that a disproportionate number of minority group members serve in the military because of inadequate economic opportunities in civilian life, studies of Native veterans tend to diminish, if not erase, this crucial motivating factor. Kathleen Roberts claims that "the cultural value of 'defending one's home' is invoked repeatedly by these veterans as the driving force behind their choice to enlist in the armed forces," and dismisses economic reasons as "inaccurate and condescending," thus upholding the exotic stereotype of the spiritually idealistic warrior.[26] Yet, when I asked about their motivations, none of the veterans I interviewed with open-ended questions stated that they had signed up in order to defend their home or due to spiritual obligation; instead, they were looking for better economic opportunities. Ivan Star Comes Out notes, "The main reason I went was because there was no opportunity for me here. I was seventeen years old, I didn't have a high school education, and I saw the military as an opportunity. And I had a plan. I was going to earn my GED while in the military. And serve my enlistment, which was just three years, get out, and use the educational benefits to go on to college. . . . That's how I ended up in the military." While briefly stationed in Germany, he finished two high school GED courses. "I still have the certificates, and those mean more to me than any medal the military gave me."[27] His son Ivan Starr also reports that his specific reasons for enlisting included the prospect of receiving certain field training and using the GI Bill: "I knew if I served I'd get a GI Bill that would help me get through college." Another father-and-son pair I interviewed was Bryan Charging Cloud[28] and his oldest child Bryan Kelly Charging Cloud,[29] from the Cheyenne River Sioux Tribe in South Dakota. Their experiences differ from the Star Comes Out veterans in that their deployments never included active war zones. Nevertheless, they also named job security and educational benefits as their primary rationale to enlist. The younger Charging Cloud stated that he was used to military life, having been raised on bases in the United States and Europe, and that he was well aware of the benefits. His father, Bryan Charging Cloud, kept on studying and working on the Cheyenne River and Pine Ridge reservations after he left military service; he graduated with a master's degree from Oglala Lakota College in 2012 at the age of seventy-two. As of 2017, he was still working as a Lakota language teacher at Wounded Knee District School on the Pine Ridge Reservation, aged seventy-seven.

What makes a man or a soldier who he is in today's Lakota culture? The answer is more complex than suggested by the simplistic warrior-to-soldier narrative—a representation of Lakota masculinity that holds the Lakota soldier captive in a certain time and place and reduces him to his physical attributes. Historically, the education system's portrayal of Native men was limited to their physical aspects. Their bodily strength could be exploited in sports, in the labor force, and in the military. This tendency to reduce Native men to their physicality persists in spite of their achievements in intellectual arenas. Today, the struggle for *survivance* (Gerald Vizenor) occurs on different battlefields: in the courtroom, in the hospital, in schools, in the universities, and in texts—all of which require formal education. Every veteran I interviewed mentioned the Veteran Assistance education benefit programs they were attracted by and later used to attend school or college. For some, the educational benefits were their sole reason to join the military.

Lakota people create their own meanings of their culture and specific concepts like masculinity and martial heroism. The interviews conducted with Lakota veterans indicate that their own ideas of Lakota manhood diverge from the heroic warrior stereotype. They reported that a man fulfils his role when he honors his relatives, honors the women, provides for the family and community, and leads his life according to the cardinal Lakota values mentioned earlier. Ivan Star Comes Out, in his occupation as a journalist for Lakota newspapers and as an author who theorizes posttraumatic and intergenerational stress, interacts with these discourses and challenges them. In his writing, Ivan Star Comes Out encourages the younger generation to think critically about the scripts they have inherited. He is projecting stories that are different from those presented in mainstream culture. He shows the real-life impact the intellect can have on behalf of the community, while counteracting the ongoing erasure of Indigenous knowledge—giving voice to perspectives that are often silenced. In this sense, he is out on the front lines, protecting and serving the people in a manner similar to the way so many veterans used military status to earn income, to further their education, and to provide for their families and the community.

THE TALE OF THE NATURAL WARRIOR

Most explanations for their overrepresentation in the armed forces portray Natives as naturally belonging on the battlefield. Although Kathleen Glenister Roberts indicates that she is primarily concerned with the construction of Native American masculinity, her data and her argument reveal that seemingly, only dancing and praying are required for the essentialist Native "warrior" to lead his people into a healed future. She backs her claims that "the warrior ideal runs the gamut through both time and space, from the Ghost Dance through the fancy dance," and that it stemmed from an "ancient" perspective, with quotes from white anthropologists' outdated publications on Native warrior traditions, a summary of Leslie Marmon Silko's 1977 novel *Ceremony*, and impressions from a few visits to commercial powwows.[30] Evidently, her research is not on par with today's Native American and Indigenous studies, but it is worth a critical reading because her chapter is included in the prominent 2011 anthology *Global Masculinities and Manhood*, edited by Ronald Jackson and Balaji Murali. Several problems with Roberts's claims should not go uncommented. They start with her portrayal of contemporary Native soldiers as continuing warrior traditions that existed prior to settler contact, as if there were no difference between Indigenous warrior societies and the U.S. military. Disparities have been obscured through media portrayals of a specific kind of military masculinity that was not tempered by communal decision making. Yet, the differences are substantial. Lakota interviewees report that basic training is designed to break personal identity, remove it, and turn soldiers into "killing machines." Although this trait was unheard of in prereservation times, Ivan Star Comes Out and Ivan Starr had experienced equally hierarchical institutions on the reservation before joining the U.S. military. The father, Ivan Star Comes Out, quit his Catholic boarding school despite his good grades in order to escape its oppressive structures. He indicates that the boarding school was based on military protocol, noting that "the military was hardly any different."[31] His son joined the Marines after having been a tribal police officer; "basic police school," he stated, "is paramilitary." Father and son encountered their own disappointments in the military. Ivan Star Comes Out envisioned becoming a mechanic and having a quiet time in the garage, but was flown to Vietnam soon after boot camp. Ironically, his son expected lots of action but instead was sent to automotive school, where he became a motor transport mechanic. Starr reports: "When I first joined I was expecting a high-speed-low-drag, doing something exciting every day. I remember thinking I'm gonna [be shooting] machine guns, kicking doors open, doing military operations on urban terrain, all the stuff you see on TV and on the internet." Reality confronted him with seemingly endless hurry-up-and-wait situations and countless cleaning assignments. "They had nothing else for us to do, so that was pretty much all we did: cleaning. We're pretty much janitors."

The persisting inscription of stereotypes of the natural warrior still affected soldiers in Vietnam. Ivan Star Comes Out had to perform certain tasks stereotypically expected of Natives. An officer kept assigning him to walk point, though he had not received any training in that task. "I was just absolutely terrified," he reminisced about this dangerous assignment. In conversations with other Native veterans, he found that many had experienced similar situations. "These military officers more than likely thought that we, being Native, could see in the dark, hear better than everybody else, maybe we were impervious to pain, and that we were natural-born fighters, natural-born killers." He could not identify with these stereotypes: "I was just as scared as everybody else. And I knew that I would die just like everybody else. Bleed just like everybody else. . . . Somehow, I survived. But I don't think it has anything to do with being Native. I am human, you know. I am not a superman." These reports of placing Native American soldiers into more dangerous situations that non-Native soldiers may explain their greater exposure to combat in Vietnam and their comparatively high rates of post-traumatic stress disorder.[32] Winona LaDuke links high rates of PTSD to her findings that "the impact of military service on individual Native people is dramatic—and all too often traumatic," particularly for inductees from rural areas or with limited experience spending extended periods of time away from their family and community.[33] Roberts's and other scholars' portrayals of Native servicewomen and -men as "unique," "tragic," and inherently "traditional," as well as "spiritual," reflect a view that is still rooted in colonial thinking in which the Other can be defined, exoticized, and interpreted at will.[34] Against the backdrop of such thinking, the vast majority of the interviewees reveal themselves to be far from unique, but rather average human beings who lead ordinary lives as tribal members and as citizens of the United States.

During the Vietnam War era, Native veterans were seen as different not only by anthropologists and comrades, but also by the enemy. Ivan Star Comes Out recalls two instances when Vietnamese were directly addressing him. In one instance, an elderly woman pushed him angrily, placed her arm next to his, and said something that Star Comes Out understood as "We're the same. Why are you doing this?" Tom Holm noted something similar in an early survey, reporting that several Indigenous soldiers were addressed by Vietnamese with "You-me, same-same."[35] The ideology of nationalism seeks to bind people together in support of state power. In the late nineteenth and early twentieth centuries, more than anything else, declarations of war against foreign enemies prompted Americans to think more about what they had in common. For Native Americans in Vietnam, however, their enemies frequently reminded them of what set them apart from fellow U.S. citizens, since they became aware of similarities between their own situation in the United States and that of the Vietnamese population in Southeast Asia. But as the interviews show, Lakota soldiers rarely thought about their patriotic obligations when fighting in Vietnam. Describing it as a fight for survival, Star Comes Out recalled: "When we were in Vietnam we didn't actually fight for that flag because in reality we fought to get out of there, to make it out of there alive, in one piece. And we helped each other in that goal, in that mission."

Over longer passages of Roberts's text, she reiterates findings of Tom Holm's early investigations into the phenomenon of Native soldiers' willingness to serve in the U.S. military. Holm sees a major difference between traditional warriorhood and modern Western-style soldiering in that the former represented a relationship with the rest of the community, while in the latter, soldiers are servants of a very impersonal institution. "Soldiering is playing a role; warriorhood is a relationship," Holm writes.[36] While the U.S. military is clearly a much more hierarchical institution than traditional *akicita* societies, the interviews I conducted suggest that Lakota soldiers are not playing a role; rather, they are doing their job. Many report that they embrace the military as a chosen community with which they establish and maintain relationships. While the shared experience of serving (in a war) together may have not erased ethnic and racial lines, it did bring Americans of different backgrounds closer together.

Masculinity, as a social interactional determination, is grounded not in principles of exactitude but in principles of perceptional expectedness—perceptions that are fluid and limited to the larger possibilities of performing gender and embodied presence. Likewise, Native men are expected to perform masculinity and Nativeness. Yet, Native veterans do not perceive themselves as only the product of a warrior culture, but as complex human beings in contemporary times. One can read and write about the continuation of the "warrior-to-soldier" grand narrative, but I regard it as necessary to take into account local histories and oral testimonies that, although far less easily accessible, tell a different story. In contrast to the oversimplifying warrior-to-soldier narrative, Native American military heroism is much more multifaceted and requires taking into account traditional Indigenous values in a contemporary context.

HEALING THROUGH CEREMONIES

In a number of publications, Tom Holm has emphasized the importance of the social absorption of stress by families, especially through ceremonial process.[37] His texts examine the meanings and effects of sweat lodge ceremonies and powwows—two quite different occasions that Holm treats in an undifferentiated manner. The latter is a social gathering, while the former is an intimate ceremony, and its content should not necessarily be discussed and shared publicly.[38] Tom Holm is regarded as an authority—if not a "hero"—on the study of Native American veterans. Unfortunately, he is often cited and read uncritically. For instance, when Holm "acknowledges the role powwows play in fulfilling tribal obligations to the Creator," the implied spiritual aspect of powwows is taken at face value.[39] Yet, among most Indigenous nations, powwows are social, not spiritual or ceremonial.[40] Kathleen Roberts reiterates the misconception of white anthropologists that "the modern-day powwow has grown out of a tradition of war dancing," and that "continuities between warrior societies, warrior traditions, and powwow competitions are clear"—an inaccurate conclusion that ignores the intricate aspects of social life among Plains tribes, while clinging to and perpetuating the "Indian warrior" stereotype.[41] Part of the problem may have to do with when and where Roberts collected her ethnographic data: at a large commercial and competitive powwow, not a community powwow. She might have interpreted it as a "ceremonial competition"—an oxymoron in the Native American context—and a powwow dancer as a "competitive 'warrior.'"[42]

Still drawing on Tom Holm, Roberts argues that Indigenous people can overcome traumatic experiences of war through their ceremonial life.[43] A number of norms in Native cultures, Holm and his followers declare, encourage better healing practices and results than Anglo norms could achieve. One of the Lakota norms is to welcome the warriors back into civilian life. For example, after his return from Vietnam to the reservation, Ivan Star Comes Out knew that his community would honor him. Yet, he could not appreciate it when they did so during the New Year's powwow after his return. "They didn't know what was going on in my head. They didn't know that people were still dying over there. War's not over yet. . . . I felt so outta place. . . . They honored me with my brother-in-law, Larry He Crow. . . . They had us sitting out in the middle on chairs with star quilts on them. . . . I was getting upset and angry, especially when people started shaking our hands. I felt like I didn't deserve that." Trauma research suggests that veterans can succeed in overcoming the gap between the experiences of war and their civilian life when they regard themselves as part of the collective. The honoring at powwows reminds veterans that they are part of the community. While cultural practices of precontact times may have been successful in addressing war experiences of that time, the interviews suggest that they are not necessarily superior in all contexts.

Moreover, it is doubtful that these ceremonies would serve the same purpose they serve in Native communities if they were copied and transferred into a non-Native context, as Lawrence Gross and his colleagues have suggested.[44] Psychologists have proposed and actually appropriated Indigenous rituals to develop treatment programs to benefit veterans of various ethnic backgrounds.[45] While white veterans have reportedly appreciated this treatment, this appropriation of cultural and intellectual property is problematic in the light of the American Indian Arts and Crafts Act and the United Nations Declaration of the Rights of Indigenous Peoples (UNDRIP).[46] By the 1970s, it had become a "tradition" in white American culture to take pleasure in and consume Indigenous traditions in the form of art, music, and cultural tourism. Twenty years later, questions were raised as to whether the profits from the art and tourism industry were fairly returned to Indigenous communities. The history of expropriation dates back to the first encounters between Natives and settlers. The Lakota word for the settlers, after having observed their conduct, was *wasicu* literally, "takes the fat," or "he takes what is of value."[47] In the military context, appropriation of Native worth starts with declarations about "our American Indian warriors" and continues with material appropriation and expropriation of Indigenous resources and lives, leading to the exploitation of Native terms and images in the cultural and intellectual domain.[48] Lawrence Gross finds it shameful that "no work has been done to examine how lessons drawn from American Indian experiences can be applied in mainstream society beyond the realm of psychological treatment, particularly in regard to religion."[49] He proposes, "It would be well for American Indians to work with various non-Indian religious groups to develop rituals and other practices appropriate to the non-Indian traditions to help non-Indian veterans recover from post-traumatic stress disorder and to honor them for their service."[50] His postulation that "I view working with non-Indian religious groups in this regard as one of the most important tasks facing Native peoples"[51] sounds cynical when taking into account the long history of white people effectively destroying Indigenous cultures—including their healing rituals. As Gross is surely aware, the U.S. federal government—in league with Christian missionaries, executed in part by the U.S. military—implemented policies under which Native Americans were stripped of many of their tribal land, their lives, rights, sovereignty, customs, ceremonies, and institutions. These issues transcend America's military heroism discourse, but are inextricably intertwined with its racial ramifications.

CONCLUSION: EMBRACING NATIVE WORTH

Whereas postcolonial scholars have suggested that colonial domination worked by inspiring in subjects a desire to identify with their colonizers, multicultural agendas embrace the Other. As the military stretches out its hands to Native Americans, Indigenous subjects are called on to perform an "authentic difference" in exchange for the nation's appreciation. I argue that the warrior-to-soldier narrative—with its legacy of intertribal powwows on bases and miliblogs[52] written by Native service members—is supposed to consolidate the imperial and genocidal history of the U.S. military. Yet, the social consequences of "the nation" embracing Indigenous traditions are quite different from the consequences of Indigenous people embracing them. The example of the celebration of Native American service members suggests that multicultural domination works by inspiring minority subjects to identify with the impossible objects of an authentic self-identity—that is, with a domesticated, nonconflictual, "traditional" war chief. The celebration of Native worth remains inflected by the conditional. Native warrior traditions are celebrated as long as this recognition is disconnected from the specificity of actual Native struggles, from differing tribal social agendas, and from the demands made on the contemporary nation-state. White America's celebration of Native American heroism, too, is conditional and ignores Indigenous traditions that directly challenge the white warrior hero ideal.

NOTES

1. When possible, I use the self-referential term *Indigenous nations*; in this case, Oglala Lakota. In transnational contexts, I prefer the terms *Indigenous* and *First Nations*, emphasizing land and sovereignty rights.
2. Stuart Hall, "The Work of Representation," in *Representation: Cultural Representations and Signifying Practices*, ed. Stuart Hall, vol. 2 (Thousand Oaks, CA: Sage/Open University, 2009), 15.

3. Patrick Wolfe, "Settler Colonialism and the Elimination of the Native," *Journal of Genocide Research* 8, no. 4 (2006): 387–409.
4. United States v. Sioux Nation of Indians, 448 U.S. 371, 376 (1980).
5. Herman J. Viola and Ben Nighthorse Campbell, *Warriors in Uniform: The Legacy of American Indian Heroism* (Washington, DC: National Geographic, 2008); Gary Robinson and Phil Lucas, *From Warriors to Soldiers: A History of American Indian Service in the United States Military* (New York: !Universe, 2010). On miliblogs, see Frank Usbeck, "The Power of the Story: 'Popular Narratology' in Pentagon Reports on Social Media Use in the Military," in *Poetics of Politics: Textuality and Social Relevance in Contemporary American Literature and Culture*, ed. Sebastian M. Herrmann, Carolin Alice Hofmann, Katja Kanzler, Stefan Schubert, and Frank Usbeck (Heidelberg: Winter, 2015), 313–333.
6. Glen S. Coulthard, "Subjects of Empire: Indigenous Peoples and the 'Politics of Recognition' in Canada," *Contemporary Political Theory* 6, no. 4 (2007): 437–460.
7. Elizabeth A. Povinelli, *The Cunning of Recognition: Indigenous Alterities and the Making of Australian Multiculturalism* (Durham, NC: Duke University Press, 2002), 16.
8. Ibid., 176.
9. George R. Goethals and Scott T. Allison, "Making Heroes: The Construction of Courage, Competence, and Virtue," *Advances in Experimental Social Psychology* 46 (2012): 186.
10. Hugh Gash and Paul F. Conway, "Images of Heroes and Heroines: How Stable?" *Journal of Applied Developmental Psychology* 18, no. 3 (1997): 349–372; Michael P. Sullivan and André Venter, "Defining Heroes through Deductive and Inductive Investigations," *Journal of Social Psychology* 150, no. 5 (2010): 471–484; Scott T. Allison and George R. Goethals, *Heroes: What They Do and Why We Need Them* (New York: Oxford University Press, 2011).
11. Ella Cara Deloria, *Waterlily* (Lincoln: University of Nebraska Press, 1990), 98.
12. Niigaanwewidam James Sinclair, "After and Towards: A Dialogue on the Future of Indigenous Masculinity Studies," in *Masculindians: Conversations about Indigenous Manhood*, ed. Sam McKegney (East Lansing: Michigan State University Press, 2014), 235.
13. Taiaiake Alfred, "Reimagining Warriorhood: A Conversation with Taiaiake Alfred," in McKegney, *Masculindians*, 78.
14. Ivan Star Comes Out, "Is It Time to Rethink the Warrior Tradition?," *Native Sun News*, April 23, 2015, http://www.indianz.com/News/2015/017221.asp.
15. Bruce E. Johansen, ed., *American Indian Culture: From Counting Coup to Wampum* (Santa Barbara, CA: Greenwood, 2015), 214.
16. Joseph Campbell, *The Power of Myth* (New York: Anchor Books, 1988), 156.
17. Exploring the involvement and celebration of veterans during the 2015–2016 protest camp at the Standing Rock occupation could add insights to the U.S. military heroism discourse.
18. Kevin R. Kemper, "'Geronimo!' The Ideologies of Colonial and Indigenous Masculinities in Historical and Contemporary Representation about Apache Men," *Wicazo Sa Review* 29, no. 2 (2014): 41.
19. Kathleen Glenister Roberts, "War, Masculinity, and Native Americans," in *Global Masculinities and Manhood*, ed. Ronald Jackson and Balaji Murali (Urbana: University of Illinois Press, 2011), 141–160. This text is in the tradition of the warrior-to-soldier narrative, as previously expressed in, for example, Tom Holm, *Wounded Souls: Native American Veterans of the Vietnam War* (Austin: University of Texas Press, 1996); Viola and Campbell, *Warriors in Uniform*; Robinson and Lucas, *From Warriors to Soldiers*; and Steven Clevenger, *America's First Warriors: Native Americans and Iraq* (Santa Fe: Museum of New Mexico Press, 2010).

20. Winona LaDuke, *The Militarization of Indian Country* (East Lansing: Michigan State University Press, 2012), 9.

21. I have complicated our understanding of the local memorializing practices at Wounded Knee and the ways in which this event and its memory are intertwined with the historiography of a settler state whose nationalist project continues to rest on stolen land in Sonja John, "Das nicht-existierende Museum in Wounded Knee: Eine Bestandsaufnahme (Teil 2)," *Magazin für Amerikanistik* 1 (2013): 14–20.

22. Personal interview with Ivan Starr, January 27, 2012; all quotes by him are from this interview.

23. See http://www.marines.com/faq (accessed September 9, 2017).

24. Karl-Markus Kreis, "Indians Playing, Indians Praying: Native Americans in Wild West Shows and Catholic Missions," in *Germans and Indians: Fantasies, Encounters, Projections*, ed. Colin Calloway, Gerd Gemuenden, and Susanne Zantop (Lincoln: University of Nebraska Press, 2002), 195–212.

25. Personal interview with Gerald Ice, March 1, 2015; all quotes by him are from this interview.

26. Roberts, "War, Masculinity, and Native Americans," 141, 148.

27. He received the National Defense Service Medal, the Vietnam Campaign Medal, the Vietnam Service Medal, two Bronze Stars, two Army Commendation Medals, a Gallantry Cross, and the Air Medal.

28. Personal interview with Bryan Charging Cloud, March 3, 2015; all quotes by him are from this interview.

29. Personal interview with Bryan Kelly Charging Cloud, March 1, 2015; all quotes by him are from this interview.

30. Roberts, "War, Masculinity, and Native Americans," 158, 141.

31. Personal interview with Ivan Star Comes Out, March 7, 2015; all quotes by him are from this interview.

32. Lawrence W. Gross, "Assisting American Indian Veterans of Iraq and Afghanistan Cope with Posttraumatic Stress Disorder: Lessons from Vietnam Veterans and the Writings of Jim Northrup," *American Indian Quarterly* 31, no. 3 (2007): 377.

33. LaDuke, *Militarization of Indian Country*, 20.

34. Roberts, "War, Masculinity, and Native Americans," 143, 144, 155, 156.

35. Tom Holm, "The National Survey of Indian Vietnam Veterans," *American Indian and Alaska Native Mental Health Research* 6, no. 1 (1994): 24.

36. Tom Holm, "PTSD in Native American Vietnam Veterans: A Reassessment," *Wicazo Sa Review* 11 no. 2 (1995): 84.

37. Tom Holm, "Culture, Ceremonials, and Stress: American Indian Veterans and the Vietnam War," *Armed Forces and Society* 12, no. 2 (1986): 247; Tom Holm, "American Indian Veterans and the Vietnam War: Restoring Harmony through Tribal Ceremony," *Four Winds* 3, no. 10 (1982): 34; Tom Holm, *Strong Hearts, Wounded Souls: Native American Veterans of the Vietnam War* (Austin: University of Texas Press, 1996), 192.

38. Audra Simpson, *Mohawk Interruptus: Political Life across the Borders of Settler States* (Durham, NC: Duke University Press 2014), 95.

39. Gross, "Assisting American Indian Veterans," 383.

40. Severt Young Bear and Ronnie D. Theiss, *Standing in the Light: A Lakota Way of Seeing* (Lincoln: University of Nebraska Press 1994).

41. Roberts, "War, Masculinity, and Native Americans," 145, 156.

42. Ibid., 152, 154.

43. Ibid., 144.

44. Gross, "Assisting American Indian Veterans of Iraq and Afghanistan Cope with Posttraumatic Stress Disorder," 373–409.

45. John P. Wilson, Alice J. Walker, and Bruce Webster, "Reconnecting: Stress Recovery in the Wilderness," in *Trauma, Transformation, and Healing: An Integrative Approach to Theory, Research, and Post-Traumatic Therapy*, ed. John P. Wilson (Philadelphia: Brunner/Mazel, 1989): 159.

46. Raymond M. Scurfield, "Healing the Warrior: Admission of Two American Indian War-Veteran Cohort Groups to a Specialized Inpatient PTSD Unit," *American Indian and Alaska Native Mental Health Research* 6, no. 3 (1995): 18.

47. Later, Lakota people also used the self-referential term of the "white man," *ska wicasa*.

48. Gross, "Assisting American Indian Veterans," 373. For an exploration of why the military locates potentially dangerous military test facilities in or close to Native American reservations, see LaDuke, *Militarization of Indian Country*.

49. Gross, "Assisting American Indian Veterans," 400.

50. Ibid., 401.

51. Ibid.

52. Praised as a continuation of Indigenous story-telling and connectedness to the reservation, I view miliblogs as purely strategic public relations measures. See Frank Usbeck, "The Power of the Story," 313–333.

10 • VIRTUAL WARFARE

Video Games, Drones, and the Reimagination of Heroic Masculinity

CARRIE ANDERSEN

The story of the video game in American culture begins not with *Pong* or *Super Mario*, but with the military. During the Cold War era, the U.S. defense community devoted substantial resources to developing computer systems that could contend with a wide array of potential threats from the Soviet Union.[1] One of the unexpected outgrowths of this technological investment in computing was the development of the video game. When a Pentagon-funded collective of graduate students in MIT's electrical engineering department acquired a new computer in the early 1960s, they created a video game called *Spacewar!*, where two players would pilot spaceships and try to blow each other up. Although the game was primitive by contemporary standards, its development ushered in two transformative shifts in the ongoing relationship between military and cultural industries, now described as the military-entertainment complex: the material collaboration between military entities and the nascent game industry, and narrativization of war in video games.[2] Since the invention of the video game, the war game has become a popular genre of the video game realm, in which players have, for years, virtually played soldier.

Video games have long promoted themes of conquest and manliness—what Stephen Kline, Nick Dyer-Witheford, and Greig de Peuter call "militarized masculinity"—and in doing so, have reified traditional visions of the masculine heroic warrior for millions of players.[3] These war games are close cousins of war films and television shows, which are well known for telling vivid stories of their heroic male protagonists. As Kyle Kontour describes, first-person shooter (FPS) war games (that is, those in which players wield guns and witness action through the eyes of a character in the game) borrowed from contemporary cultural representations of heroism in other media: "Stylistically, FPS have borrowed heavily from existing popular culture motifs. This includes cinematic fodder such as action movies (stoic, hypermasculine tough guys with dry, cool wits), war films (with their themes of honor, nobility, sacrifice, and heroism), and film noir (taciturn antiheroes, femme fatales)—all heavily laden with heteronormative and homosocial themes."[4] Visions of Rambo and John Wayne, in other words, have not remained confined to the silver screen. The logic of the masculine heroic warrior has infused virtual representations of warfare in popular video games, chiefly through constructing video games' protagonists as enacting a particular model of military service rooted in bravery, sacrifice, and physical prowess. These video game characters espouse several qualities described elsewhere in this collection of essays, especially those associated with masculine power.

Yet, as the introduction to this volume reminds us, masculine identities, as well as notions of martial heroism, are continually in flux, subject to historical context and contingency. As a result, video games have not presented an unchanging vision of the masculine heroic soldier over time. Nor have they portrayed static qualities as being virtuous, particularly in moments when the demands of war are shifting, and soldiers are subject to new tasks and requirements in the conduct of war. Consequently, in the last decade, video games have taken new cues from a changing approach to real-world warfare, and have begun to reimagine the character of war as increasingly futuristic. This war is driven less by humans and more by sophisticated unmanned technologies.

This chapter contends with the fluctuating nature of military heroism and masculinity in contemporary video games, especially those that reflect recent conflicts like the War on Terror and ongoing skirmishes against pockets of terrorists overseas. Two defining traits of this kind of warfare are that, instead of nation-states combating nation-states, U.S. military units seek smaller bands of rogue terrorists hiding around the world; and that more new technologies were introduced onto the battlefield than ever before. Less than one year after 9/11, the military began deploying unmanned vehicles, commonly known as "drones," to gather intelligence through surveillance operations and to launch remote attacks against enemies. Instead of sending troops on the ground into dangerous situations, military officials increasingly send a drone, often operated by a pilot far from the front lines. Today, with drone flights increasing in frequency, the military is hungry for more drone pilots to fill their ranks, rather than boots-on-the-ground infantrymen.[5] Gregoire Chamayou, however, questions the heroism of drone pilots, whose avoidance of physical harm in enacting violence against enemies "is still seen as the highest degree of cowardice and dishonor."[6]

Elsewhere, in a close reading of *Call of Duty: Black Ops II,* I have analyzed the potential disruptions that drone warfare poses to military heroism, arguing that the game challenges traditional visions of heroism and, in doing so, ideologically trains players to cope with the new psychological challenges of military drone operation.[7] Yet, an additional component of heroism left unexamined in that piece is the role of masculinity in shaping orthodox visions of what it means to be heroic. To examine the ways that drone warfare has reimagined masculine military heroism, I analyze three games in the popular *Call of Duty* series that feature a future laden with terrorists, where drones are deployed to stop them. These games construct the ongoing War on Terror as a "hunt" for terrorists: enemies are not entire nations, but individuals who must be found and captured or killed. Consequently, in assessing these games' alignments with and departures from traditional narratives of heroism, I draw on heroic virtues that have historically been associated with the activity of hunting, where men solidified their masculine identities while also, in some cases, preparing for war. The use of drones in the hunt, however, ultimately limits the opportunities players have to develop the virtues that have come to define heroism in battle. This emerges principally from the expansion of the violent power of drone technology and the consequential reduction of the dangers that a human soldier faces. Instead of heroism emerging from fortitude and strength on the dangerous front lines, *Call of Duty* gestures toward technological power as a masculine virtue of war—contributing to what Chamayou describes as "a vast redefinition of warrior virtues."[8]

HISTORICIZING THE HEROIC IDEAL IN VIDEO GAMES

Twenty years after *Spacewar!* made its debut, the military was fully invested in the video game realm, whether they modified the games for military purposes, collaborated with commercial game designers, or left war games as is, imagining them as both a source for new training simulations for their soldiers and a form of soft power to align public sentiment in favor of military power.[9] Yet, these early simulations rarely featured avatars of human soldiers; more often, early representations of virtual war offered opportunities to drive tanks or pilot planes—situations where human soldiers were visually absent.[10]

The early 1990s saw the launch of two particular games that ushered in a new era of masculine heroism in the video game space, centering on the stories of human protagonists endowed with power and courage—and a propensity for violence. *Wolfenstein 3D*, launched in 1992, tells the story of an Allied spy during World War II who charges through a Nazi prison to kill enemies with a slew of different weapons. This spy is defined by his propensity to enact violence and, according to the game's cover art, by his chiseled masculine physique. The following year saw the release of a game called *Doom*. *Doom* featured a manly and physically imposing protagonist—a Marine described as a "lonely hero" and a "lone hero" by Hartmut Gieselmann and Ed Halter, respectively—charged with killing enemy aliens in a distant future.[11] Although, as Carl Thierren notes, first-person shooter games predated the launch of both of these games, together, *Wolfenstein 3D* and *Doom* popularized the first-person shooter video game genre, which went on to become one of the most popular genres in the history of video games.[12] These games also directly linked the genre to video games about war and combat.

More recent war games have continued to traffic in these themes, and they have more fully articulated war as a space for the heroic masculine soldier to exercise power and save the nation. Such video games have promoted sanitized and even laudatory visions of war in which soldiers are honorable heroes fighting righteously. One of the best known of these video games, *America's Army,* was created by the military in 2003 to recruit gamers into the ranks of the U.S. Army, and now boasts fifteen games in the series in which players guide soldiers to kill enemy soldiers. Games in the *America's Army* series requires that players engage in "acts of (virtual) heroism" that link enacting violence against enemies with preserving freedom.[13] The fact that *America's Army* games typically require players to operate male avatars further links the virtues of war promoted in the game with masculine identities.[14] Moreover, the game's popularity—the most recent iteration of the game, *America's Army: Proving Grounds,* was released in 2013 and, as of July 2017, boasts "more than 1.3 million player accounts and 935 years of play time"—suggests that the game's vision of military heroism reaches broad audiences.[15]

This interrelationship between war and masculinity in video game narratives was driven not only by cultural narratives, but also by stereotyped visions of the identity of the video game player, which is partly promoted by the game industry. Scholars have discussed at length the ways that the "gamer" is gendered and culturally constructed as a young male, even when demographic data about people who play video games indicate a much more diverse audience.[16] These war games, in offering a space for players to virtually enact violence as heroic and buff soldiers, resonated with "the ethos of men and boys . . . who became the 'gamer' demographic."[17] We should not be surprised, then, that the dominant protagonist in video games—even those that do not present narrative visions of war—continues to be the white male. Anna Everett and S. Craig Watkins, and Dmitri Williams et al. posit that between 70 and 80 percent of protagonists in video games are white males.[18] Other scholarly analyses have produced similar findings in which white men dominate video game narratives.[19] Moreover, with respect to the first-person shooter genre, Michael Hitchens found that of 566 video games surveyed, players were required to operate a male avatar in 81 percent of them.[20] These findings, in line with Kontour's assessment cited earlier, suggest that video games are coterminous with broader cultural narratives that link military heroism and masculinity.

Yet, I question the notion that video games still squarely present an unabashed vision of martial heroism centered on chiseled, brave men willing to sacrifice themselves for the good of the nation. If visions of heroism and masculinity are both in flux, examining the transformations of both concepts in the wake of the transformations in war—the growing use of unmanned aerial vehicles, for example, or the shift away from wars between nations and toward war on specific individuals—is worth considering. In this vein, Debra Ramsay analyzes games representing World War II, and, looking specifically at the first game in the *Call of Duty* series, concludes that the game's preoccupation with military technology "counters the archaic notion that the actions of the individual matter on the industrial battlefield and instead emphasizes how the destructive impartiality of mechanized warfare renders obsolete the skill and prowess of the lone soldier."[21] As a result, the game celebrates the spectacle of war rather than the heroic soldier himself. Similarly, I question whether later iterations of games in the *Call of Duty* series—those that represent near futures emerging from the War on Terror, laden with drones and sophisticated military hardware, rather than World War II narratives—similarly overshadow the heroic warrior.

HUNTING FOR HEROISM IN THE WAR ON TERROR

In this chapter I focus on a particular iteration of martial heroism that was prevalent after 9/11, but drew from earlier visions of masculine power in the nineteenth century. In the aftermath of the September 11 attacks, one of President Bush's first remarks to the public was a sober vow to "hunt down and punish those responsible for these cowardly acts," and this and other thematic statements about a global hunt for evil were echoed throughout his administration.[22] In this post-9/11 hunt for terrorists, the icon of the heroic hunter ascended into the public consciousness—a manly figure who fought terrorists and, according to Susan Faludi, "was less Batman than Daniel Boone."[23] This heroic figure circulated through popular culture and political rhetoric. While thousands of warfighters were confronting dangerous enemies in Afghanistan and Iraq in the first few years after 9/11, President Bush and his opponent in the 2004 presidential election, Senator John Kerry, frequently secured photo ops in which they were shown hunting in the wilderness, donning camouflage and taking down geese and pheasants. The hero that America needed in this moment—when it was "vulnerable to the enticements of protection fantasies"—was the masculine hunter.[24] In exploring the status of masculine heroism in games about terrorism, this chapter engages with these ongoing constructions of the War on Terror as a "hunt" for terrorists and, thus, builds on definitions of heroism that emerged from practices of hunting in America.

If the War on Terror and the ongoing search for terrorists are also conceived as a hunt, then these conflicts' heroic warriors can be construed as martial hunters. As such, understanding the celebration of the mythologized manly hunter informs how we understand the virtues that comprise heroism in this contemporary context.

Historical narratives of hunting have not only constructed the practice as a utilitarian means to acquire food; they have also imbued the practice with symbolic value.[25] Scholars have explored various ways that the American hunter throughout history has embodied heroic, laudable qualities that were at once culturally valued and practically useful on both the frontier and the front lines of war. In describing the heroism of the hunter, some scholars have emphasized his skill at surviving in the depths of the wilderness.[26] According to Richard Slotkin, for example, President Theodore Roosevelt advocated for public hunting parks where men could develop "vigorous manliness" in an approximation of the frontier experience.[27] Other scholars focus more narrowly on the ways hunting links masculinity, the acquisition of power, and dominance. Charles Bergman, for instance, emphasizes the links between hunting and imperial conquest, where "the hunter as hero in his conquest of the beast . . . naturalizes discourses of conquest" globally.[28] In that vein, according to Matt Cartmill, alongside the figure of the romantic hunter living in the wilderness there exists a more aggressive hunter who delivers "an assertion of his competitive superiority" over native peoples and nature—an imperial gesture of violent cultural dominance.[29] These ideologies of hunting and domination also took root in the nineteenth-century American South, where the hunter displayed his masculine identity through his hunting prowess. As Nicolas Proctor notes, hunting represented an opportunity for the gentry to develop and flaunt their skills with weapons to their fellow hunters, which constructed an "intricate conception of masculinity based on the display of prowess, self-control, and the multifaceted concept of mastery."[30]

Taken together, these scholars offer a comprehensive vision of the hunter whose heroism merges masculinity, dominance, and self-actualization. He thrives in the dangerous wilderness, and enjoys the invigorating effects of confronting danger. He is self-reliant, skilled with a gun, and assertive of his power over others—particularly those deemed savage or more animal than human. These attributes, as several of these scholars also note, reflect the masculine American hunter hero, with hunting comprising an essential activity that would provide opportunities to develop mastery and power for young men. To be a good hunter was to be a good man, so said this cultural mythology.

Beyond the cultural symbolism that was attached to hunting, hunting was historically a precursor for military service—another realm of masculine development and expression. In colonial India, for example, where hunters tracked tigers, elephants, and other creatures, "the dangerous pursuit of big game by the officer-hunter served as a harbinger of sterner tests on battlefields" due to the danger that inhered in confronting threatening beasts.[31] Narratives of the brave hunter against wild animals were widely circulated in nineteenth-century books and magazines, legitimizing imperial claims to foreign power over native lands and lives while also invigorating masculine power through violence.[32] Hunting could teach men martial ideals such as courage, physical fitness, confidence, self-sacrifice, and ruthlessness—qualities that comprised "masculine virtues" at war.[33] Or hunting could teach skills that were specifically applicable on the battlefield, like marksmanship, leadership, and land navigation.[34] Imagining the hunt as a form of war "drew it further into the male domain," strengthening the links between both practices and masculine visions of military service.[35] Ultimately, these scholarly accounts reveal how hunting, masculinity, and war have become bound up in American culture since the nineteenth century, when hunting at once prepared men for war and confirmed and strengthened their masculine identities.

The masculine, heroic hunter of American myth, narrative, and history is thus a close cousin of the heroic soldier. Yet, because masculinity is a dynamic identity, subject to historical context and social construction, the virtues and celebrated feats of future wars may not correspond to these earlier visions of heroism. In other words, we must explore the virtues of modern war that video games put forth, particularly in their increasing attention to the qualities of contemporary conflict: a war increasingly driven by unmanned machines.

THE DRONE HUNT

In line with George W. Bush's continual reminders that America would "hunt down" its terrorist enemies, drones have been rhetorically constructed as technological agents of hunting. Hunting-related names of military drones notwithstanding—the Predator, the Global Hawk, and the Stalker are the monikers for widely used unmanned military vehicles—political figures, military officials, and journalists have described how drones hunt terrorists and criminals.[36] As a result, an ideological vision of the War on Terror and subsequent military efforts against terrorism as power-driven, technologically sophisticated manhunts was quickly co-opted into video games such as those in the *Call of Duty* series. These games contributed to what Roger Stahl describes as a surge in "insurgent hunting games" due to the escalation of the War on Terror.[37] Particular moments of three games in the *Call of Duty* series engage, in various degrees of subtlety, with metaphorical linkages among drone warfare, hunting, heroism, and masculinity. The games reveal how the terrorist hunt plays out when drones are integrated into the practice of tracking down enemies, challenging historic linkages between the aforementioned virtues of war and contemporary practices of drone combat. In doing so, the games present new virtues of war that rely on linkages between masculinity and technological power.

As Proctor notes, hunting historically provided opportunities for southern men to display their prowess with weapons. Skill with a weapon likewise comprises a key element of narratives of heroism in these video games. I turn first to *Call of Duty: Ghosts*. Released in 2013, *Ghosts* explores a near-future conflict between a powerful collective of terrorists from South America, known as the Federation, and the few North American servicemen who remain in action following a devastating series of attacks on several North American cities. These servicemen band together to form a paramilitary group called the Ghosts, who seek to eradicate Federation forces before they invade the United States. The game thus projects the Ghosts, and consequently the player, as both the hunter and the hunted. The player participates in this hunt in a variety geographic regions and styles of combat, including using drones to defend a Santa Monica beach from waves of encroaching troops in the style of D-Day, covertly navigating a South American forest saturated with enemies that the player must pick off one by one with a knife, and swimming through the deep ocean amidst fish and sharks to destroy a Federation ship.

In considering how drones are used in this battle against the Federation, and thus how their deployment engages with heroic masculine virtues, I turn to a level titled "Homecoming," which constructs drone combat as lacking in the empowering qualities of hunting and killing (e.g., self-control, precision, mastery) articulated in historical accounts and narratives. In this level, Federation troops invade a U.S. base in Santa Monica, California, complete with trenches, barbed wire, ramshackle outposts, and a large Ferris wheel in the background—a vulnerable homeland. The player must attempt to stave off this invasion using guns and, eventually, a drone.

The level presents a vision of drone combat as imprecise slaughter rather than an opportunity to display prowess with a weapon. In addition to firing at enemies with a gun, as is typical in a first-person shooter game, the player must also use a drone to kill these enemies storming the beach. Rather than pinpointing a particular enemy to kill, however, the drone is used to carpet-bomb an expansive region of the battlefield to kill as many enemies as possible. The quantity of the kill is more important than which individuals or vehicles are targeted, as the game lauds the player for killing high numbers of enemies. This form of blanket violence marks a significant departure from the way Cartmill describes the mythic hunt as "an act of loving communion with nature."[38] With the targets barely recognizable as humans in the screen interface, appearing as merely abstracted pixels outlined in orange, the drone attack becomes an act of technological conquest, not intimate connection.[39]

Such powerful, albeit imprecise, drone kills are necessary to prevent the Federation from taking over the beach. When the enemies destroy the drone's control tower, leaving the U.S. troops toothless except for their infantry, the troops are ordered to retreat and cede the beach to the Federation. This mode of killing differs from the way a player in a first-person shooter game would typically conduct violence; that is, from the vantage point of a warfighter with a gun, where the gun's limited geographic reach requires greater precision to kill.[40] In this case, a player might track and pick off each enemy rather than spray bullets indiscriminately in the vague direction of enemy territory—a mode of violence that would produce few consistent kills and waste a slew of bullets.

The violence that the drone produces in this level presents a counterpoint to political rhetoric outside of the video game space that lauds the incredible precision of drone combat. Weaponized drones are frequently idealized in military discourse as technological implements that can kill with astonishing precision, thus preventing innocent noncombatants from becoming "collateral damage" in these hunter-killer missions. In 2012, White House counterterrorism adviser John Brennan praised the drone's "surgical precision—the ability, with laser-like focus, to eliminate the cancerous tumor called an al-Qa'ida terrorist while limiting damage to the tissue around it."[41] If Brennan's framing of drone warfare applied to *Ghosts*, drone combat would afford opportunities to develop skill with a weapon—an essential quality of heroic hunting and the fulfillment of an idealized masculine identity. Yet, this "surgical precision" is not what the player experiences while using the drone in *Ghosts*; at least, not in the "Homecoming" level. Instead, the player has an opportunity to kill without restraint.

Indiscriminate and imprecise hunting has met with criticism over the course of American history, as this form of violence was not indicative of the skill that defined the heroic hunter. Proctor, for example, notes that in genteel hunting outings in the old South, "the advocates of sport insisted that true sportsmen placed proper form above indiscriminate slaughter. The advocates of sport insisted that real men (that is, those welcome in their fraternities) killed in certain specific ways."[42] Appropriate expressions of manhood emerged from skillful and restrained violence, not from destroying all life with their powerful weapons.

This distaste for slaughter was one of the reasons that Henry David Thoreau often decried hunting in mid-nineteenth-century America, even as he celebrated the sport's capacity to bring man closer to nature. The dangers of indiscriminate killing, for Thoreau, were especially problematic because they could transfer to man-on-man violence, rather than violence enacted against animals only. According to Thomas L. Altherr, who discusses Thoreau's conflicted vision of hunting, "The matter of the hunters' indiscriminate killing forced Thoreau to ponder the issues of innocence and barbarity regarding animals, but the savage urge to hunt men as animals especially incensed him."[43] These imprecise forms of violence transform human enemies into animals and rob the hunt of any moralizing or culturally energizing qualities it otherwise had, particularly when those hunters began attacking other humans. In *Ghosts*, the drone kills are not presented as a virtuous expression of masculine power in line with past narratives that celebrated precision, skill, and personal mastery. Here, a drone kill does not require acuity or restraint; the player simply presses a button to annihilate scores of enemy troops in one fell swoop.

These critiques of hunting as an expression of indiscriminate violence align with contemporary anxieties about the violence that drones afford. Writing for *Foreign Policy* in 2016, Micah Zenko, a senior fellow at the Council on Foreign Relations, and Amelia Mae Wolf, a research associate for the same organization, aggregated data from three separate NGO reports on drone strikes that illustrates that one civilian is killed for every 1.6 drone strikes.[44] Although the lack of transparency in the Pentagon and in the intelligence community regarding civilian casualties makes it impossible to discern how many are actually killed, these reports suggest that drone attacks are far less precise than advisers like Brennan have suggested. Concerns about drones' imprecision have begun to inform cultural orientations toward drone warfare itself. Even as a majority of Americans support the use of drone strikes, a 2015 Pew poll showed that 80 percent of Americans were very or somewhat "concerned that U.S. drone attacks endanger[ed] the lives of innocent civilians."[45] Games like *Ghosts* coincide with and potentially extend this cultural concern about drones' imprecision by allowing players to enact indiscriminate violence and by demonstrating how drone technology does not necessarily produce a targeted killing. As a result, cultural notions of military heroism are threatened in the wake of a growing awareness of the imprecise violence that drone pilots enact.

Ghosts, in line with a trend in insurgent hunting games, includes segments that require players to use drones to hunt and kill enemies in the insecure post-9/11 milieu. No realm is completely safe from conflict: this is a world in which a space of leisure and entertainment, the Santa Monica beach, has been transformed into a war zone, articulating an ongoing fear of domestic terrorist attacks that require substantial military intervention and violence. In this case, that violence is supplied in large part by drone technology. This in-game drone hunt, however, is presented as an opportunity to kill indiscriminately, with no apparent skill, robbing drone combat of the benefits that emerged in heroic hunting practices and transforming the agent of violence from a virtuous masculine hero into an ostensibly bloodthirsty barbarian.

A later game in the series, *Call of Duty: Advanced Warfare*, presents a counterexample with respect to the ways narratives of drone combat encourage precise or imprecise violence. Released in October 2014 and set in the mid-twenty-first century, *Advanced Warfare* celebrates a slew of futuristic military technologies, drones included. The game's narrative is not meant to be fantastic or outlandish, but rather anticipates the technologies that are close to being deployed on real-world battlefields. *Advanced Warfare* follows the story of Jack Mitchell, a former Marine who joins a private military company called Atlas as a contracted fighter. After a series of deadly terrorist attacks that leave Atlas the primary source of global security, the company's CEO is revealed to have ulterior motives: he has become a dictator, and rather than keeping the world safe, he hopes to achieve world domination, principally through his advanced technologies. Mitchell must stop the company from exacting global destruction.

In a level called "Manhunt," Mitchell, as an Atlas employee, is tasked with finding a terrorist inside a building in Santorini, Greece. In order to provide cover and intelligence for Atlas's ground troops who are entering the building, he deploys a sophisticated aerial drone, called a WASP, which provides aerial surveillance and directs firepower toward the terrorists guarding the building. When Mitchell uses the drone to take out enemies one by one, the violence he directs differs starkly from that of *Ghosts*: the player must shoot precisely, or the enemies under attack will become aware of Atlas's presence and retaliate in kind. The game rewards stealth and meticulous violence, where only one bullet is used to take down a target. A later phase in the operation requires Mitchell to pick off a certain number of enemies scattered throughout the building within a thirty-second span, or the player fails the mission. Each shot must be fatal, and thus accurate, in order for the player to complete the killings within that limited timeframe. Here, then, idealized fantasies of drone combat as "surgically precise" are realized, and are more akin to Proctor's description of the heroic hunt in the mid-nineteenth century.

Although this form of violence does more closely resemble the narrative elements of heroism described earlier, it does, nonetheless, depart in a different way from the ways heroic hunts were imagined years ago. The heroic hunter of historic narratives *directly* confronted the dangers of the hunt, whether that was charging forth into the uncertain, dangerous frontier or attacking violent big-game animals abroad. This mythologized hero of the hunt subjected himself to the risk of death. Mitchell, when piloting the WASP, experiences no such risk, nor does he have any opportunity to sacrifice himself for some external good, such as his fellow soldiers or the nation-state as a whole.

In addition to combat drones, players have opportunities to deploy surveillance drones to secretly capture intelligence that is essential for mission objectives. These surveillance drones further remove avatars from the front lines, as they can send the drones into dangerous spaces to acquire information without incurring risk to their own lives. In this section, I focus on two games, *Call of Duty: Black Ops II* and *Advanced Warfare*, both of which expand the distance between the game's protagonist and the dangers of combat. *Black Ops II*, set in

2025, presents war as driven by drone power, but reliance on unmanned military technologies soon becomes a liability for the United States. When a terrorist hacks into the United States' massive arsenal of networked drones, he takes control of the entire stock of drones and deploys them against cities worldwide in order to stoke a new world war. The player's objective is to stop the attack and to kill or detain the terrorist.

Both games require players to use drones to conduct surveillance operations and gather intelligence necessary to find terrorists. One of the missions in *Black Ops II*, "Karma," requires the player's character to infiltrate a city called Colossus that is floating in the sea and secretly acquire intelligence essential to capturing the terrorist. The player controls a character named Mason, who deploys a handheld robotic spider drone called "Ziggy" to record conversations among the city's security forces, who have been compromised by enemy private military forces, or PMCs. Mason can direct Ziggy through a series of vents, and the game tells the player through on-screen text, "Ziggy can cling to most surfaces," in addition to being able to jump over large gaps in the vent system. While controlling Ziggy, Mason learns that security forces are planting explosives in the city's interior, putting thousands of Colossus residents and visitors in danger.

As small as Ziggy is, the drone still packs a punch against enemies. Upon reaching an elevator, the player is instructed to use a "zapper"—a tool like a taser—to disable a member of the enemy security forces. Ziggy can then scan the disabled man's retina in order to unlock biometrically secured doors and acquire more intelligence. Unfortunately for Mason, one of the security forces finds Ziggy and stomps on it, ending the drone's surveillance efforts. The player returns to controlling Mason, who is now pursued by enemy security forces.

This part of the mission spent operating Ziggy introduces another quality of the drone hunt that rubs against the cherished ideals of the heroic hunt in American culture: safety. While directing Ziggy through the city's vents and into dangerous territory, Mason cannot be killed, in spite of the fact that Mason's fellow operative, Harper, says the PMC forces are headed his way. Although danger seems imminent, Mason is invincible while operating the drone—a reminder that remotely conducted combat, in myths and narratives of modern war, does not require soldiers to incur any bodily risk.[46] The same is true in other levels throughout *Black Ops II*.[47] This experience of violence is a stark departure from the dangers of the hunt that Mangan and McKenzie and Cartmill describe. The dangers of the frontier are absent in this moment; consequently, there are few opportunities to exercise the bravery and courage that have defined the heroic hunter in historical narratives.

Similarly, in *Advanced Warfare*'s "Manhunt," which I described earlier, Mitchell cannot die while operating the WASP and gathering information about the terrorist's location in the building. He incurs no risk in this military operation until the drone is no longer used. Once Mitchell and his fellow Atlas troops discover the terrorist in the building was a body double rigged with explosives, the building goes up in flames and the drone is destroyed. Only when the drone is gone does Mitchell return to being a vulnerable body: the enemy's gunshots can, once again, pierce his skin and wound him. Much as the level rewards drone-driven precision violence, it also reduces the risk and danger that Mitchell experiences while conducting that violence. This narrative has little room for self-sacrifice, an element of war that is no longer required when a drone, in lieu of human soldiers, conducts dangerous military operations.

Arguments against warfare conducted at a distance circulated in American culture long before drones entered the battle arena, and for reasons that gesture more specifically toward historic visions of heroic battle. According to Drew Gilpin Faust, during the Civil War era, sharpshooters, or early snipers, were criticized for firing at enemies from distances of nearly a half-mile because "the asymmetry of risk involved in sharpshooting rendered it even more threatening to principles of humanity than the frenzied excesses of heated battle."[48] These sharpshooters were no heroic soldiers, according to contemporary critics. This experience is replicated in the *Call of Duty* narrative: in both games, Mitchell and Mason need not subject themselves to any danger to complete a mission, making them ideological descendants of the Civil War era's sharpshooters, decried for their lack of heroism.

The same logic has infused critiques of the lopsidedness of drone combat, where the lack of danger that drone pilots confront results in fewer combat deaths and thus may make war easier to tolerate.[49] Chamayou notes that the asymmetrical risk between the drone pilot and the drone target challenges conventional understandings of martial heroism, and he questions whether drone pilots can ever be heroes as a result. As I have discussed elsewhere, there is perhaps no greater example of the misalignment between traditional visions of military heroism and drone warfare than the Pentagon's failed introduction in 2013 of a medal honoring drone pilots, called the Distinguished Warfare Medal. Because the medal would have been ranked higher than medals earned in military combat, opposition to it surged immediately after its announcement, and centered on the notion that drone piloting could not be heroic because it involved no danger to a soldier's physical body, and no opportunity for self-sacrifice. Due to extensive pushback from public officials and veterans' organizations, the medal was canceled.[50] The *Call of Duty* games that I analyze here reflect the notion that the safety of drone piloting could forestall the possibility that operating a drone could constitute a demonstration or enactment of heroic acts.

Beyond precise violence and a willingness (if not a desire) to confront danger, the heroic hunter was historically defined in part by his ability to conquer his prey, making hunting a practice of exacting masculine power and dominance. In the nineteenth century, for example, hunting was a practice that would allow men to reinforce "the subordination of white women, slaves, children, and the natural world" to preserve patriarchal institutions and norms.[51] These games do indeed present strong linkages between drone combat and power. But they also transform the agent of power from the man to the machine, in turn troubling the linkage between masculine heroism and the human soldier. Rather than completely jettisoning the notion of heroism, these games instead articulate an alternate vision of masculine martial heroism rooted in the deployment and display of extreme technological power in the service of dominance.

Scholars have previously linked technology and masculine power outside of the military arena, where mastering and using an array of technologies provides opportunities for men to display their masculinity in ways that depart from pure physical strength.[52] This frame likewise applies to the three games that I analyze. In the aforementioned level of *Ghosts*, for example, the player can ward off invading enemy troops only by deploying the drone's ever-powerful missiles; without its aid, the level cannot be completed successfully. The power dynamic here is clear, with the level reflecting Chamayou's assessment of drones' lopsided power in the real world. For Chamayou, technologies extend "imperial power from the center over the world that constitutes its periphery," where drones become a means to "project power" outwardly.[53] The result, Chamayou observes, is that "what could still claim to be combat is converted into a campaign of what is, quite simply, slaughter."[54] Absent here are the self-improving, moralizing benefits of the heroic hunt. Nonetheless, drones do offer an opportunity for conquest through violence—not unlike historic hunts. After all, as Proctor notes, violence offered a "popular and potent" display of masculinity in early America.[55] Where these narratives depart from Proctor's is in the notion that the drone hunt is an act of dominance emerging from technological might rather than from a human agent. As such, in the case of *Ghosts*, martial masculinity is more a product of technological muscle than of bravery and sacrifice on the front lines.

Surveillance technologies manifest power in different ways than weapons and missiles do, but they ultimately contribute to the conquest of bodies by producing superior knowledge of the enemy. Outside of the video game realm, scholars have described how surveillance technologies like drones can supply power to the person or institution that gazes on a target. Michel Foucault, for example, describes how the expansiveness of a surveillance apparatus—the metaphorical panopticon—can manage entire populations by projecting the idea that those populations are always being watched.[56] Even if one may not see the watcher in a given moment, the ongoing pervasiveness of surveillance technologies, like drones, suggests that subjects are continually visible and thus controlled and managed.

By conducting surveillance operations on these targets in games like *Black Ops II* and *Advanced Warfare*, the player's characters acquire intelligence that affords them greater power in these otherwise dangerous situations. Put differently, knowing where threats lie enables both Mason and Mitchell opportunities to mitigate those threats. Through their capacity to gather intelligence and conduct surveillance operations, drones like Ziggy and the WASP transform the power of historic hunts from violent conquest over enemy bodies through gunfire into a form of power endemic to the War on Terror and subsequent conflicts against terrorists and insurgents: the total knowledge of enemy subjects gleaned through advanced technologies.

Yet, this knowledge also poses risks to those who hold it. A rising concern about drone warfare outside of the video game space involves the wounding psychological effects of drone combat on the soldiers who launch strikes, emerging in part from the thorough knowledge they have of their targets. A report in *GQ* about former drone pilot Brandon Bryant reflects on the uncanny intimacy between drone pilot and target that develops when the former is charged with watching the latter for days, if not weeks, at a time:

> Sitting in the darkness of the control station, Bryant watched people on the other side of the world go about their daily lives, completely unaware of his all-seeing presence wheeling in the sky above. If his mission was to monitor a high-value target, he might linger above a single house for weeks. It was a voyeuristic intimacy. He watched the targets drink tea with friends, play with their children, have sex with their wives on rooftops, writhing under blankets. There were soccer matches, and weddings too. He once watched a man walk out into a field and take a crap, which glowed white in infrared.[57]

Such intimacy may be partly responsible for the high levels of depression, anxiety, and PTSD that drone pilots are diagnosed with, and it disrupts the notion that total knowledge of the enemy, gleaned through technology, is a source of power and heroism.[58] Yet, the military's response to this growing health issue is telling. One proposed option in the military is to introduce a voice-activated system in the drone interface, where instead of enacting the violence himself or herself with a joystick, the pilot could simply tell the drone to launch a strike, absolving himself or herself of some moral responsibility by displacing the action to the machine, albeit to a limited extent.[59] In this scenario, the fighter burrows more deeply into the machine. Affording unmanned military vehicles more power and agency may ameliorate the harms caused by watching the violence they direct on screens. Perhaps, again, the future of military heroism lies in technological prowess and machine power.

These forms of power, derived from the drone's unique technical capabilities, gesture toward virtues of drone combat that are built on conquest, destruction, and superior intelligence—all derived from technology, rather than human physical strength. Although more traditional understandings of military heroism persist in the national consciousness as well as in the video game arena, here, in an age of increasingly unmanned warfare, an alternative is developing that merges martial masculinity with the vast power of the machine.

CONCLUSION: THE FUTURE OF MASCULINITY AND TECHNO-WAR

Ultimately, narratives of drone warfare in the *Call of Duty* series challenge and reimagine manly forms of heroism that emerged from the hunt. These games offer ambiguous representations of precision violence; reduce opportunities for characters to incur risk or danger, thus limiting opportunities for courage or self-sacrifice; and offer opportunities for new expressions of heavily technologized power. Although the mythologized figure of the masculine hero at war remains prominent in the public consciousness—indeed, some of the virtues of the heroic warrior are retained even in narratives of drone combat—these games also present an alternative vision of the principal values of modern warfare that are rooted in technological power. Technological power is vaunted as both a reflection of state power and a means of masculine domination, reimagined from traditional visions of masculine heroism centered on the soldier's conduct on the literal battlefield.

These games ultimately suggest that such powerful unmanned technologies are not only useful, but also desirable, fetishizing the technology into an awesome and symbolic technical reflective of righteous state power.[60] The fetishization of military technology is not new to this recent era of pervasive drone warfare. Robin Luckham, for example, suggests that the Cold War's celebration of technology in popular culture idealized martial activity as the solution to Cold War anxieties, where nuclear fear was abated through clinging to American technological supremacy.[61] In addition to linking technological power and national security, the fetishization of weaponry also challenges contemporary constructions of martial masculinity. Michael Salter discusses the ways law enforcement agencies have fetishized drone technology, elevating the machines to positions of extreme power and sophistication in spite of evidence that drones are not the technological panacea that these state bodies claim.[62] Moreover, he notes that drones are "embedded within a pervasive cultural code of military signs and symbols promising the rush and thrill of masculine conflict and, ultimately, victory," fueled by desires for masculine martial domination.[63] Building on Robin Luckham's argument, Salter concludes that weapons "promise individual and collective renewal through violence," a particularly desirable outcome in an era where heroic martial masculinity is perceived to be threatened.[64]

These video games ultimately present unmanned technologies as a means to experience an alternative iteration of masculine power when the conditions of the battlefield that previously allowed for traditionally heroic actions are inaccessible. In the twenty-first century, traditional manifestations of masculine heroism that revolved around courage, skill, and power have transformed and merged with the fetishization of military drone technologies in the Pentagon and elsewhere. Moreover, as war is increasingly driven by not just unmanned, but automated technologies, where human pilots would not need to direct these machines to fly over particular areas, the human element of war is in danger of decreasing.[65] These games will perhaps become harbingers of a new world in which our vaunted heroes are no longer soldiers at all: they are machines.

NOTES

1. See, for example, Stuart W. Leslie, *The Cold War and American Science: The Military-Industrial-Academic Complex at MIT and Stanford* (New York: Columbia University Press, 1993).
2. For a detailed history of the links between the military and the video game industry, see Corey Mead, *War Play: Video Games and the Future of Armed Conflict* (New York: Houghton Mifflin Harcourt, 2013).
3. Stephen Kline, Nick Dyer-Witheford, and Greig de Peuter, *Digital Play: The Interaction of Technology, Culture, and Marketing* (Montreal: McGill-Queen's University Press, 2003).
4. Kyle Kontour, "The Governmentality of Battlefield Space: Efficiency, Proficiency, and Masculine Performativity," *Bulletin of Science, Technology, and Society* 32, no. 5 (2012): 355.
5. Gordon Lubold, "Air Force Will Offer Bonuses to Lure Drone Pilots," *Wall Street Journal*, July 14, 2015, http://www.wsj.com/articles/air-force-will-offer-bonuses-to-lure-drone-pilots-1436922312.
6. Gregoire Chamayou, *A Theory of the Drone* (New York: New Press, 2015), 98.
7. Carrie Andersen, "Games of Drones: The Uneasy Future of the Soldier-Hero in *Call of Duty: Black Ops II*," *Surveillance and Society* 12, no. 3 (2014): 360–376.
8. Chamayou, *A Theory of the Drone*, 101.
9. Mead, *War Play*.
10. See, for example, *Missile Command* (1980), *Defender* (1981), *Galaxian* (1979), and *Battlezone* (1980).
11. Hartmut Gieselmann, "Ordinary Gamers—The Vanishing Violence in War Games and Its Influence on Male Gamers," *Eludamos* 1, no. 1 (2007); Ed Halter, *From Sun Tzu to Xbox: War and Video Games* (New York: Thunder's Mouth Press, 2006), 163.
12. Carl Thierren, "Inspecting Video Game Historiography through Critical Lens: Etymology of the First-Person Shooter Genre," *Game Studies* 15, no. 2 (2015), http://gamestudies.org/1502/articles/therrien.
13. David Nieborg, "Training Recruits and Conditioning Youth: The Soft Power of Military Games," in *Joystick Soldiers: The Politics of Play in Military Video* Games, ed. Nina B. Huntemann and Matthew Thomas Payne (New York: Routledge, 2010), 61.
14. Mark B. Salter, "The Geographical Imaginations of Video Games: *Diplomacy, Civilization, America's Army,* and *Grand Theft Auto IV*," *Geopolitics* 16, no. 2 (2011): 359–388.

15. "*America's Army: Proving Grounds* Released on PS4™," *America's Army*, July 17, 2017, http://www.americasarmy.com/press.

16. See, for example, Kline, Dyer-Witheford, and de Peuter, *Digital Play*; Benjamin Paaßen, Thekla Morgenroth, and Michelle Stratemeyer, "What Is a True Gamer? The Male Gamer Stereotype and the Marginalization of Women in Video Game Culture," *Sex Roles* 76, no. 7–8 (2017): 421–435; Adrienne Shaw, "What Is Video Game Culture? Cultural Studies and Game Studies," *Games and Culture* 5, no. 4 (2010): 403–424.

17. Kontour, "The Governmentality of Battlefield Space," 355.

18. Anna Everett and S. Craig Watkins, "The Power of Play: The Portrayal and Performance of Race in Video Games," in *The Ecology of Games: Connecting Youth, Games, and Learning*, ed. Katie Salen Tekinbaş (Cambridge, MA: MIT Press, 2008), 141–166; Dmitri Williams, Nicole Martins, Mia Consalvo, and James D. Ivory, "The Virtual Census: Representations of Gender, Race, and Age in Video Games," *New Media and Society* 11, no. 5 (2009): 815–834.

19. See, for example, Jeroen Jansz and Raynel G. Martis, "The Lara Phenomenon: Powerful Female Characters in Video Games," *Sex Roles* 56, no. 3–4 (2007): 141–148; Tracy Dietz, "An Examination of Violence and Gender Role Portrayals in Video Games: Implications for Gender Socialization and Aggressive Behavior," *Sex Roles* 38, no. 5–6 (1998): 425–442.

20. Michael Hitchens, "A Survey of First-Person Shooters and Their Avatars," *Game Studies* 11, no. 3 (2011), http://gamestudies.org/1103/articles/michael_hitchens.

21. Debra Ramsay, "Brutal Games: *Call of Duty* and the Cultural Narrative of World War II," *Cinema Journal* 54, no. 2 (2015): 98.

22. Gerry J. Gilmore, "U.S. 'Will Hunt Down and Punish' Terrorists, Bush Says," *American Forces Press Service*, September 11, 2001, http://archive.defense.gov/news/newsarticle.aspx?id=44914; Erin Steuter and Deborah Wills, *At War with Metaphor: Media, Propaganda, and Racism in the War on Terror* (Lanham, MD: Lexington Books, 2008).

23. Susan Faludi, *The Terror Dream: Myth and Misogyny in an Insecure America* (New York: Henry Holt and Company, 2007), 148.

24. Ibid., 151.

25. Charles Bergman, "Obits for the Fallen Hunter: Reading the Decline—and Death?—of Hunting in America," *American Literary History* 17, no. 4 (2005): 819.

26. Matt Cartmill, *A View to a Death in the Morning: Hunting and Nature through History* (Cambridge, MA: Harvard University Press, 1996), 121.

27. Richard Slotkin, *The Gunfighter Nation: The Myth of the Frontier in Twentieth-Century America* (New York: Atheneum, 1992), 56.

28. Bergman, "Obits for the Fallen Hunter," 819.

29. Cartmill, *A View to a Death in the Morning*, 137.

30. Nicholas Proctor, *Bathed in Blood: Hunting and Mastery in the Old South* (Charlottesville: University Press of Virginia, 2002), 39.

31. J. A. Mangan and Callum McKenzie, "Martial Conditioning, Military Exemplars and Moral Certainties: Imperial Hunting as Preparation for War," *International Journal of the History of Sport* 25, no. 9 (2008): 1134.

32. Ibid., 1134.

33. Ibid., 1159.

34. Proctor, *Bathed in Blood*, 72–73.

35. Ibid., 73.

36. See David Axe, "Will the Navy's New Killer Drones Hunt Terrorists or Fight China?" *Wired*, May 15, 2013, http://www.wired.com/2013/05/navy-drone-bet/; Joseph Trevithick, "U.S. Air Forces Drones Spend Weeks 'Man-Hunting,'" *Medium*, January 5, 2015, https://medium.com/war-is-boring/u-s-air-force-drones-spend-weeks-man-hunting-f8204f4534c8.

37. Roger Stahl, "Have You Played the War on Terror?," *Critical Studies in Media Communication* 23, no. 2 (2006): 118.

38. Cartmill, *A View to a Death in the Morning*, 137.

39. I have argued elsewhere that the lack of precision required of players in this level of *Ghosts* serves as training for the real-world boredom that characterizes contemporary drone warfare. See Carrie Andersen, "Securing America: Drone Warfare in American Culture after 9/11" (PhD diss., University of Texas at Austin, 2017), 160.

40. Mark Claypool and Kajal Claypool, "Latency and Player Actions in Online Games," *Communications of the ACM* 49, no. 11 (2006): 40–45.

41. John O. Brennan, "The Ethics and Efficacy of the President's Counterterrorism Strategy," speech delivered at the Woodrow Wilson International Center for Scholars in Washington, D.C., on April 30, 2012, https://www.c-span.org/video/?305721-1/us-counterterrorism-strategy.

42. Proctor, *Bathed in Blood*, 88.

43. Thomas Altherr, "'Chaplain to the Hunters': Henry David Thoreau's Ambivalence toward Hunting," *American Literature* 56, no. 3 (1984): 356.

44. Micah Zenko and Amelia Mae Wolf, "Drones Kill More Civilians than Pilots Do," *Foreign Policy*, April 25, 2016, http://foreignpolicy.com/2016/04/25/drones-kill-more-civilians-than-pilots-do/.

45. "Public Continues to Back U.S. Drone Attacks," *Pew Research Center*, May 28, 2015, http://www.people-press.org/2015/05/28/public-continues-to-back-u-s-drone-attacks/.

46. For further discussion of the significance of invincibility in *Black Ops II*, see Andersen, "Securing America," 138; Andersen, "Games of Drones," 369.

47. Andersen, "Games of Drones," 369.

48. Drew Gilpin Faust, *This Republic of Suffering: Death and the American Civil War* (New York: Vintage Books, 2008), 42.

49. See, for example, Mark Coeckelbergh, "Drones, Information Technology, and Distance: Mapping the Moral Epistemology of Remote Fighting," *Ethics and Information Technology* 14, no. 2 (2013): 87–98; John Williams, "Distant Intimacy: Space, Drones, and Just War," *Ethics and International Affairs* 29, no. 1 (2015): 93–110.

50. Chamayou, *A Theory of the Drone*, 98; Andersen, "Games of Drones," 367.

51. Proctor, *Bathed in Blood*, 63.

52. See, for example, Cynthia Cockburn, *Brothers: Male Dominance and Technological Change* (London: Pluto Press, 1983); Judy Wacjman, *Feminism Confronts Technology* (University Park: The Pennsylvania State University Press, 1991).

53. Chamayou, *A Theory of the Drone*, 12.

54. Ibid., 13.

55. Proctor, *Bathed in Blood*, 71.

56. Michel Foucault, *Discipline and Punish: The Birth of the Prison* (New York: Vintage Books, 1977).

57. Matthew Power, "Confessions of a Drone Warrior," *GQ*, October 22, 2013, https://www.gq.com/story/drone-uav-pilot-assassination?printable=true.

58. James Dao, "Drone Pilots Are Found to Get Stress Disorders Much as Those in Combat Do," *New York Times*, February 22, 2013, http://www.nytimes.com/2013/02/23/us/drone-pilots-found-to-get-stress-disorders-much-as-those-in-combat-do.html?mcubz=0.

59. David Axe, "How to Prevent Drone Pilot PTSD: Blame the 'Bot," *Wired*, June 7, 2012, https://www.wired.com/2012/06/drone-pilot-ptsd/.

60. For further discussion of the fetishization and desirability of drone technologies, see Andersen, "Securing America."

61. Robin Luckham, "Armament Culture," *Alternatives: Global, Local, Political* 10, no. 1 (1984): 1–44.

62. Michael Salter, "Toys for the Boys? Drones, Pleasure, and Popular Culture in the Militarization of Policing," *Critical Criminology* 22, no. 2 (2014): 171.

63. Ibid., 173.

64. Ibid., 166.

65. Nafeez Ahmed, "How the Pentagon's Skynet Would Automate War," *Motherboard*, November 24, 2014, https://motherboard.vice.com/en_us/article/8qxvvg/how-the-pentagons-skynet-would-automate-war.

ACKNOWLEDGMENTS

The essays collected in this volume are revised versions of papers that were first presented at the conference "Race, Gender, and Military Heroism in U.S. History," which took place at the Goethe University of Frankfurt in March 2015. I gratefully acknowledge the financial support of the German Research Foundation, which funded said conference and the related research project "Marginalized Masculinities and the American Nation: Native American and African American Military Heroism, 1941–1978." I would also like to thank Michael Voigt for co-organizing the conference. Alex Popa and Rebecca Roessling are to be thanked for providing important research and administrative assistance. I am also indebted to Styles Sass, who copyedited the first version of the manuscript. Brian D. Behnken deserves my gratitude for helping me come up with a catchy book title. Finally, I am grateful to Leslie Mitchner for gracefully ushering this book through the review and publication process at Rutgers University Press.

NOTES ON CONTRIBUTORS

CARRIE ANDERSEN is a lecturer in American studies at the University of Texas at Austin. In 2017, she received her Ph.D. in American studies from the University of Texas at Austin. Her dissertation on drone warfare in American culture won the 2017 Michael H. Granof Award for the best dissertation at UT Austin in any field of study. Her work has been previously published in *Game Studies* and *Surveillance and Society*.

STEVE ESTES is professor of history at Sonoma State University, where his teaching and research focus on the cultural history of the United States in the twentieth century. He is the author of *I Am a Man: Race, Manhood and the Struggle for Civil Rights* (2005), *Ask and Tell: Gay and Lesbian Veterans Speak Out* (2007), and *Charleston in Black and White: Race and Power in the South after the Civil Rights Movement* (2015). Estes is currently working on a cultural history of surfing in the American South.

SIMON HALL is professor of modern history at the University of Leeds. His research interests focus on the American civil rights and black power movements, the 1960s, and global protest during the Cold War. His most recent book is *1956: The World in Revolt* (2016).

SONJA JOHN is assistant professor of political science at Bahir Dar University, Ethiopia, where she continues her work on indigenous sovereignty and decoloniality. Her seminars at the American Studies Institutes at Humboldt University of Berlin and Technical University of Dresden revolve around contemporary political and cultural issues in Native North America. She holds a Ph.D. in political science and earned master's degrees in Lakota leadership and management from Oglala Lakota College and in political science from Free University of Berlin. She is the author of *Enacting Empowerment: Implications from the Oglala Oyate Woitancan Empowerment Zone* (2011) and has cowritten and coedited books on democracy theory. Her current research project investigates refusal and willfulness from an intersectional perspective.

GEORGE LEWIS is head of the School of History, Politics, and International Relations at the University of Leicester, UK, where he previously served as director of the Centre for American Studies. He has published two monographs, *The White South and the Red Menace: Segregationists, Anti-Communism and Massive Resistance, 1945–1965* (2004) and *Massive Resistance: The White*

Response to the Civil Rights Movement (2006), and is the editor of a special issue of the *Journal of American Studies* on un-Americans. He has published essays in a range of books and journals, including the *Journal of Southern History, Patterns of Prejudice,* and *Radical Americas,* and is currently completing a book manuscript on the long history of un-Americans and un-Americanism.

AMY LUCKER is currently completing a Ph.D. in American studies at Rutgers University–Newark. Her dissertation focuses on the work of artists who contemporaneously repurposed new images of the Vietnam War in their work. From 2006 until her retirement in 2018, she worked as a librarian at New York University, where she served for eleven years as Head of the Library at the Institute of Fine Arts. Previously she worked in the libraries of Harvard University, the Museum of Fine Arts in Boston, Columbia University, and the Brooklyn Museum of Art.

SARAH MAKESCHIN is assistant professor of American studies at the University of Passau, Germany. Her research interests include war and memory, political culture and political communication, and media literacy studies. She has completed a book manuscript on political communication in Barack Obama's 2008 presidential campaign and has published articles on the same topic. She is currently supervising a research project on information and media literacy in educational contexts.

MATTHIAS VOIGT is a doctoral student at the Goethe University of Frankfurt, Germany. His research focuses on Native American history, gender, and memory. In his dissertation, he examines how Native Americans reinvented cultural and warrior traditions within the larger context of U.S. colonial domination and modernity.

SIMON WENDT is assistant professor of American studies at the Goethe University of Frankfurt. His research interests revolve around African American history, gender history, memory, nationalism, and the history of heroism. He is the author of *The Spirit and the Shotgun: Armed Resistance and the Struggle for Civil Rights* (2007) and editor or coeditor of a number of books, including *Black Intellectual Thought in Modern America: A Historical Perspective* (2017), *Masculinities and the Nation in the Modern World: Between Hegemony and Marginalization* (2015), and *Globalizing Lynching History: Vigilantism and Extralegal Punishment from an International Perspective* (2011). Simon Wendt is currently completing a book manuscript on the history of the Daughters of the American Revolution.

ELLEN D. WU is associate professor of history and director of the Asian American studies program at Indiana University, Bloomington. Her research and teaching interests focus on Asian/Pacific America, immigration, and race in the United States. Her monograph *The Color of Success: Asian Americans and the Origins of the Model Minority* (2014) received the Immigration and Ethnic History Society's First Book Award (2015) and was a finalist for its Theodore Saloutos Memorial Award (2015), as well as for the Association for Asian American Studies History Book Award (2016). Her writing has appeared in the *Pacific Historical Review*, the *Journal of American Ethnic History*, *Chinese America: History and Perspectives*, and *Race and Retail: Consumption across the Color Line* (2015), the *Los Angeles Times*, and on NPR's *Code Switch* blog. Wu's research has been supported by fellowships from the National Endowment for the Humanities, the Ford Foundation, and the University of Texas at Austin's Institute for Historical Studies. She is currently at work on *Overrepresented: Asian Americans in the Age of Affirmative Action*, a history of race making, policy making, and migration in recent times.

INDEX